CLINICAL STUDIES IN
NEURO-PSYCHOANALYSIS

CLINICAL STUDIES IN NEURO-PSYCHOANALYSIS
Second Edition

Introduction to a Depth Neuropsychology

Karen Kaplan-Solms & Mark Solms

Foreword

Arnold Z. Pfeffer

New York
London

First published in 2000 by H. Karnac (Books) Ltd., 6 Pembroke Buildings, London NW10 6RE, a subsidiary of Other Press LLC, New York.

Extracts from Sigmund Freud, *The Standard Edition of the Complete Psychological Works of Sigmund Freud, Vol. XXIII: An Outline of Psychoanalysis*, London, 1964, reproduced by arrangement with Mark Paterson & Associates.

Extracts from A. R. Luria, *The Man with a Shattered World: A History of a Brain Wound* (1972), by permission of Random House UK, London.

Library of Congress Cataloging-in-Publication Data

Kaplan-Solms, Karen.
  Clinical studies in neuro-psychoanalysis : introduction to a depth neuropsychology / Karen Kaplan-Solms & Mark Solms ; foreword, Arnold Z. Pfeffer.—2nd. ed.
    p. cm.
  Includes bibliographical references and index.
  ISBN 1-59051-026-7 (pbk.)
  1. Neuropsychiatry.   2. Psychoanalysis.   3. Neurobehavioral disorders.
  I. Solms, Mark.   II. Title.
  [DNLM: 1. Psychoanalysis.   2. Biological Psychiatry.   3. Neuropsychology.
  4. Psychoanalytic Therapy—methods—Case Report. WM 460 K177c 2001]
  RC341 .K293 2001
  616.89'17—dc21

                                                                    2001050012

CONTENTS

PART II
Observations

PART III
Integration

ABOUT THE AUTHORS

Karen Kaplan-Solms is a speech and language pathologist and neuropsychologist. She was an Honorary Lecturer in Neurosurgery at the London Hospital Medical College at the time she conducted this research. She is an Associate Member of the British Psycho-Analytical Society. She has published broadly in neuropsychological and psychoanalytic journals.

Mark Solms is an Associate Member of the British Psycho-Analytical Society and an Honorary Member of the New York Psychoanalytic Society. He is an Honorary Lecturer in Neurosurgery at St Bartholomew's & the Royal London School of Medicine and a Lecturer in Psychology at University College London. His books include *A Moment of Transition* (co-edited with M. Saling, 1990) and *The Neuropsychology of Dreams* (1997), and he is a co-editor of the new interdisciplinary journal *Neuro-Psychoanalysis* (with E. Nersessian). He is currently editing and translating the forthcoming *Complete Neuroscientific Works of Sigmund Freud* (4 vols), the *Revised Standard Edition of the Complete Psychological Works of Sigmund Freud* (24 vols), and *The Brain and the Inner World: An Introduction to the Neuroscience of Subjective Experience* (with Oliver Turnbull).

PREFACE

The research described in this book was conducted over a long period of time, starting in 1985. From the outset, we had a lot to learn about both of the fields that we wanted to combine in this research. We trust readers will not judge these early steps too harshly, especially with respect to our handling of psychoanalytic technique. For this reason also, we wish to express our appreciation to the patients described in this book, whose misfortune became the basis of our learning. We hope that our efforts were of some personal benefit to them. We also hope that through this book their suffering will contribute something to the advancement of knowledge and will thereby benefit others. Lastly, we would like to thank very sincerely the following people, all of whom contributed fundamentally, in different ways, to making this work possible: Cecil Kaplan, Lotte Köhler, Baljeet Mehra, Percy Miller, Arnold Pfeffer, the late Sydney Press, Dorothy Tobiansky, Oliver Turnbull, and Clifford Yorke.

This research was supported by a generous grant from the Köhler-Stiftung, Munich.

May 2000

FOREWORD

The present volume is based loosely on a selection of papers that were presented during four series of lectures and clinical presentations, delivered monthly during 1993–94, 1994–95, 1997–98, and 1998–99, at the New York Psychoanalytic Institute. The theoretical lectures were presented by Dr Mark Solms and the clinical cases by Dr Karen Kaplan-Solms (then both Hon. Lecturers in Neurosurgery at St. Bartholomew's and the Royal London Hospital School of Medicine). These presentations formed part of an ongoing scientific programme at the New York Psychoanalytic Institute, which began in September 1990, when Dr James Schwartz (Professor of Neuroscience at the Columbia University School of Medicine) arranged for ten distinguished neuroscientists in each of the years 1990–91 and 1991–92 to lecture on and discuss their work with a selected group of psychoanalysts. This study group continued to meet through 1992. In 1992–93, Dr Jason Brown (Clinical Professor of Neurology at New York University Medical Center) arranged a third series of ten lectures by distinguished neuroscientists. There are now 50 members in the Neuro-Psychoanalysis group, including members of the Columbia

University, New York University, and New York Psychoanalytic
Societies. This group formed the nucleus of the Solms' audience,
which consisted of a larger number of psychoanalysts and neuroscientists from various centres. The material they presented, and
therefore the contents of this volume, represents the fruition of one
aspect of mind–brain correlation.

Freud, in his 1895 "Project for a Scientific Psychology", attempted to join the emerging discipline of psychoanalysis with
the neuroscience of his time. But that was 100 years ago, when the
neuron had only just been described, and Freud was forced—
through lack of pertinent knowledge—to abandon his project. We
have had to wait many decades before the sort of data which
Freud needed finally became available. Now, these many years
later, because of advances in clinical methods and scientific technology, contemporary neuroscience allows for the resumption
of the search for correlations between the findings of the two disciplines.

The method of study used by Karen Kaplan-Solms and
Mark Solms is in the clinical tradition of Aleksandr Romanovich
Luria: the correlation of localized brain lesions, such as tumours
and strokes and surgical resections, with the results of extensive
psychoanalytic exploration, to discern changes in deep psychology. In this way, the neurological organization of various mental
functions of interest to the psychoanalyst may be determined.

The Drs Solms are uniquely qualified for this task, having
trained in both psychoanalysis and the neurosciences, and the
work described in this volume ushers in a new era for our field.

Arnold Z. Pfeffer, M.D.
Chairman, Neuro-Psychoanalysis Center
New York Psychoanalytic Institute

PART I

FOUNDATIONS

CHAPTER ONE

The historical origins of psychoanalysis in neuroscience

Introduction

The aims of this book are modest but far-reaching. They are modest in the sense that the book aims to introduce (and illustrate) a new scientific method, which consists in nothing more than a combination of two existing methods. The far-reaching aims of the book arise from the scope of the opportunities that are created by this new method, for we firmly believe that it paves the way for an integration—on a sound empirical basis—of psychoanalysis and neuroscience, the two major approaches to the study of mental life which characterized the twentieth century.

It is easy to forget that psychoanalysis is a young science. According to its pioneer, it was born "in 1895 or 1900 or somewhere in between". These dates mark the period during which Sigmund

This chapter and parts of chapters two and four are based on a lecture entitled "The Origins of Psychoanalysis in Neuroscience", delivered by Mark Solms at the Neuro-Psychoanalysis Center of the New York Psychoanalytic Institute on 2 October 1993. A version of these chapters appeared in Solms (1998a).

Freud abandoned the relative security of the neuroscientific methods passed down to him by his teachers for an entirely new approach to mental science. This new approach—psychoanalysis—arose directly out of the mystery of the mind–body problem. The essence of that mystery was (and always has been) this: how is subjective awareness—consciousness—produced by the anatomical structures and physiological functions of the brain? By the time that Freud confronted this problem, he had studied the physical side of the mind–body equation (the structures and functions of the nervous system) for almost 20 years. Starting in 1877 with the problem of the fine structure of spinal ganglion cells in a lowly animal, Freud had moved gradually through the animal series from crustacea and fishes to the human being, up the nervous system via the spinal cord and brainstem to the cerebral cortex, and from the structure of individual nerve cells to the functions of the brain as a whole, until he finally reached the prototypical problem of human neuropsychology: the cerebral localization of language (i.e. the interpretation of the aphasias).

During this gradual transition from histology to neuropsychology, Freud had also moved from the orderly world of laboratory medicine to the disorders of the clinic. There, in his everyday medical work, like other neurologists of his day, he was forced to grapple with what was then one of the most difficult problems of clinical medicine: the physiologically inexplicable symptomatology of hysteria and the other neuroses. This confrontation completed the shift from the physical end of the psycho-physical equation to its psychic end: to subjective experience.

It was these two problems—aphasia and the neuroses, which began to dominate Freud's scientific attention from the winter of 1885—that brought him face to face with the mysteries of the mind–body relationship, and ultimately it was these two problems that prompted him, in 1895 or 1900 or somewhere in between, to abandon neuroscientific methods for psychoanalysis.

It will be well worth our effort, in view of the task that we have set ourselves—namely, the integration of psychoanalysis and neuroscience—to consider precisely why, in the first place, these problems forced Freud to abandon the one approach for the other. This will identify the significant obstacles we have to overcome if we are going to reunite these apparently antithetical approaches in a sustainable way—that is, if we are going to unite psychoanalysis and neuroscience in a way that pays due regard to the considerable differences that have divided them for the past 100 years.

The clinico-anatomical method

It is no accident that Freud shifted from neuroscience to psychoanalysis at a point when he had redirected his scientific attention from comparative neuroanatomy to the problems of human neuropsychology, and when he had exchanged laboratory methods for those of the clinic. Just as it is easy to forget that psychoanalysis is a young science, so too it is easy to forget that the term "neuroscience" covers a wide range of activities and methods. If one surveys the literature that has begun to accumulate in recent years on the possible physical correlates of the psychological functions and mechanisms that have been brought to light by psychoanalysis, it is surprising to note how many authors seek their physical correlates directly in the basic concepts or discoveries of neurophysiology, or functional anatomy, or even in molecular biology.[1] What these authors ignore is the fact that psychoanalysis is, first and foremost, a *clinical* science and, furthermore, a *psychology*.

How is one to bridge the gap between the clinically derived, psychological concepts of psychoanalysis and the experimentally derived concepts of physiology and anatomy without having recourse to what Freud once described in the same connection as "imaginings, transpositions and guesses" (Freud, 1950a [1887–1902])? Moreover, these attempts to integrate psychoanalysis and neuroscience via the basic sciences of anatomy and physiology ignore the fact that a discipline *already exists* within the broad ambit of neuroscience which, like psychoanalysis, is both a clinical and a psychological discipline, and which is devoted precisely to the problem of correlating the phenomena of mental life with the structures and functions of the brain. This is the science of *neuropsychology*, which evolved gradually over the past 50 years

---

[1] See the bibliography electronically archived at www.neuro-psa.com for a nearly complete listing of this literature.

out of the clinical discipline of behavioural neurology. The probability that this discipline, neuropsychology, provides the most serviceable point of contact between psychoanalysis and the neurosciences is underlined by the fact that it was precisely this discipline—or at least its progenitor, behavioural neurology—that spawned psychoanalysis in the first place.

This is how it happened. When Freud decided to specialize in neurology, it was still a relatively young discipline, which rested almost entirely on one scientific method. That was the method of *clinico-anatomical correlation*, which was carried over to the new speciality of neurology by some of the ablest practitioners of the art of internal medicine. As its name suggests, internal medicine concerned itself with the diagnosis and treatment of diseases in the interior of the body, which could for that reason not be apprehended directly in the living case and had to be inferred from their indirect clinical manifestations—external symptoms and signs. The physician had to wait for the death of the patient and the pathologist's report before he could determine conclusively whether or not his clinical diagnosis had been correct. But with the accumulation of experience, over generations, regarding which clinical presentation during life tended to correlate with which pathological-anatomical findings at autopsy, it gradually became possible for the internal physician to recognize pathognomonic constellations of symptoms and signs and thereby to predict with reasonable accuracy the nature and location of the underlying disease, and to conduct the treatment accordingly. This was the origin of the concept of clinical *syndromes*, about which we shall have much to say in the pages to follow.

Neurology became a separate speciality within internal medicine as it became increasingly evident not only that the brain—like all other organs—was subject to its own special pathologies peculiar to its own special tissues, but also that damage to different parts of the brain produced widely different clinical syndromes. On this basis, a specialized subgroup of internal physicians gradually came into being who mastered the art of recognizing the nature and location of the externally invisible diseases of the nervous system on the basis of their pathognomonic external symptoms and signs. When Freud trained in clinical neurology in the early

1880s, this was the art that he learned: rational diagnosis and treatment of neurological diseases by the syndrome method, which was based on medical knowledge obtained by the method of clinico-anatomical correlation. In fact, we are told that Freud was a particularly gifted practitioner of this art. In his *Autobiographical Study* he wrote:

> I was able to localize the site of a lesion ... so accurately that the pathological anatomist had no further information to add. ... The fame of my diagnoses and of their post-mortem confirmation brought me an influx of American physicians to whom I lectured upon the patients in my department. [Freud, 1925d, p. 12]

Freud also published a series of clinical articles at the time, attesting to his skill, which Jelliffe (another neurologist/psychoanalyst) later described as "models of good neurological deduction" (1937, p. 702).

Localizationism

The application of the clinico-anatomical method in neurology was, in these respects, no different from its application in other aspects of internal medicine. The aim was to describe typical clinical presentations (syndromes) that were pathognomonic of particular diseases affecting particular parts of the nervous system. This knowledge, in turn, became the basis for experimental research into the pathophysiological mechanisms of the diseases in question, and likewise for their treatment. This knowledge was also useful for the development of models of the *normal* functions of the nervous system. However, in one respect clinico-anatomical correlation in neurology was quite different from other aspects of internal medicine. Diseases of the brain—unlike those of any other organ—do not only produce physical symptoms and signs, they also have immediate and direct effects on the *mind* of the patient. The celebrated case of Phineas Gage, reported by Harlow in 1848 and followed up for twenty years, is classically cited in this con-

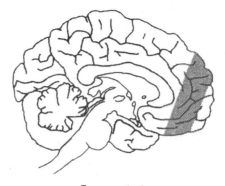

FIGURE 1-1

text. A tamping rod passed through the left frontal lobe of his brain (the shaded area in Fig. 1–1), with the following results:

> His physical health is good, and I am inclined to say that he has recovered ... [but] the equilibrium or balance, so to speak, between his intellectual faculties and animal propensities, seems to have been destroyed. He is fitful, irreverent, indulging at times in the grossest profanity (which was not previously his custom), manifesting but little deference for his fellows, impatient of restraint or advice when it conflicts with his desires, at times pertinaciously obstinate, yet capricious and vacillating, devising many plans of future operation, which are no sooner arranged than they are abandoned. ... In this regard his mind was radically changed, so decidedly that his friends and acquaintances said that he was "no longer Gage." [Harlow, 1868, p. 327]

This case, and countless others like it, made it abundantly clear to the early neurologists (as, indeed, had been clear to physicians throughout the ages) that neurological disease changes the patient as a *person*, and therefore that the human mind (or soul) was somehow represented in the physical tissues of the brain. Moreover, it soon became clear that, as was the case with the physical symptoms and signs of brain disease, damage to different *parts* of the brain also gave rise to different mental changes. On this basis, the clinico-anatomical method soon came to be put to a new and radically different use in the nascent field of neurology—namely, the *localization of mental functions*.

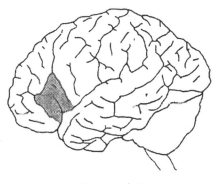

FIGURE 1-2

In the early 1860s, a French neurologist by the name of Pierre Paul Broca demonstrated that damage in a particular part of the brain, now known as Broca's area (Fig. 1-2), produced a highly characteristic mental syndrome (Broca's aphasia)—namely, loss of the power of speech despite normal functional capacity in the physical organs of articulation. (A case of this type is described in chapter five.) On the basis of this clinico-anatomical observation, the physical seat of an unequivocally mental function—symbolic vocalization—was identified for the first time, and henceforth the faculty of articulate speech was *localized* in a specific part of the brain. Ten years later, a German neurologist, Carl Wernicke, demonstrated that damage to a different part of the brain, now known as Wernicke's area (Fig. 1-3), produced a different mental syndrome—namely, loss of the capacity to *comprehend* spoken lan-

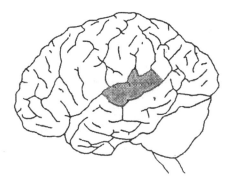

FIGURE 1-3

guage, despite preservation of a normal sense of hearing (Wernicke's aphasia)—and he localized the function of speech comprehension accordingly. (A case of Wernicke's aphasia is described in
chapter six.)

Broca's and Wernicke's seminal discoveries were followed by
a rapid series of clinico-anatomical correlations with regard to a
variety of other mental functions such as reading, writing, skilled
movement, and visual recognition, and on this basis a wide range
of psychological faculties were localized in a mosaic of so-called
centres on the surface of the human brain. This was the origin of the
sub-speciality of behavioural neurology, mentioned above, which
later developed into the modern discipline of neuropsychology.

We know from Freud's writings of that time that he was thoroughly versed in the methods and discoveries of this exciting new
branch of science. In fact, there is abundant evidence to suggest
that the clinico-anatomical localization of mental functions was a
subject of special interest to him. Clearly, then, Freud was aware,
long before he made the breakthrough into psychoanalysis, that
there was an established method available to the clinical neurologist by means of which it was possible to identify, on an empirical
basis, the physical seat of mental functions. But if that was so, it
raises the question: why did he not use this method to identify the
neurological correlates of the psychological processes that he later
discovered? And why do *we* not use it today?

The French and German schools of classical neurology

As we have said, Freud was a gifted physician, and it did not take
him long to master the syndrome method in his diagnostic work
and the clinico-anatomical method in his ongoing research. It also
did not take him long to discover the *limits* of this method. Freud
rapidly came to the conclusion that the neurology of his time was
just "a silly game of permutations" (Bernfeld, 1951). The decisive
shift appears to have occurred in the winter of 1885–86, just at the
point, ironically, when Freud decided to immerse himself fully in
the problems of clinical neurology. Although it is true that the
clinico-anatomical method was to all intents and purposes the only

method available to the late-nineteenth-century neurologist—and especially to the neurologist interested in the localization of mental functions—it was used in subtly different ways within two distinct schools of Continental neurology. In the *German* school (i.e. in the German-language medical schools), in which Freud was initially trained, the emphasis fell squarely on the *anatomical* side of the clinico-anatomical equation. According to this school, the primary aim of neurological science was not simply to describe which syndromes correlated with which lesions, but rather to *explain* the mechanisms of the clinical phenomena—and thereby the corresponding *normal* functions—on the basis of existing anatomical and physiological theory. In short, the primary aim of German neurological science was to develop anatomical and physiological theory. Clinical material served the secondary purpose of demonstrating and confirming existing anatomical and physiological theory. Accordingly the clinical facts were subordinated to the anatomical and physiological theories. This approach reflected the broader ideals of the Helmholtz school of medicine, which had pledged the following scientific oath in 1848:

> No other forces than the common physical and chemical ones are active within the organism. In those cases which cannot at the time be explained by these forces one has either to find the specific way or form of their action by means of the physical-mathematical method or to assume new forces equal in dignity to the chemical-physical forces inherent in matter, reducible to the forces of attraction and repulsion. [Du Bois Reymond, 1842, emphasis added]

In the *French* school of neurology, on the other hand, the emphasis fell very much upon the *clinical* side of the equation. According to this school, which collected around the personality of Charcot and the famous wards of the Salpêtrière Hospital, the primary task of neurological science was to establish new clinical facts, regardless of anatomical and physiological theory.[2] The goal

---

[2] The tension between the German and French schools of neurology, part of a broader trend in the history of science, is expressed in the conflicts between "classical" versus "romantic" science, "nomothetic" versus "ideographic" psychology, "hospital" versus "laboratory" medicine, and so on. (See Sacks, 1990.)

of French neurology, therefore, was not so much to *explain* the
various clinical pictures on the basis of existing theory, but rather
to identify, classify, and *describe* them. French neurology was, first
and foremost, nosology:[3]

> In the case of the . . . [German approach] the clinical picture
> and the [clinical] type play no principal part; on the other
> hand, another characteristic comes into prominence, which is
> explained by the evolution of the German clinicians: a ten-
> dency to make a physiological interpretation of the clinical
> condition and the interrelation of the symptoms. The clinical
> observation of the French undoubtedly gains in self-suffi-
> ciency in that it relegates physiological considerations to a
> second place. Their removal, however, may be the chief expla-
> nation of the puzzling impression made by the French clinical
> methods on the uninitiated. In this, incidentally, there is no
> neglect, but a deliberate exclusion which is considered expedi-
> ent. [Freud, 1892–94, pp. 134–135][4]

The following quotation graphically illustrates the difference between these two ways of applying the clinico-anatomical method:

> Charcot . . . never tired of defending the rights of purely clini-
> cal work, which consists in seeing and ordering things, against
> the encroachments of theoretical medicine. On one occasion
> there was a small group of us, all students from abroad, who,
> brought up on German academic physiology, were trying
> his patience with our doubts about his clinical innovations.
> "But that can't be true," one of us objected, "it contradicts the

---

[3] "The word *nosological* in English refers to the nomenclature and classification of disease, but [in French neurology] it is the clinical method of
investigation in its widest sense which is . . . that method of investigation
which argues from effect to cause, commencing with a study of the disease at
the bedside, as distinguished from the converse [German] method of *a priori*
reasoning, with the teachings of physiology for its basis" (Savill, in Charcot,
1889, p. 9).

[4] Strachey appended the following footnote to this passage: "It may be
remarked that Freud himself followed the French method to a large extent, at
all events in his earlier classificatory work. See in particular his first paper on
anxiety neurosis (1895b)." A similar viewpoint is expressed by Levin (1978, p.
64): "Freud's early writing on hysteria was devoted largely to establishing the
existence of standard patterns of symptoms . . . a uniform clinical pattern."

Young–Helmholtz theory [of vision]." He did not reply "So much the worse for the theory, clinical facts come first" or words to that effect; but he did say something which made a great impression on us: ["*Theory is good; but it doesn't prevent things from existing.*"] [Freud, 1893f, p. 13][5]

This was one of Freud's favourite anecdotes. Its affinity with the lines attributed to Mephistopheles in Goethe's *Faust* (Part 1, Scene 4), which Freud also cited more than once with approval (e.g. 1924b, p. 149), is noteworthy: "*Grey, dear friend, is all theory, / And green alone Life's golden tree.*"

As is well known, during a period of study at the Salpêtrière in 1885–86, Freud moved from being under the direct, personal influence of some of the leading figures of the German school of neurology (Theodor Meynert in particular) to being under the direct, personal influence of Charcot. This shift had a decisive influence on his thinking, and especially on his attitude to clinico-anatomical localization.

What can only be called a "conversion" from mechanistic physiology to clinical medicine occurred during Freud's travelling fellowship to the Salpêtrière (1885 to 1886), when he fell under the influence of the great neurologist Charcot . . . his contact with Charcot breathed life into his previously sterile clinical expertise. [Accardo, 1982, p. 452]

The reason for this shift was simple. Although the differences between the German and French schools of neurology complemented each other well in regard to most neurological disorders, with the one school emphasizing the anatomical and the other the clinical side of the equation, there was one group of diseases—which were considered at the time to fall under the domain of neurology—that threw the differences between the two approaches into sharp relief. These were the *neuroses*, and hysteria

---

[5] Similar sentiments are expressed in the following statement attributed to Claude Bernard, quoted in the English edition of Charcot's clinical lectures (1889): "Set up first the medical problem which arises from the observation of a malady, and afterwards seek for a physiological explanation. To act otherwise would be to risk overlooking the patient, and distorting the malady" (p. 8).

and neurasthenia in particular, for which no demonstrable lesion of the nervous system could be found at autopsy to account for the clinical symptomatology observed during the life of the patient.

The lack of a demonstrable lesion posed no serious problems for the French school of neurology: Charcot simply proceeded to *describe* the pathognomonic clinical syndromes of hysteria and neurasthenia, as he had done with countless other "nervous" diseases. The neuroses were for Charcot, as Freud (1893f) wrote at the time, "just another topic in neuropathology".[6] However, for the German neurologists the problem was wellnigh insoluble. How was one to explain in anatomical and physiological terms the physiological mechanism of a clinical syndrome that had no pathological–anatomical basis? As a result, some German neurologists, Freud's teachers among them, developed elaborate but completely unconvincing speculative theories, while others simply declared that the neuroses were not fit subjects for serious scientific attention; if there was no anatomical lesion, then there was no disease.[7]

During the crucial period that Freud studied under Charcot, this was the subject that most interested him. By then, Charcot believed that clinico-anatomical knowledge of the major structural diseases of the nervous system was more or less complete; what

---

[6] Freud's endorsement of this viewpoint is evident from the following passage: "Hysteria is a neurosis in the strictest sense of the word—that is to say, not only have no perceptible changes in the nervous system been found in this illness, but it is not to be expected that any refinement of anatomical techniques would reveal any such changes. Hysteria is based wholly and entirely on physiological modifications of the nervous system and its essence should be expressed in a formula which took account of the conditions of excitability in the different parts of the nervous system. A physio-pathological formula of this kind has not yet, however, been discovered; we must be content meanwhile to define the neuroses in a purely nosographical fashion by the totality of symptoms occurring in it, in the same sort of way as Graves' disease is characterized by a group of symptoms—exopthalmos, struma, tremor, acceleration of the pulse and psychical change—without any consideration of the closer connection between these phenomena" (1888b, p. 41).

[7] Meynert, for example, wrote the following in the preface to his (1884) textbook on psychiatry: "The reader will find no other definition of 'Psychiatry' in this book but the one given on the title page: 'Clinical Treatise on *Diseases of the Fore-Brain.*' The historical term psychiatry, i.e. 'treatment of the soul,' implies more than we can accomplish, and transcends the bounds of accurate scientific investigation" (p. v).

was needed next was a thorough clinical study of hysteria and the other neuroses. Freud concurred with this opinion, and he even went so far as to inform his faculty that he had "nothing more to learn from the German medical schools" (1956a [1886]). Accordingly, he soon became a devoted pupil of Charcot—his "unqualified admirer"—and upon his return to Vienna he expounded his views whenever and wherever he could, much to the irritation of his old teachers. It is important to notice, however, that this shift of allegiances was not a shift away from neurology and towards psychology. It applied equally to Freud's work with conventional neurological disorders as it did to his work on the neuroses. Similarly, it is important to note that for Freud the neuroses were not non-physical, *psychological* disorders; rather, they were non-anatomical—that is to say, non-localizable—*physiological* disorders.[8] At that point in his scientific development, Freud did not distinguish at all between psychology and physiology.[9] We will return to this point shortly.

---

[8] This is evident, for example, from the following two quotations, the second of which was quoted above: "Neurasthenia is not a clinical picture in the sense of textbooks based too exclusively on pathological anatomy: it should rather be described as a *mode of reaction of the nervous system*" (1887a, p. 35, emphasis added). "Hysteria is a neurosis in the strictest sense of the word—that is to say, not only have no perceptible changes in the nervous system been found in this illness, but it is not to be expected that any refinement of anatomical techniques would reveal any such changes. Hysteria is based wholly and entirely on *physiological modifications of the nervous system* and its essence should be expressed in a formula which took account of the conditions of excitability in the different parts of the nervous system" (1888b, p. 41, emphasis added).

[9] Freud's writings from the late 1880s make it abundantly clear that he drew no distinction between physiology and psychology (cf. Levin, 1978; Stewart, 1969). For the young Freud, like so many of his contemporaries (Amacher, 1954), psychology was simply the physiology of the cerebral cortex. This is demonstrated, for example, by the following remarks on hypnotism: "The question might still be asked whether all the phenomena of hypnosis must *somewhere* pass through the psychical sphere; in other words—for the question can have no other sense—whether the changes in excitability which occur in hypnosis invariably affect only the region of the cerebral cortex. . . . We possess no criterion which enables us to distinguish exactly between a psychical process and a physiological one, between an act occurring in the cerebral cortex and one occurring in the subcortical substance" (Freud, 1888–89, p. 84).

Freud's critique
of narrow localizationism:
dynamic functional systems

Gradually, with increasing clinical experience, and under the theoretical influence of the English neurologist John Hughlings Jackson, Freud began to edge away from Charcot and to develop a viewpoint that was at the time rather unique. Charcot was content to describe the clinical syndromes of hysteria and neurasthenia— on the assumption that their pathological–anatomical correlates (which, he believed, had a hereditary aetiology) would eventually yield to advances in microanatomical and other laboratory techniques:

> When Charcot turned to autopsy studies, he found no lesion in hysteria, but, undaunted, he continued his studies in this purely anatomical perspective, seeking for "an analogy to anatomical lesions." [Goetz, Bonduelle, & Gelfand, 1995, p. 129]

Freud, on the other hand, came to the view (sometime between 1888 and 1893) that a basis for the clinical syndromes of the neuroses would *never* be found in pathological anatomy:

> What might be the nature of the lesion in hysterical paralysis, which dominates the situation, without regard to the localization or extent of the lesion or of the anatomy of the nervous system? We have several times heard from M. Charcot that it is a cortical lesion, but one that is purely dynamic or functional. [However] . . . if one reads that "there must be a hysterical lesion" in such and such a centre, the same centre in which an organic lesion would produce a corresponding organic syndrome, and if one recalls that one is accustomed to localize a hysterical dynamic lesion in the same manner as an organic lesion, one is led to believe that behind the expression "dynamic lesion" there is hidden the idea of a lesion like oedema or anaemia, which are in fact transitory organic affections. I, on the contrary, assert that the lesion in hysterical paralyses must be completely independent of the anatomy of the nervous system, since *in its paralyses and other manifestations it behaves as*

though anatomy did not exist or as though it had no knowledge of it.
[Freud, 1893c, pp. 168–169][10]

The alternative theory that Freud proposed in order to account for hysterical paralyses asserted that the hysterical "lesion" should be conceived of as a *psychological* disturbance (described in *functional* terms), the physiological correlate of which consisted of "associations" that existed *between* the anatomical elements of the nervous system:

> The lesion in hysterical paralyses consists in nothing other than the inaccessibility of the [paralysed] organ or function concerned to the associations of the conscious ego; . . . [a] purely functional alteration. [p. 172]

He based this conclusion on two major observations, which he had first made in regard to *another* subject in neurology, the subject that had first revealed to him the limits of the clinico-anatomical method: the problem of *aphasia*. This is, of course, precisely the subject to which the clinico-anatomical method had first been applied for the localization of mental functions—by Broca and Wernicke—twenty or so years before. Freud's two critical observations were the following. First, he observed that psychological faculties break down according to the logic of *their own functional laws*, not according to the laws of cerebral anatomy. For this reason, Freud concluded that psychological syndromes needed to be both described and explained in their own *psychological* terms. To do otherwise "would be to risk overlooking the patient, and distorting the malady" (see fn. 5 above). Second, Freud observed that psychological faculties are never *destroyed* by localized brain lesions—they are not simply removed like pieces from a jigsaw puzzle. Rather, they are distorted and changed in *dynamic* ways that reflect a mutual interdependence with other faculties. Freud concluded that psychological faculties, which have their own functional laws, were complicated things arising out of complex interplays of forces that exist between more elementary compo-

---

[10] In his obituary of Charcot, Freud (1893f) remarked that his master "did not make a sufficiently sharp distinction between organic nervous affections and neuroses, either as regards their aetiology or in other respects" (p. 23).

nent functions. Such complex processes are the products of dynamic functional systems, which are capable of constantly organizing and adapting themselves to changing circumstances, and therefore they must be conceived of as distributed *between* the static elements of the nervous system and cannot be localized *within* discrete anatomical centres.[11] Freud concluded, therefore, that the clinico-anatomical method—which localized mental functions within a mosaic of centres on the surface of the hemispheres of the brain—was wholly incapable of accommodating the essential attributes of mental activity. He held to this view for the rest of his life: "The psychical topography that I have developed . . . has nothing to do with the anatomy of the brain, and actually only touches it at one point.[12] What is unsatisfactory in this picture— and I am aware of it as clearly as anyone—is due to our complete ignorance of the *dynamic* nature of the mental process" (Freud, 1939a [1937-39] p. 97).

It is of crucial importance for us to note that Freud first reached these conclusions not in relation to hysteria or any other neurosis, but, rather, in relation to *aphasia*—that is, in relation to a syndrome that only occurs in the context of a definite organic lesion. In other words, these were conclusions that Freud arrived at while he was still a fully fledged *neurologist*. They did not mark a break with neurology, but, rather, a break with a particular research tradition

---

[11] "In psychology the simple idea is to us something elementary which we can clearly differentiate from its connection with other ideas. This is why we are tempted to assume that its physiological correlate, i.e., the modification of the nerve cells which originates from the stimulation of the nerve fibres, be also something simple and localizable. Such an inference is, of course, entirely unwarranted; the qualities of this modification have to be established for themselves and independently of their psychological concomitants. What then is the physiological correlate of the simple idea emerging and re-emerging? Obviously nothing static, but something in the nature of a process . . . it starts at a specific point in the cortex and from there spreads over the whole cortex and along certain pathways" (Freud, 1891b, pp. 55–56).

[12] This refers to the primary perceptual modalities of consciousness [the system Pcpt.-Cs.], which Freud always localized in the cerebral cortex (see, for example, Freud, 1920g). From his aphasia monograph onward, Freud (1891b) argued that only the functions of early unimodal cortices—which he described as the "cornerstones" of the speech apparatus—were localizable.

within neurology (the narrow localizationist tradition), which, he believed, was incapable of accommodating the complex clinical reality that Charcot had taught him to respect above all else. The fact that Freud's break with this localizationist tradition did not represent a break with neurology is underlined by the fact that he went on to make similar observations with regard to other complex functional systems of the brain which were entirely non-psychological in nature. In his writings on the disorders of voluntary movement that occur in cerebral palsy, for example, Freud went out of his way to demonstrate that the relevant functions could not be localized. In a series of monographs on the subject, as in his book on aphasia, Freud appealed to dynamic and genetic—that is to say, developmental—factors, rather than static and anatomical ones, to explain the various movement disorders in terms of a regression in the complex functional apparatus that supports them (cf. Schott, 1981).

It was only *later*—between 1893 and 1900—that Freud applied these principles to psychopathology, when he made a further theoretical innovation (discussed in chapter three). This is when the new science of psychoanalysis was born. The fact that Freud's critique of narrow localizationist neurology in favour of a neurology based on dynamic principles places him in a particular tradition *within* neurology is of critical importance for us, because in chapter two we want to show how that tradition has developed and expanded since Freud's death, and how *a neuroscientific method for studying the cerebral organization of mental functions was established on precisely the principles that Freud adumbrated in his critique.* This is obviously of great relevance to us in our quest for a method by means of which we may rejoin psychoanalysis with neuroscience.

Between 1893 and 1900, then, Freud *the neurologist* generalized the conclusions that he had reached with regard to speech and voluntary movement to the whole field of higher mental functioning, and he wrote these fateful words in *The Interpretation of Dreams*, which marked the actual parting of the ways between psychoanalysis and neuroscience:

> I shall entirely disregard the fact that the mental apparatus with which we are here concerned is also known to us in the

form of an anatomical preparation, and I shall carefully avoid the temptation to determine psychical locality in any anatomical fashion. I shall remain upon purely psychological ground, and I propose simply to follow the suggestion that we picture the instrument which carries out our mental functions as resembling a compound microscope or a photographic apparatus, or something of the kind. On that basis, psychical locality will correspond to a point inside the apparatus at which one of the preliminary stages of an image comes into being. In the microscope or telescope, as we know, these occur at ideal points, regions in which no tangible component of the apparatus is situated.[13] [Freud, 1900a, p. 536]

This was a radical rejection of the narrow localizationism of classical German neurology. What Freud retained, however, and carried over into the new field of psychoanalysis, was almost everything else that he had learned as a neurologist. That is, he continued to rely on the clinical method of the French school of neurology, with its special emphasis on the careful descriptive study of individual clinical cases, with the aim of identifying regular clinical patterns with particular pathological significance; he continued to explain

---

[13] Consider also the following passages:

We can avoid any possible abuse of this method of representation by recollecting that ideas, thoughts and psychical structures in general must never be regarded as localized *in* organic elements of the nervous system but rather, as one might say, *between* them. . . . Everything that can be an object of our internal perception is *virtual*, like the image produced in a telescope by the passage of light-rays. But we are justified in assuming the existence of systems (which are not in any way psychical and can never be accessible to our psychical perception) like the lenses of the telescope, which cast the image. [Freud, 1900a, p. 611, emphasis added]

It will soon be clear what the mental apparatus is; but I must beg you not to ask what it is constructed of. That is not a subject of psychological interest. Psychology can be as indifferent to it as, for instance, optics can be to the question of whether the walls of a telescope are made of metal or cardboard. We shall leave entirely on one side the *material* line of approach, but not so the *spatial* one. For we picture the unknown apparatus which serves the activities of the mind as being really like an instrument constructed of several parts (which we speak of as "agencies"), each of which performs a particular function and which have a fixed spatial relation to one another. [Freud, 1926e, p. 194]

the clinical phenomena in terms of natural forces and energies, as he had been taught to do by his original masters in the Helmholtz school of medicine; and he continued to believe that these forces and energies were ultimately *somehow* representable as physical–chemical processes. The very existence of his "Project for a Scientific Psychology" (1950 [1895])—with its aspiration to "represent psychical processes as quantitatively determinate states of specifiable material particles, thus making those processes perspicuous and free from contradiction" (p. 295)—attests to this fact. All that he abandoned was the narrow localizationist notion that psychological processes, which have complex, dynamic, functional organizations, can be concretely located in discrete anatomical structures. Under the influence of Charcot's teachings, Freud was able to approach clinical phenomena without having to force upon them a preconceived physiological–anatomical scheme.[14] On this basis, Freud resolved to "content myself with the *clinical* explanation of the neuroses" (Freud, 1950a [1887–1902], p. 137 [letter dated 12 December 1895]). Henceforth, rather than attempt to explain a clinical syndrome by correlating it with hypothetical damage to one or another anatomical region, Freud investigated the internal psychological structure of the syndrome and explained it by refer-

---

[14] The meticulous observation of the individual clinical case that Charcot recommended gradually led Freud to the realization that particular clinical presentations tend to co-occur with particular psychological events in the *history* of these cases. Thus, he came to associate particular clinical syndromes with particular *developmental* factors, and clinico-anatomical correlation, which sought to localize the pathological/aetiological factor within the tissue of the brain, gave way to clinico-psychological correlation, which sought to "localize" the pathological/aetiological factor within the developing mind. Then, as is well known, with increasing clinical experience Freud gradually moved away from the identification of actual traumatic events in the past life of the patient (whereby different neuroses were linked to different types of trauma, occurring at different stages of development) towards a fuller understanding of the effects of the complex interplay of constitutional and environmental factors upon the internal structure of the developing mind. Thus, to an ever-increasing degree, the search for an aetiological *event* gave way to the elucidation of underlying pathogenic *factors*. This transition is exemplified, for instance, by a comparison of Freud's early nosographic studies on obsessional ideas (ca. 1895) with his later writings on anal character types (ca. 1908).

ence to a functional system that he pictured as being dynamically represented *between* the elements of the brain.

That is why Freud continued to acknowledge throughout his scientific life that the mental apparatus that he hypothesized to account for his clinical observations was a *provisional* construct, a system of *functional relations* which must be represented *somehow* in the tissues of the brain, and why he always continued to insist that we should "not mistake the scaffolding for the building" (1900a) and so on. Freud's many comments to the effect that psychoanalysis must someday be rejoined with neuroscience are well known.[15] But he insisted that this would not be possible until neu-

---

[15]Consider, for example, the following passages (which are just a few from among many):

It would have to be possible in some manner which cannot *yet* be indicated to represent [psychical] paths by organic elements of the nervous system. [1905c, p. 148, emphasis added]

The [psychoanalytic] theory does not by any means fail to point out that neuroses have an organic basis—though it is true that it does not look for that basis in any pathological anatomical changes, and *provisionally* substitutes the conception of organic functions for the chemical changes which we should expect to find but which we are at present unable to apprehend. [1905e, p. 113, emphasis added]

We must recollect that all our *provisional* ideas in psychology will presumably some day be based on an organic substructure. [1914c, p. 78, emphasis added]

The theoretical structure of psycho-analysis is in truth a superstructure, which will *one day* be set upon its organic foundation. But we are still ignorant of this. What distinguishes psycho-analysis as a science is not the material which it handles but the technique with which it works. [1916–17, pp. 388–389, emphasis added]

The indefiniteness of all our discussions on what we describe as metapsychology is of course due to the fact that we know nothing of the excitatory process that takes place in the elements of the psychical systems, and that we cannot feel justified in framing any hypotheses on the subject. . . . The deficiencies in our description would probably vanish if we were *already* in a position to replace the psychological terms by physiological or chemical ones. . . . Biology is truly a land of unlimited possibilities. We may expect it to give us the most surprising information and we cannot guess what answers it will return in a few dozen years to the questions we have put to it. They may be of a kind which will blow away the whole of our artificial structure of hypotheses. [1920g, pp. 30, 60]

In view of the intimate connection between the things that we distinguish as physical and mental, we may *look forward* to the day when

roscience developed a method that was capable of accommodating the complex and dynamic nature of the human mental process. Until that was possible, Freud insisted, psychoanalysis should continue to investigate and clarify the internal organization and functional principles of the mental apparatus in its own terms, using a purely clinical method, and disregarding its anatomical representation.

Therefore, after making his final attempt to sketch the psychological dynamics of the brain in quasi-anatomical terms in his 1895 "Project",[16] Freud disregarded the neuroanatomical viewpoint, pending future developments:

> Research has given irrefutable proof that mental activity is bound up with the function of the brain as it is with no other organ. We are taken a step further—we do not know how much—by the discovery of the unequal importance of the different parts of the brain and their special relations to particular parts of the body and to particular mental activities. But every attempt to go on from there to discover a *localization* of mental processes, every endeavour to think of ideas as stored up in nerve-cells and of excitations as travelling along nerve-fibres, has miscarried completely. . . . There is an hiatus here which at present cannot be filled, nor is it one of the tasks of psychology to fill it. Our psychical topography has *for the present* nothing to do with anatomy; it has reference not to anatomical localities, but to regions in the mental apparatus, wherever they may be situated in the body. In this respect our work is untrammelled and may proceed according to its own requirements. It will, however, be useful to remind ourselves that as things stand our hypotheses set out to be nothing but graphic illustrations.

---

paths of knowledge and, let us hope, influence will be opened up, leading from organic biology and chemistry to the field of neurotic phenomena. That day still seems a distant one, and for the present these illnesses are inaccessible to us from the direction of medicine. . . . However much philosophy may ignore the gulf between the physical and the mental, it still exists for our immediate experience and still more for our practical endeavours. [1926e, pp. 231, 247, emphasis added]

[16] We say *quasi*-anatomical because, due to the lack of pertinent knowledge, Freud's language in the "Project" is in fact a *functional* language (see Solms & Saling, 1986).

[Freud, 1915e, pp. 174–175; first emphasis added, the second emphasis is Freud's own]

Freud's standpoint can be restated as follows. In order to elucidate the neurological organization of a mental process, two steps are necessary. First, the process in question must be subjected to a fully *psychological* analysis, the aim of which is to elucidate the internal structure of the functional system in question, regardless of its cerebral organization. (This is the task to which Freud himself devoted his scientific life.) Only then will it be possible to accurately and validly identify the cerebral correlates of the psychological process in question. (This is the task that Freud left to the future, as no viable methods for achieving it were available, during his lifetime, for localizing *dynamic* functional systems of the sort that his psychological research revealed.) All of Freud's remarks on the relationship between psychoanalysis and neuroscience are compatible with this simple formulation of his standpoint.

This places psychoanalysis in a very particular relationship to the neurological sciences. It places its fundamental assumptions and basic method within a well-established tradition in behavioural neurology, a tradition that has always been closely associated with the clinical-descriptive emphasis first promulgated by Charcot, and which, following Jackson, has always rejected the notion that complex mental faculties can be narrowly localized in the brain. This is the *dynamic school of behavioural neurology*, which has been associated through the years with such outstanding physicians and theoreticians as Marie, von Monakow, Pick, Head, Goldstein, Luria, and Brown (see Riese, 1959). Similarly dynamic, anti-localizationist, functional concepts have recently spawned whole new schools of theoretical neuroscience—such as the "connectionist" and "neural darwinist" schools, which currently enjoy much popularity and influence.

The influence of the dynamic school of *clinical* neurology itself has waxed and waned over the decades. Currently it is on the wane. With the enormous strides that have been made in the use of technological auxiliary aids in medicine, the art of clinical judgement is no longer so highly valued, and the human factor in medicine is being lost. Ironically, therefore, one could say that psychoanalysis stands together with this branch of neurology as one of the last outposts of the great clinical traditions of classical internal medicine.

But the important point for our purposes (looking forwards rather than backwards) is that Freud carried over from neurology into psychology a basic method—namely the clinical-descriptive method of Charcot (or the method of syndrome analysis, as it later came to be known)—and a basic conceptualization of mind–brain relationships—namely the anti-localizationist or dynamic conceptualization—which gives pride of place to psychological methods of analysing psychological syndromes *regardless of whether or not they have an organic aetiology*. This methodology, and these basic principles, have determined the object of study of psychoanalysis, the way we go about studying it, and, most important of all, the sort of knowledge that it generates.

Therefore, if we now wish to integrate knowledge of this sort with knowledge about the brain, then our natural point of contact is with that branch of neuroscience which shares our basic assumptions, and out of which psychoanalysis grew—that is, with the *dynamic* school of clinical, behavioural neurology, which shortly after Freud's death (in 1939) gave rise to the new science of *dynamic neuropsychology*. If we try to relate our clinically generated psychoanalytical knowledge with knowledge about the brain which was generated by fundamentally incompatible methods, or by methods that Freud explicitly rejected, then not only are we confronted by the insoluble problem of having to rely on speculation, just as Freud did in 1895, but we also have to recognize that we may be doing violence to the basic pillars upon which psychoanalysis was built. Surely everyone who values psychoanalysis will agree—and this was always Freud's *most* fundamental viewpoint on the matter—that there is little point in accommodating psychoanalysis to neuroscience if it means that we have to abandon all that psychoanalysis has achieved in the process.

CHAPTER TWO

Psychoanalysis and the origins of dynamic neuropsychology: the work of Luria

In this chapter we describe one of the major developments that has occurred, since Freud's death, in the branch of neuroscience out of which psychoanalysis arose. We believe that this development provides a method by means of which psychoanalysis can be rejoined with neuroscience in a way that is compatible with Freud's basic assumptions.

Luria and Soviet psychoanalysis

In 1922, a young Russian psychologist wrote to Freud to apply for formal recognition of a new psychoanalytic society he had formed in the city of Kazan. This man was Aleksandr Romanovich Luria.[1]

This chapter is based on Solms (2000).

[1] For a full discussion of Luria's psychoanalytic career, see Leon (1982), Kozulin (1984), Angelini (1988), and Van der Veer and Valsiner (1991). The present account relies heavily upon the last-mentioned work.

Freud granted the recognition, and a brief correspondence ensued, which can still be studied in Luria's family archives in Moscow.[2] During the following two years, Luria conducted extensive psychoanalytical research, published a large number of articles, monographs, and brief reports, and conducted clinical work in a local psychiatric hospital.[3] Luria then moved to Moscow and joined the Russian Psychoanalytical Society, where he continued his intensive psychoanalytic programme for the remainder of the decade.[4] Luria was drawn to psychoanalysis, he wrote, because it was the only

---

[2] Three letters from Freud can be found in the archives (see Van der Veer & Valsiner, 1991, p. 87).

[3] The intensity and scope of Luria's involvement with psychoanalysis during this period is well illustrated by the wide-ranging series of reports that he published at the time in the *Internationale Zeitschrift für Psychoanalyse* (Luria, 1922a, 1922b, 1923a, 1923b, 1923d; see also Luria, 1923c, 1923e). The meticulous notes upon which these reports were based can still be consulted in the Luria archives. During the first 17 meetings of the Kazan Psychoanalytical Society, which were held between September 1922 and September 1923, Luria himself delivered 12 lectures. On 7 September 1922, he spoke on the "Present state of psychoanalysis". On 21 October, he presented a psychoanalytic study of sexual differences in dress, a subject to which he was later to return at the All-Russian Congress on Psychoneurology in Moscow (Luria, 1923c). On 10 December 1922, he addressed the Society on "The current crisis in Russian psychology". He spoke twice on 18 February 1923, firstly on "Some principles of psychoanalysis", followed by a psychoanalytical study of Leonid Andreev's play *Savva*. On 5 March, he spoke on "Psychoanalysis in the light of the main tendencies of modern psychology." Finally, on 18 March, he presented a study of sleep-onset phantasies. In addition to these early scientific activities in Kazan, Luria analysed patients (including, it is rumoured, Dostoevsky's granddaughter) at the local Kazan Psychiatric Hospital.

[4] See Luria, 1923f, 1924a, 1924b, 1925a, 1925b, 1925c, 1925d, 1926a, 1926b, 1926c, 1926d, 1926e, 1926f, 1926g, 1927a, 1927b, 1927c, 1928; Vygotsky and Luria, 1925. By the time that Luria moved to the Russian Psychoanalytical Society in Moscow, which had been founded in 1921, its formal activities included scientific meetings, publication of a book series entitled "The Psychological and Psychoanalytical Library", clinical work at the State Psychiatric Institute, and the running of a psychoanalytic kindergarten and laboratory. Jaroshevsky (1989, p. 131) claims that Stalin's son, Vasily, was among the children attending this kindergarten. The Russian Psychoanalytical Society included among its membership Sabina Spielrein, who later played a prominent role in Swiss and Viennese psychoanalytic circles (including in the conceptual development of the death drive). She also analysed Jean Piaget for a brief period. Luria not only performed administrative duties as the Society's

branch of psychology that was both solidly rooted in materialist science and studied the living experience of real human beings. Van der Veer and Valsiner (1991) state that "it is no exaggeration to say that the institutional history of psychoanalysis in the Soviet Union was to a substantial degree determined by his efforts" (p. 79).

However, the tide of political opinion soon turned against psychoanalysis in the Soviet Union, and by the early 1930s—fearing for his academic future, if not his life—Luria resigned from the Russian Psychoanalytical Society and abruptly ceased all psychoanalytic activities. He also delivered a penitent speech in which he admitted to his ideological mistakes—namely, according to the Party line of that time, that psychoanalysis "biologized" human behaviour and ignored its social origins.[5] This was a surprisingly

---

secretary, but he also conducted clinical and scientific work; the latter included a series of studies on dream-work, wherein he implanted dream thoughts under hypnosis and then observed transformations of the thoughts in subsequent manifest dream content. He presented numerous lectures and frequently participated in discussions at scientific meetings. On 29 May 1924, for instance, he presented a talk entitled "Psychoanalysis as a system of monistic psychology" (this was subsequently translated into English: see Luria, 1925a). In the following year, he spoke on "Affect as a non-abreacted reaction" (26 May), "Experimental study of the phantasies in a boy" (16 April), and "The use of experiments for psychoanalytic goals" (12 November). On 23 February 1927, he delivered a lecture entitled "The experimental study of children's primitive thinking", and on 17 March he presented a discussion of Bykhovsky's book on Freud's Metapsychology.

[5] Less than one month after presenting a sympathetic discussion of Freud's metapsychology, Luria suddenly asked to be relieved of his duties as secretary of the Russian Psychoanalytical Society. Within two years he had resigned from the society itself. At that point, he delivered the "penitent speech" (Lobner & Levitin, 1978, p. 19), in which he disassociated himself publicly from psychoanalysis (Pappenheim, 1990). He also published an article in which he admitted to his "psychoanalytic mistakes" (Kozulin, 1984, p. 88). A few years later, he contributed an article on psychoanalysis to the Great Soviet Encyclopedia (Luria, 1940) in which he dismissed it as "a false theory" belonging to "the sphere of hostile advanced [bourgeois] science", on the grounds that it "biologizes the complex, historically-determined conscious state of the human being" (p. 510). He never again discussed the subject of psychoanalysis in his published writings—apart from in his autobiography, where he described his youthful involvement with it as "an error": "Here, I thought, was a scientific approach that combined a strongly deterministic explanation of concrete, individual behaviour with an explanation of the

naive remark coming from somebody with so complex an understanding of Freud's teachings, but that was not the point.[6]

Luria's (ostensible) abandonment of psychoanalysis was undoubtedly the result of political and ideological pressure, rather
than developments in his scientific thinking. The facts supporting
this view are well documented in numerous places and do not
need to be discussed in detail here (see, for example, Kozulin, 1984;
Lobner & Levitin, 1978). Essentially, following increasing criticism
in the scientific literature and the public press between 1924 and
1929—including direct and personal criticism of Luria himself—
"psychoanalysis became a *scientia non grata* in the Soviet Union"
(Van der Veer & Valsiner, 1991, p. 78). After Luria was denounced
and "found guilty of ideological deviations" (Kozulin, 1984, p. 20),
his resignation from the Russian Psychoanalytical Society and his
subsequent public disavowal of his views was "the only way he
would be able to continue his important work" (Pappenheim,
1990, p. 5). Many of his colleagues were blacklisted, some were
even executed, and "those who survived lived in an atmosphere of
total suspicion" (p. 22).

However, as numerous authors have pointed out, the apparent
change in Luria's scientific direction did not really affect his underlying commitment to psychoanalytic ways of conducting research

---

origins of complex human needs in terms of natural science. Perhaps psychoanalysis could serve as the basis for a scientific *reale Psychologie*, one that
would overcome the nomothetic–ideographic distinction. . . . But I finally
concluded that it was an error to assume that one can deduce human behaviour from the biological 'depths' of the mind, excluding its social 'heights'"
(Luria, 1979, pp. 23–24).

[6] The charge that psychoanalysis "biologized" mental life is ironical in
view of the later direction that Luria's research followed. Sacks (1990) writes:
"There is, indeed, a fascinating contrast here to Freud. Freud started as a
biologist, a neurologist, and only later moved up to mental life, to the psyche;
whereas Luria started as a cultural relativist and a psychologist with a predominantly social-developmental orientation, and only later moved down
into neurophysiology and biology. . . . It was only when Luria came to grasp
the biological aspects firmly—he liked to speak here of the 'neurodynamics'
of nervous activity, as analogous to the 'psychodynamics' of which Freud
was speaking—that he was able to achieve the twofold unity which he had so
long needed and sought. It was only at this juncture that the 'double science'
of neuropsychology came into being, as an enterprise analogous to psychoanalysis" (pp. 188–189).

and conceptualizing his findings. The change in direction amounted to little more than window dressing:

> [His] published papers and official records must be taken not at face value but rather as rough material for subsequent distillation and decoding. [Kozulin, 1984, p. 1]

> In the case of Luria, it is not quite clear whether his renunciation of psychoanalysis in the 1930s was a result of, or a form of resistance against, the silencing of the topic. [p. 89][7]

> In short, Luria always managed to maintain professional integrity within his discipline, while adapting himself to the requirements of the authorities without. The subtle combination of inner autonomy and outward compliance has been a characteristic feature . . . in Luria's response to . . . Stalinism. [Joravsky, 1974, p. 24]

A survey of Luria's publications following his penitent disavowal of psychoanalysis clearly demonstrates that the basic conceptual and methodological debt that he owed to Freud was now merely "buried under layers of ideological verbiage" (Kozulin, 1984, p. 1). This accounts for the fact that, despite his public disavowal of psychoanalysis and all that it stood for, Luria continued to pursue the same scientific goals, using the same fundamental methods, in his post-psychoanalytic, neuropsychological period. This is evident from the fact that although the word "psychoanalysis" no longer appeared in Luria's publications (which reported experimental studies of free association and clinical studies of the development of various mental functions in normal and abnormal children),[8] these publications (e.g. Luria, 1929, 1932a, 1936, 1961, 1968a) continued to be cited in Grinstein's (1956–1975) *Index of Psychoanalytic Writings*. The continuity is perhaps most obvious in

---

[7] This might explain why Luria's (1940) encyclopaedia article on psychoanalysis combined a neutral description of its historical development and a favourable estimation of its conceptual, methodological, and clinical importance, with a blistering critique of its ideological premises.

[8] Other works by Luria in the immediate post-psychoanalytic period included a field study of cultural differences in thinking, conducted with a group of colleagues, in which Luria himself concentrated on "visual thinking" and "self analysis and evaluation of other individuals at various stages of personality development" (Luria, 1932c, p. 242). See also Luria and Vygotsky's (1930) intriguing book *Ape, Primitive Man and Child*, which did not appear in English until 1992.

Luria's (1932a) book *The Nature of Human Conflicts*. This book was based directly on the researches that he initiated while he was a member of the Russian Psychoanalytical Society, but the name of Freud and the subject of psychoanalysis were scrupulously avoided in its pages. Instead, Luria now conceptualized his findings within a *Jacksonian* framework—just as Freud (1891b) had done before him. Luria particularly emphasized Jackson's theory to the effect that

> the higher stratum of the nervous apparatus was inhibitory, restraining the primitive reactions of the older cerebral systems; this included the restraining and organising role of the morphologically higher strata of the apparatus as well as the analogous role of the higher functional systems, creating the complex processes of biological and historical evolution. Jackson . . . working on aphasia, pointed out the primary organising role played by speech on the voluntary and emotional disturbances occurring when these complex functional strata were injured. This exposition is of vital importance to us. [Luria, 1932a, p. 370]

Any psychoanalyst would recognize this model as his or her own. Thus, Michael Cole, who studied under Luria and corresponded with him from 1962 until Luria's death in 1977, wrote:

> Read in the proper way, *The Nature of Human Conflicts* is a unique source of information; but read in isolation from his 1925 article on psychoanalysis . . . this book seems opaque because of its many theoretical positions. [Cole, 1979, p. 208]

The same could be said for Luria's other post-1930 writings:

> When I correlated the content and style of his writings with the general political and social controversies of the day, the otherwise disjointed, zigzag course of Alexander Romanovich's career began to make sense. His interest in psychoanalysis no longer appeared a curious anomaly . . . his apparent shifts of topic at frequent intervals, all took on the quality of an intricate piece of music with a few central motifs and a variety of secondary themes. [Cole, 1979, p. 198][9]

---

[9]Cf. Sacks (1990): "Luria's interest in psychoanalysis has been dismissed as a youthful [aberration]. This smacks of intellectual laziness, even arrogance . . . dismissing some of a man's enterprises and interests because we cannot see how they fit into the pattern" (p. 185).

Other authors have recognized the continued influence of Freud in Luria's life-long commitment to the clinical method and the intensive study of single cases. In his autobiography, Luria identified his approach with the clinical-descriptive tradition in classical behavioural neurology:

> The medicine of previous years had been based on the effort to single out important syndromes by describing significant symptoms. This activity was considered essential both for diagnosis and for treatment. With the advent of the new instrumentation, these classical forms of medical procedure were pushed into the background. The physician of our time, having a battery of auxiliary aids and tests, frequently overlooks clinical reality. Observation of patients and evaluation of syndromes have begun to give way to dozens of laboratory analyses which are then combined by mathematical techniques as a means of diagnosis and as a plan of treatment. Physicians who are great thinkers have gradually disappeared. It is rare now to find a really good physician who is equally adept in observing, judging, and treating. I do not intend to underrate the role of instrumentation in medicine. But I am inclined to strongly reject an approach in which these auxiliary aids become the central method and in which their role as servant to clinical thought is reversed. ... In the previous century, when auxiliary laboratory methods were rare, the art of clinical observation reached its height. One is unable to read the classical descriptions of the great physicians J. Lourdat, A. Trousseau, P. Marie, J. Charcot, [C.] Wernicke, S. Korsakoff, [H.] Head, and A. Meyer without seeing the beauty of art in science. Now this art of observation is nearly lost. [Luria, 1979, pp. 176–177]

We have seen above that Freud, too, was deeply influenced by this tradition.[10] In attempting to understand the above passage, Sacks (1990) wrote that he himself was "ineluctably drawn to [Luria's] earliest enterprises—his writing to Freud, at the age of 19; his founding, with Freud's encouragement, a psychoanalytical society in Kazan; and his first book, written as a youth of 20, an appreciation and critique of psychoanalysis" (p. 185). Similarly,

---

[10]Interestingly, Luria here (p. 174) quoted the same lines from Goethe that, as we saw in chapter one, had so impressed Freud (1924b, p. 149).

Luciano Mecacci (1988) wrote that "[Luria's] clinical approach to the study of neuropsychological disorders undoubtedly sprang from his early experience in psychoanalysis in the 1920s" (p. 268). Mecacci continued:

> Luria's involvement with psychoanalysis was deeper and more complex than he cared to show. . . . As anyone who saw Luria at work at the Burdenko Institute of Neurosurgery in Moscow would have noted, his approach to patients was purely clinical, closer to the psychoanalytic style than that of the experimentalistic attitude towards behavior. He had no fixed schedule for interviewing and testing a patient, but he employed a free-association technique, selecting the questions and the test trials according to what emerged in the session. Finally, this mode of neuropsychological investigation was unique with each patient, and might not be replicated with another patient. . . . The neuropsychological "portrait" that emerged from this clinical investigation fit[ted] in with the conception of the historical character of an individual's psychological life. [p. 269][11]

Luria's abiding interest in psychoanalysis is attested to directly by other friends and colleagues. Oliver Sacks, for example, states in a personal communication (17 March 1987) the following:

> I can give you only one direct quotation from Luria bearing on his (later) attitudes to psycho-analysis. In December '75 I sent him a tape of (the verbal and vocal ejaculations of) a patient of mine with severe Tourette's syndrome. Among these, but ejaculated with such speed as to seem at first a meaningless noise, was the word "Verboten!", uttered in a harsh (indeed parodied) "Teutonic" voice, and at times (and in a manner suggestive of) self-recrimination. This *had*, it later turned out, been spat out by the patient's German-speaking father whenever his son showed "impermissible" tics and impulses. The confirmation of this, indeed the following up of it, was initiated by Luria's letter, in early '75, when he suggested that I study ". . . the introjection of father as tic". (I will have to pull

---

[11] See also Van der Veer and Valsiner (1991), p. 88. Mecacci has made similar remarks to us in a personal communication (24 March 1992).

out and xerox the original letter).[12] I think Luria said, or felt able to say, *in letters* a good deal that he felt (externally or internally) unable to say in print—and this made me feel that he was still, at least, sympathetic to psychoanalysis as a tool and dynamic description of value.

This insight into Luria's private beliefs makes sense of his abiding commitment in his later work to the methodological and theoretical principles that originally attracted him to Freud and psychoanalysis. These principles include, among other things, (1) the priority of psychological analysis of psychological disorders, whatever their aetiology; (2) the individualized, flexible case-study approach, with its emphasis on qualitative–descriptive methods of investigation, and the method of syndrome analysis in particular; (3) the appreciation of the dynamic nature of mental life, with both normal and pathological psychological phenomena being conceptualized as resultants of functional interactions between more elementary components of the mental apparatus; and (4) the developmental and hierarchical model of that apparatus, conceived of as a complex functional system.[13]

---

[12] When he did pull out this letter, Luria's psychoanalytical attitude to the case in question was even more pronounced than Sacks had remembered. Luria referred to "the structuralization of the [patient's] super-ego" as well as to "the introjection of the father's voice as tic" (the letter was actually dated 29 January 1976; see Sacks, 1990, p. 186, n. 6). This reference by Luria to introjection and structuralization of the superego is of particular interest in view of the important role he assigned to the internalization of the spoken word in the development of the regulatory functions of the frontal lobes (see chapter nine).

[13] Evidence of a different sort can be found in the curious fact that Donald Winnicott, after meeting Luria in Copenhagen in 1958, considered him to be the appropriate person to arrange publication in the Soviet Union of his seminal psychoanalytic study, "The Theory of the Parent–Infant Relationship" (Winnicott, 1960; see Winnicott's letter to Luria, dated 7 July 1960, in Rodman, 1987, p. 130). Two letters from Luria to Winnicott can be found in the Winnicott collection at the Cornell University Medical Center Library. The first of these, dated 7 December 1958, refers to an earlier letter from Winnicott that seems to have been lost. The nature of the Copenhagen meeting is not clarified, but Luria refers to both "formal scientific" and "informal, intimate" contact in his letters.

Luria and dynamic neuropsychology

Luria was not simply a crypto-psychoanalyst, nor can all of his later work be reduced to his early interest in psychoanalysis. There is no doubt that there were other influences besides Freud upon Luria's thinking. Vygotsky is the outstanding example. Also, Luria's interest in psychoanalysis may itself have been determined by prior, more fundamental interests, which can be traced throughout his work. Luria suggested this in his autobiography, where he stated that he was attracted to psychoanalysis because he was searching for a psychology that could bridge the conflict between descriptive (ideographic) and explanatory (nomothetic) science (see Luria, 1979, pp. 21–23; cf. Luria, 1925a).[14] Also, although Luria's rejection of psychoanalysis was externally motivated, his personal commitment to Marxism–Leninism was such that he may well have gradually internalized the Party line. Personal communications from some Western colleagues suggest that his mature attitude to psychoanalysis, even in private conversation, was sometimes ambivalent.[15] These issues raise extremely complex

---

[14] In an essay on "Luria and 'Romantic Science'", Sacks (1990) writes: "Here, it seems to me, is the key to Luria's early enthusiasm for psychoanalysis, for Freud; here, too, the permanent *heuristic* effect of Freud on his thought, whatever reservations and differences were later to appear. Freud offered a principle—the general principle Luria needed" (p. 188).

[15] Karl Pribram writes that Luria considered Freud's 1895 "Project" to be "seminal and viable" but felt that "some of Freud's later work was not of this caliber and in general [Luria] wanted therefore to be disassociated from it" (personal communication, 16 June 1987). Michael Cole writes that "There is no doubt in my mind that Luria was both very sympathetic of psychoanalytic ideas and critical of certain shortcomings in the enterprise" but also that "there was severe external pressure to renounce Freud" (personal communication, 1 April 1989). Jason Brown writes that Luria was "antagonistic [to psychoanalysis], rather like most Soviet neuropsychiatrists", although his work "seems to have something in common with [Freud's] topographic theory" (personal communication, 11 March 1992). Luciano Mecacci describes (personal communication, 24 March 1992) an occasion on which a reference by a Western colleague to *The Nature of Human Conflicts* angered Luria— "perhaps because it belonged to an old story". Mecacci suggests that Luria was attracted to psychoanalysis because he wished to study "the human psyche through the human being in itself and not in its distinct psychological

questions that extend beyond the scope of the present study. However, the intricate thread of psychoanalytic influence through the "disjointed, zigzag course" of Luria's career (Cole, 1979) is secondary in the present context to another aspect of his work—namely, his basic contributions to *neuropsychology*. The following pages demonstrate that Luria's fundamental concepts and methods *with regard to brain–behaviour relationships* were entirely compatible with those of Freud.

It is a remarkable fact that Luria's work in this field began where Freud's left off—with the study of *aphasia*. He began to investigate the problem of aphasia shortly after he resigned from the Russian Psychoanalytical Society,[16] and he eventually published his findings in a celebrated monograph, *Traumatic Aphasia* (Luria, 1947). Considering the fact that he ostensibly turned his back on psychoanalysis because it "biologized" human behaviour, it is striking indeed that after resigning from the Russian Psychoanalytical Society, he proceeded to study medicine and then to explore directly, for the remainder of his scientific life, the neurobiological bases of behaviour.

Luria introduced his book on aphasia with a discussion of the historical background to the subject. After a brief review of the classical theories of Broca, Wernicke, Lichtheim, and others, he concluded that the localization of complex psychological processes in discrete brain "centres" was untenable. Referring to Jackson, he distinguished between the localization of symptoms and the localization of functions. Psychological functions, he insisted, were not "lost" with focal brain lesions; rather, they were distorted in complex, dynamic ways. He applauded Jackson's anti-localizationist, evolutionary approach to the problem—and (in a glaring omission of Freud) noted that his ideas were not taken up by his colleagues until well into the present century. However, Jackson's views, he argued, resulted in an *excessive* swing away from localization, to-

---

elements". He concludes: "I think that Luria was not directly influenced by psychoanalysis from a strict theoretical point of view, except for what regards Freud's theory of aphasia, but this is another point". Mecacci's last remark is of considerable interest in the present context (see text below).

[16] Luria (1979, p. 136) states that he defended a thesis on aphasia for his medical degree.

wards psychological and biological theories that neglected the un-
equal role played by different parts of the brain. Luria, in his own
study, aimed to bridge the divide between localizationism and
equipotentialism. In all of these respects, Luria's (1947) analysis of
the problem of aphasia was identical to that of Freud (1891b).

The solutions that Luria proposed, too, were almost identical to
those of Freud. He conceived of speech and language as products
of a hierarchical functional system, subserving a psychological
process, with a complex structure and genesis, which was distributed *between* the basic sensorimotor centres of the brain. A functional system of this sort, Luria argued, could not be localized in
the conventional sense of the word.[17] However, the elementary
component parts of the functional system—like the "cornerstones"
of Freud's speech apparatus—*could* be localized:

> "Localization of function" in this case becomes another prob-
> lem, viz., the problem of the *dynamic distribution of functional
> systems in central regions of the nervous system* and especially in
> the cerebral cortex. Instead of conceptions of "centres" for
> complex psychic processes there arise the concepts of *dynamic
> structures or constellations of cerebral zones,* each of which com-
> prises part of the cortical portion of a given analyser and
> preserves its specific function, while participating in its own
> way in the organisation of one or another form of activity.
> [Luria, 1947, p. 20]

Lesions within the speech field which affect the different component zones (sensorimotor analysers) lead to the characteristic
aphasic syndromes. In the conceptualization of these syndromes,
however, the secondary effects of the lesion on the functional system as a whole also have to be considered. Luria went to great
lengths to emphasize that this system subserved a *psychological*
function, and that its symptomatology therefore required a fully

---

[17] Consider the striking similarity between Freud's (1900a) suggestion that
we should view the mind as a complex optical instrument, in which psychic
locality corresponds to an ideal point in which no tangible component of the
apparatus is situated, with the following statement by Luria (1987): "all attempts to postulate that . . . images, or ideas, could be found in single units of
the brain were as unrealistic as trying to find an image inside a mirror or
behind it" (p. 489).

psychological analysis. On this conceptual basis, he examined the structure of aphasic disturbances in large numbers of patients and correlated the disturbances with the underlying lesions. He then proposed a new classification of the aphasias, based on a new theory of speech, in which he took care to localize only the *elementary component parts* of the functional system, and not the functional system of speech as a whole.

The similarities between this model and Freud's (as reviewed, for example, by Solms & Saling, 1986, 1990) will be immediately obvious to those familiar with Freud's writings on aphasia. However, there was one important difference between the two models. Whereas Freud believed that only the primary sensorimotor functions that lie at the *periphery* of the speech apparatus could be localized, Luria believed that *every stage* in the complex psychological process of speech could be localized, so long as one respected the fundamentally *dynamic* nature of the process as a whole. He localized not only the peripheral components, but all components of the speech process, *including those performed by structures lying deep within the apparatus*. This represented a major advance.

The question arises: how did Luria manage to achieve this step—which Freud had always acknowledged must be possible in principle, but which he could not carry out in practice? There were two essential factors. First, Luria's (1947) work was based on a more sophisticated theory of the psychology of language than was Freud's work. This enabled him to identify the (localizable) component parts of the functional system supporting language—that is, to discern its *internal* workings. The details of Luria's neuropsychology of language, which owed much to the structuralist linguistics of Roman Jakobson, are not elaborated here (for a comprehensive account, see Luria, 1976a).[18] However, it is important to recognize that Luria's approach to the problem was fundamentally compatible with Freud's approach. Freud (as we discussed in chapter one), always argued that it was essential to gain a comprehensive understanding of the internal psychological structure of a mental process before it would be possible—or even useful—to localize it.

---

[18] See Marshall (1974) for a summary of Freud's psychology of language.

The second (and more important) advance that Luria introduced was a methodological one: that is, *he modified the classical clinico-anatomical method to accommodate the essentially dynamic nature of the mental process.* This, the reader will recall, was the step—indeed the breakthrough—that Freud had always insisted was necessary before psychoanalysis could be rejoined with neuroscience.

In view of the obvious importance of this advance for the purposes of the present study, Luria's methodological proposals will now be examined in detail. However, the problem of speech will no longer be our sole concern, for Luria applied this same method to a wide range of human mental functions (see Luria, 1966, 1973, 1976b, 1980).

Luria's method of "dynamic localization"

Luria's method involved two stages: (1) *qualification of the symptom* and (2) *syndrome analysis.* He described the first stage as follows:

Symptoms evoked by disturbances of different factors have complicated structures and can have different causes. For this reason, symptoms must be carefully analyzed and "qualified". The "qualification of the symptom" depends on a careful [psychological] analysis of the patient's defects. This is the basic goal of the Soviet neuropsychologist's approach. He is never content with merely finding a certain defect. . . . The singling out of a symptom is not the end but rather the beginning of his work, which continues in depth. He attempts the elucidation of the disturbed structure, attempting to find distinct psychological factors underlying the symptom. This must occur first, in order to make the symptom's inner structure lucid and to allow the formulation of a hypothesis as to its relationship with a local brain lesion. [Luria & Majovski, 1977, p. 963][19]

---

[19] Luria was, incidentally, fully aware of the fact that a psychological analysis of this sort is, of necessity, *theory-driven* (Luria & Majovski, 1977, *passim*). See text below.

In view of the importance of this latter task for the purposes of the present study, two further passages are quoted here in which Luria describes this aspect of his method:

> In order to progress from establishment of the *symptom* (loss of a given function) to the *localization* of the corresponding mental activity, a long road has to be travelled. Its most important section is the *detailed psychological analysis of the structure of the disturbance and the elucidation of the immediate causes of collapse of the functional system*, or, in other words, a *detailed qualification of the symptom observed*. [Luria, 1973, p. 35]

The purpose of this "detailed psychological analysis" is the formulation of a hypothesis as to the nature of the fundamental disturbance underlying the manifest symptom:

> The investigator's immediate task is to study the *structure of the observed defects and to qualify the symptoms*. Only then, by work leading to the *identification of the basic factor lying behind the observed symptom*, is it possible to draw conclusions regarding the localization of the focus lying at the basis of the defect. [p. 38]

It is easy to see—as Mecacci saw (1988)—that this part of Luria's clinical method—the "qualification of the symptom"—coincides with Freud's psychoanalytic approach. It could be said that Luria's method is to neurology what Freud's is to psychiatry. *The aim is not to identify and designate the symptom, but, rather, to obtain a detailed picture of its internal psychological structure in order to elucidate its fundamental psychological basis.*

This leads directly to the second stage of Luria's method—namely, syndrome analysis:

> The qualification of the symptom is only the first step in the analysis of the cerebral organization of mental processes. So that the results of this analysis ... can serve as the basis for reliable conclusions regarding both the structure of mental processes and their "localization" in the human cerebral cortex, the next step must be from the qualification of the single symptom to the description of the complete symptom-complex or, as it is generally called, to the *syndrome analysis* of changes in behaviour arising in local brain lesions. [Luria, 1973, p. 38]

It is necessary not only to identify the factor underlying the disturbance of the functional system under investigation (qualification of the symptom), but also to identify which other functional systems are disturbed by the same lesion and what factors underlie those other disturbances. This enables the investigator to identify *the single, basic factor that underlies all of the symptoms produced by the one particular lesion.* The common underlying factor, in turn, points to *the basic function of that particular part of the brain.*

The next step is to study the different ways in which each functional system is disturbed by lesions to *different parts of the brain.* Lesions in different parts of the brain will disturb the functional system in different ways. The different types of disturbance are identified by a repetition of the above procedure—that is, a qualification of the symptom arising from each site of lesion, followed by a syndrome analysis of the complex of other symptoms arising with the same lesion. This step-by-step process identifies the *various basic factors* that contribute to the functional system, and at the same time it identifies the *various basic functions* of the different parts of the brain.

In this way, the *component parts* of each functional system are identified and localized in the tissues of the brain. These are the elementary components of the functional system *between* which the mental process itself is localized. This is the meaning of the term "dynamic localization". It is not the function *itself* that is localized, but, rather, the component parts of the apparatus that supports it. This is something quite different from the localization of whole mental faculties (i.e. the narrow localizationism of classical neurologists):

> It will easily be seen that syndrome analysis sheds considerable light on the *cerebral organization of mental processes* and also gives *considerable insight into their internal structure,* something which for many centuries psychologists have been unable to do. . . . The fact that every complex mental activity is a functional system which can be disturbed in different components and which can be impaired by brain lesions in different situations (even though it is impaired differently) means that we can get closer to the description of the *factors* composing it and thereby discover new ways of neurophysiological analysis

of the internal structure of mental processes. . . . From all the foregoing remarks it will be clear that the use of observations on the changes in mental processes arising in local brain lesions can be one of the most important sources of our knowledge of the cerebral organization of mental activity. However, the correct use of this method is possible only if *the attempt is resisted to seek the direct localization of mental processes in the cortex*, and only if this classical task is replaced by another—*by analysis of how mental activity is altered in different local brain lesions and what factors are introduced into the structure and complex forms of mental activity by each brain system.* [Luria, 1973, p. 42]

The way in which Luria's approach differs from the classical method of clinico-anatomical localization is best conveyed by the following analogy:

Most investigators who have examined the problem of cortical localization have understood the term *function* to mean the "function of a particular tissue". . . . It is perfectly natural to consider that the secretion of bile is a function of the liver and the secretion of insulin is a function of the pancreas. It is equally logical to regard the perception of light as a function of the photosensitive elements of the retina and the highly specialized neurons of the visual cortex connected with them. However, this definition does not meet every use of the term *function*. When we speak of the "function of respiration," this clearly cannot be understood as the function of a particular tissue. The ultimate object of respiration is to supply oxygen to the alveoli of the lungs to diffuse it through the walls of the alveoli into the blood. The whole process is carried out, not as a simple function of a particular tissue, but rather as a complete functional system, embodying many components belonging to different levels of the secretory, motor, and nervous apparatus. Such a "functional system" . . . differs not only in the complexity of its structure but also in the mobility of its component parts. [Luria, 1979, pp. 123–124]

Freud, too, recognized that it was only possible to localize *elementary perceptual processes* by the classical clinico-anatomical method. The essence of Luria's advance was to devise a method that could accommodate the more complex processes—that is, those that occur *deep within the mental apparatus*.[20] This method clearly is, as Freud insisted it had to be, capable of accommodating the *dynamic* nature of complex mental processes.

Once one has studied, by this method, the full series of different ways in which a complex psychological faculty breaks down with damage to different parts of the brain, then one will have discovered its dynamic neurological representation, by identifying which parts of the brain contribute, and in what way they contribute, to the complex functional system underlying that faculty. In so doing one will not have localized that faculty in any one part of the brain, but will have identified the various components *between* which, by dynamic interaction, the physiological processes representing that psychological faculty are produced.

If our description of Luria's method is sufficiently lucid, the reader will have noticed that his method achieves something else besides: it teaches us something new about the structure of psychological faculties. *It identifies, from a physical point of view, the elementary component functions out of which each mental faculty is constructed.*

We believe that this method of Luria's represents a major step forward, because it enables us to identify the neurological organization of *any* mental faculty, no matter how complex, without contradicting the fundamental assumptions upon which psychoanalysis was built. By this method, psychological functions are still understood in their own, psychological terms; their essential, dynamic nature is respected and accommodated; they are not *reduced* to anatomy and physiology, although their neurological representation is laid bare; and something new is learned about their internal structure.

In the next chapter, we illustrate this method by means of a concrete example.

---

[20] Psychoanalysis, too, is a method of syndrome analysis. Indeed, it was in this sense that Freud's clinical method transcended that of Charcot and moved from the level of description to that of explanation. (Cf. Solms & Saling's comment that "psychoanalysis could almost be called a provisional neuropsychology of personality": 1986, p. 413.)

CHAPTER THREE

An example:
the neurodynamics of dreaming

In this chapter, we illustrate how Luria's method of dynamic localization—which we are recommending is the natural method for rejoining psychoanalysis and neuroscience—works in practice. We have chosen for our example a piece of research that we recently completed into the neurological organization of a subjective mental process that is of special interest to psychoanalysts: the function of dreaming (Solms, 1997a).

In order to lay bare the neurological organization of a complex mental function like dreaming, it is necessary first of all to identify the different ways in which dreaming is disordered by lesions to different parts of the brain, and then to subject these disorders to detailed psychological analysis. As stated in chapter two, Luria called this analytic process the "qualification of the symptom". It is not enough to state simply that dreaming is disrupted by damage to such-and-such part of the brain; we need to know in exactly *what way* the psychological structure of dreaming is changed with each lesion. This is done by attempting to isolate the fundamental factor that accounts for the disturbance of function, combined with an analysis of the *other* mental functions that are disordered along with the primary symptom of interest. Luria called this process "syndrome analysis". All the different mental faculties that are disrupted by a single circumscribed brain lesion should have something in common, and this common factor represents the underlying basic function of the part of the brain that is damaged by the lesion. In identifying this underlying factor, we reveal not only how but also why dreaming broke down with damage to the region in question. This ultimately clarifies the fundamental components of the functional system supporting dreaming.

Using this method to study the dreams of patients with focal brain lesions, we learned that dreaming is disturbed in various different ways by damage to six different parts of the brain. These regions are identified by the coloured zones in Figure 3-1 (facing p. 52), which is based on CT (computerized tomography) scans and shows horizontal slices through the brain, from the base (top left slice in the figure) to the vertex (bottom right slice in the figure).

If the brain is damaged in the regions identified as zones A, B, or C (see key to Fig. 3-1)—that is, the inferior parietal region of either hemisphere, or the deep ventromesial frontal region—the conscious experience of dreaming stops completely. *This does not mean that the function of dreaming can be narrowly localized within these parts of the brain.* Rather, it tells us that the component functions localized in these three parts of the brain are fundamental to the whole process of dreaming, for when any one of them is damaged, the conscious experience of dreams becomes impossible. Why that should be the case is revealed by an identification of the functional properties of those components and the parts they play in the process of dreaming as a whole. This can only be done by means of an analysis of the effects of the lesions on *other* functions that are not completely obliterated by the lesions. That is, the functional contributions that these three regions make to the overall process of dreaming can only be discerned by means of an analysis of the psychological *syndromes* within which the loss of dreaming is embedded in each case. What does syndrome analysis reveal in each of these cases?

First syndrome:
cessation of dreaming (left parietal damage)

The loss of dreaming caused by left inferior parietal-lobe lesions (zone A, Figure 3-1) is associated with the symptoms of *left/right disorientation* (inability to distinguish spatially between right and left) and *finger agnosia* (inability to identify and distinguish between fingers on a hand). Psychological analysis of these symptoms—which form part of the classical Gerstmann syndrome—suggests that the fundamental component function here is *the ability to derive abstract concepts from spatially organized heteromodal information* (a function that Luria called "quasi-spatial synthesis"). A disorder of this elementary function results in an inability to represent perceptual information *symbolically* (Luria, 1973, 1980). There is nothing wrong with the primary perceptual abilities of these patients, but they lose the ability to extract higher-order abstractions from perceptual information in all modalities—that is, to *conceptualize* concrete information and perform symbolic operations on it. (A case in which these functions were severely impaired is reported in chapter seven.) The fact that loss of dreaming caused by damage in the left inferior parietal lobe is embedded within this syndrome demonstrates that abstraction, conceptualization, and symbolization are fundamentally important component functions in the complex process of dreaming. Of additional interest is the fact that the quasi-spatial nature of left inferior parietal-lobe mechanisms implies that the mental processes occurring in this region are represented in the form of *simultaneous* patterns rather than *sequential* processes (which is how they are represented in the frontal lobes [zones C and H in Fig. 3-1]; see Luria, 1966, 1973).

Note that the fact that processes such as abstraction, concept formation, and symbolization are disturbed by damage in the left inferior parietal region *does not imply that these functions can be narrowly localized within that part of the brain*. It means only that the elementary function contributing to mental activity by the left inferior parietal region *participates in* all of these complex functions. For that reason, all of these functions (and dreaming, too) break down with damage in this area. However, just as the function of dreaming involves the participation of many other elementary functions contributed by other brain regions (see below), so too functions like "abstraction", "concept formation", and "symbolization" involve the concerted action of many different component functions, each of which is contributed by a different brain region.

Second syndrome:
cessation of dreaming (right parietal damage)

Loss of dreaming caused by right inferior parietal-lobe lesions (zone B, Fig. 3-1) is accompanied by deficits of *visuospatial working memory* (i.e., inability to hold visuospatial information in mind for short periods of time). This suggests that the fundamental factor contributed by this region to the complex function of dreaming is the ability to *concretely represent information mentally in a visuospatial medium*. These patients, too, do not suffer primary perceptual deficits in any modality; however, they cannot hold perceptual information *in consciousness*, in simultaneous visuospatial patterns. This applies equally to internally *and* externally generated information. It comes as little surprise to learn that this elementary psychological function, too, is essential for the conscious experience of dreams

Once again, note that this does not imply that "visuospatial working memory" is narrowly localizable within the right parietal lobe, any more than it implies that "dreaming" is localized there. It implies only that dreaming and visuospatial working memory *share* the elementary component function that is contributed by this part of the brain.

Third syndrome:
cessation of dreaming (deep bifrontal damage)

In the case of bilateral white-matter lesions in the ventromesial frontal region (zone C, Fig. 3-1), psychological analysis reveals that loss of dreaming is accompanied by various mental symptoms, the most conspicuous of which is *adynamia* (i.e. lack of spontaneous motivational impetus). Careful analysis of this symptom (which is well known to neuropsychologists) suggests that the *fundamental component function* that is disordered by damage to this part of the brain—that is, the common factor that underlies both adynamia and (this form of) loss of dreaming—affects spontaneous *motivation*.

This is an important piece of evidence for Freud's arguments against the view that "dreams are froth" (Freud, 1900a)[1] and for the alternative view that dreams are meaningful psychological events. This finding alone demonstrates the value of the neuro*psychological* approach, for it corrects a major misconception concerning the function of dreams—that dreams are "motivationally neutral" events (McCarley & Hobson, 1977, p. 1219)—a misconception that has dominated neuroscientific thinking about dreams for almost 50 years and arose from the use of physiological and anatomical methods that are incapable of answering psychological questions (see Solms, 1995a, 1999s, in press [a]).

It is interesting to note that the site of the lesion that produces this syndrome (the ventromesial white matter of the frontal lobes) is precisely the region that was targeted surgically in the modified prefrontal leucotomy procedure that was so popular during the middle of the previous century as a treatment for severe mental illness. Whatever it was that prevented leucotomized patients from sustaining their neurotic and psychotic symptoms also prevented them from generating dreams.[2]

Again, it must be said that these findings do not in any way imply that the function of "motivation" (or the "libidinal drive") can be *localized* in the deep white matter of the ventromesial frontal region. All one can say is that the fibres of this region contribute an elementary function that is crucial to human motivation.

Damage to other parts of the brain produces more subtle disturbances of dreaming that shed further light on the neuropsychological organization of the overall process. In these cases, the fundamental psychological deficit is easier to discern from a qualification of the primary symptom. Syndrome analysis merely confirms or elaborates the initial conclusions.

---

[1] Cf. McCarley and Hobson's (1977) remarks to this effect.

[2] Cessation of dreaming was a common side-effect of prefrontal leucotomy (see Solms, 1997a, in press [a]).

Fourth syndrome:
non-visual dreaming (occipito-temporal damage)

Damage in the ventromesial occipito-temporal region (zone D, Fig. 3-1) results in a very strange syndrome. These patients continue to experience dreams that are normal in every respect apart from the fact that they are devoid of *visual imagery*, or of particular *aspects* of visual imagery (such as the ability to visualize faces or colours or movements). This highly selective disorder of dreaming is accompanied by equally selective disturbances of waking imagery—that is, by a symptom known to neuropsychologists as *irreminiscence* (i.e. inability to form mental images). Here, the fundamental component function that accounts for the disorder of both waking and dream imagery is known as *visual pattern activation* (Kosslyn, 1994)—an essential prerequisite for what Freud (1900a) called "visual representability". This function is thought to involve the *endogenous activation of perceptual representations*. Unlike the inferior parietal cases described above, in these (occipito-temporal) cases the disorder affects the patients' ability to represent visual perceptual information *concretely*. This is not a disorder of *symbolic* cognition. Again, it should come as no surprise to learn that this component function is implicated in the visual hallucinatory process of dreaming.

What is especially interesting, however, is the fact that visual pattern activation is thought by contemporary neuropsychologists to be closely related to a process known as "backward projection" (Kosslyn, 1994)—a process that is identical to the mechanism that Freud described as "topographical regression". These facts, together with the fact that the dreams of these patients are in every respect normal (apart from their non-visual character), suggest that the "pattern-activation" component of dreaming should be placed at the *terminal* end of the hallucinatory process. This implies that, in dreams, the stage of abstract, symbolic cognition and conceptualization *precedes* the stage of concrete perceptual representation (i.e. dreams reverse the normal sequence of perceptual cognition).[3]

---

[3] Cf. Freud's remark to the effect that in dreams "the fabric of the dream-thoughts is resolved into its raw material" (1900a, p. 543).

Fifth syndrome:
dream/reality confusion (frontal limbic damage)

Damage in the frontal limbic region (zone E, Fig. 3-1)[4] results in an equally strange, but completely different syndrome. Patients with damage in this region continue to dream—indeed they dream *excessively* and sometimes seem to dream all night—but *they lose the ability to distinguish between dreams and real experiences*. Psychological study of these patients reveals that their judgement in regard to other aspects of reality monitoring is also impaired. Consequently, they present with a wide range of related symptoms, such as anosognosia (unawareness of illness), neglect (inattention to the left-hand side of space), reduplicative paramnesia (conflated experience of two different realities), confabulatory amnesias, and the like. Syndrome analysis reveals that the underlying common factor in these cases is a disturbance of *reality-testing*, which further neuropsychological analysis suggests is attributable to "equalization of the excitability of traces" (Luria, 1973). This is a fundamental deficit of *mental selectivity*, which results in an inability to differentiate between perceptions, thoughts, memories, fantasies, and dreams. The following excerpt from a clinical interview vividly illustrates the deficit (Solms, 1997a, p. 186):

> [*Patient:*] I wasn't actually dreaming at night, but sort of thinking in pictures. It's as if my thinking would become real—as I would think about something, so I would see it actually happening before my eyes and then I would also be very confused and I wouldn't know sometimes what had really happened and what I was just thinking.
>
> [*Examiner:*] Were you awake when you had these thoughts?
>
> [*Patient:*] It's hard to say. It's as if I didn't sleep at all, because so much was happening to me. But of course it wasn't really happening, I was just dreaming these things; but they weren't like normal dreams either, it's as if these things were really happening to me . . .
>
> [An example:] I had a vision of my [deceased] husband; he came into my room and gave me medicine, and spoke some

---

[4]This zone includes the basal forebrain nuclei, medial paralimbic frontal cortex, anterior cingulate gyrus, and anterior and mediodorsal thalamic nuclei.

kind things to me, and the next morning I asked my daughter: "Tell me the truth, is he really dead?" and she said "Yes Mama". So it must have been a dream . . .

[Another example:] I was lying in my bed thinking, and then it sort of just happened that my husband was there talking to me. And then I went and bathed the children, and then all of a sudden I opened my eyes and "Where am I?"—and I'm alone!

[*Examiner:*] Had you fallen asleep?

[*Patient:*] I don't think so, it's as if my thoughts just turned into reality.

In these cases, therefore, we are apparently dealing not so much with a disorder of dreaming as with a factor that normally *inhibits* dreaming and dream-like thinking (i.e. inhibits regression)—with the result that waking cognition and dreaming become indistinguishable.

Sixth syndrome:
recurring nightmares (temporal-lobe seizures)

The syndrome associated with discharging lesions affecting the temporal limbic region (zone F, Fig. 3-1) takes the form of *recurring stereotyped nightmares*. These nightmares are associated with complex partial epilepsy and, indeed, may reasonably be described as *seizure equivalents*. This equivalence is demonstrated, for example, by the fact that the stereotyped dream scenes that these patients experience also appear in the form of waking seizures or aurae. Moreover, the fact that the same dream scenes can be generated artificially by means of temporal-lobe stimulation—and the fact that the recurring nightmares disappear following successful pharmacological or surgical treatment of the underlying seizure disorder—demonstrates that the limbic discharges actually play a *causal* role in the generation of these dreams. This suggests that a factor of *affective arousal* should be added to our picture of the overall functional matrix of the dream process. It also suggests that this factor should be placed at the initiatory, *generative* end of the process—that is, at the opposite end of the process from the visuo-spatial *representational* mechanisms discussed previously.

Conclusions: the functional anatomy of dreaming

Having completed these six clinico-anatomical syndrome analyses, we are now in a position to sketch the neurodynamic localization of the function of dreaming. It is apparent that the process of dreaming unfolds over a functional system that has six fundamental component parts: the left inferior parietal region, the right inferior parietal region, the deep ventromesial frontal region, the ventromesial occipito-temporal region, the frontal limbic region, and the temporal limbic region (zones A through F, Fig. 3-1).

Note that the function of dreaming cannot be localized *within* any of these regions; rather, it must be thought of as a dynamic process that unfolds *between* these different component parts of the functional system as a whole. This *process* may be dynamically localized as follows (cf. Fig. 3-1). Dreaming begins with an arousal stimulus, originating either in the ventral midbrain (the source nuclei of the fibres that are severed by a lesion in zone C) or in the temporal limbic region (zone F, the location of the discharging lesions that cause recurring nightmares). The fact that dreaming so frequently accompanies the physiological state known as REM sleep (a state that is known to be generated by pontine brainstem mechanisms, located in zone G, Fig. 3-1) suggests that this region, too, should be included among the triggering mechanisms of the dream process. This and other evidence (Solms, in press [a]) suggests that it is possible that *anything* that arouses the sleeping brain has the potential to trigger the dream process. However, the fact that among these regions only damage in the deep ventromesial frontal region results in a complete cessation of dreaming suggests that this part of the brain is the final common path that initiates the dream process proper (the "dream work", in the terminology of Freud, 1900a).

We have seen that the deep ventromesial frontal region is essential for normal motivation. The fact that dreaming ceases when the deep fibres in this region are severed suggests that dreaming is

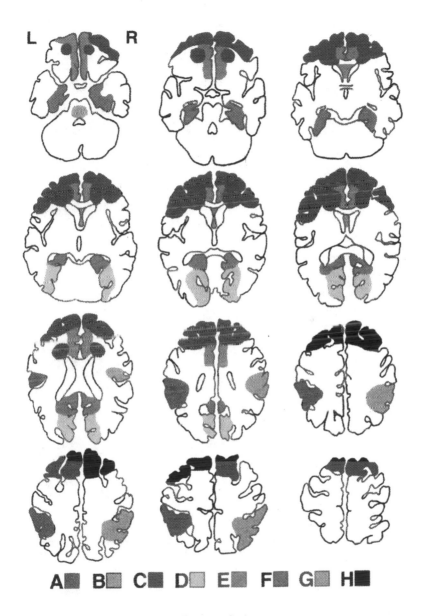

L   R

A ■ B ▨ C ■ D ▨ E ▨ F ▨ G ▨ H ■

Figure 3-1

a *motivated* process, driven by the same forces that initiate normal waking cognition and spontaneous behaviour. This, combined with the other evidence regarding the triggers of the dream process, just reviewed, suggests that activation of these motivational systems is a *response* to the stimulus that aroused the sleeping brain in the first place (e.g. REM activation). The fact that dreaming stops completely if these systems are incapacitated but not when the arousal systems themselves are damaged suggests further that dreaming *only* occurs when an arousal stimulus during sleep attracts motivational interest. Due in part to the fact that the motor systems (zone H, Fig. 3-1)—or at least, their output channels[5]—are inhibited during sleep, the motivational programmes activated in this way cannot terminate in volitional *motor* activity. That is to say, voluntary action and the state of sleep are mutually incompatible states. For this reason, it appears, the motivational programme terminates in a *perceptual* rather than a motor act.[6] This implies that the sequential programmes normally contributed by the frontal region are replaced by the simultaneous patterns that are characteristic of parietal-lobe functioning; and the response to the arousing stimulus is represented symbolically (zone A) in a spatial medium (zone B).[7] The resultant dream is due also to the fact that reflective judgement is weakened, because of the functional conditions that prevail during sleep in the frontal limbic region (zone E). Consequently, attentional cathexis is directed uncritically during dreaming towards the perceptual regions, where the mnestic pat-

---

[5] It was established long ago—by neurophysiological methods—that spinal motoneurons are inhibited by pontine brainstem mechanisms during REM sleep. However, recent research using neuropsychological methods suggests that the cortical end of the motor system, too, might be inhibited during dreaming sleep (Braun et al., 1997; Solms, 1997a). If this finding is confirmed, it has important implications for the psychology of dreaming, for this part of the brain (zone H, Fig. 3-1), more than any other, might legitimately be described as the "scene of action" of normal ideational activity (to paraphrase Fechner, 1860). The fact that this part of the brain does not appear to participate in the process of dreaming goes a long way towards explaining the irrationality and credulity of dreaming thought, for the contribution that it makes to normal waking ideation is absolutely fundamental.

[6] This is consistent with the sleep-protection function of dreams, postulated by Freud (1900a).

[7] This might be a neurodynamic medium for the psychological processes of condensation and displacement.

terns activated in the parietal zones are projected backwards onto the visual buffer (zone D). Thus the process ends in a concrete perceptual representation, which is hypercathected by the reflective systems (zone E) as if it were a real experience. This accounts for the delusional and hallucinatory quality of dreams.

This example should have conveyed to the reader at least something of how Luria's method of dynamic localization works in practice. For a fuller account, the reader should consult the original study on which this brief synopsis is based (Solms, 1997a). Hopefully, despite its brevity, the synopsis makes clear why we believe that this method is capable of overcoming the objections that Freud levelled at the classical clinico-anatomical method of narrowly localizing mental functions. The picture of the dream work that emerges from an application of Luria's method is entirely compatible with Freud's assumptions to the effect that "psychical structures in general must never be regarded as localized *in* organic elements of the nervous system but rather, as one might say, *between* them" (1900a, p. 611). It is also compatible with his recommendation that we should

> picture the unknown apparatus which serves the activities of the mind as being really like an instrument constructed of several parts (which we speak of as "agencies"), each of which performs a particular function and which have a fixed spatial relation to one another [Freud, 1926e, p. 194].

What Luria's method reveals about the neurodynamics of dreaming also provides some important initial indications as to how the entire mental apparatus described by Freud (1900a) might be dynamically localized in the tissues of the human brain (see chapter ten).

A gateway from psychology to basic neuroscience

We said in chapter one that neuroscience encompasses a wide range of subsidiary disciplines, each with its own special methods which are used to study different aspects of the nervous system (e.g. neuroanatomy, neurophysiology, neuropsychology, clinical neurology) and different levels of its biological organization (from the level of functional activity of the system as a whole to the level of molecular biology of the individual cell). What we have argued is that the appropriate point of contact between psychoanalysis and neuroscience is the discipline of neuropsychology—and, more specifically, the dynamic tradition within neuropsychology—which studies the nervous system from the viewpoint of its functional organization, using fully psychological methods, with the aim of laying bare the neurological representation of human mental functions.

However, the correlation of psychoanalytic and neuroscientific knowledge does not *end* at the neuropsychological level of analysis. By identifying the fundamental component parts of the functional system supporting a complex mental function using the method of dynamic localization, one has in fact established a *gateway*—a conceptual *bridge*—between psychological and neurological science. Thereafter it becomes possible to take advantage of the numerous well-established methodological and conceptual links between the various subsidiary disciplines within neuroscience. This makes it possible to shift seamlessly between psychoanalytical concepts and their neurophysical correlates, from the global level of neurodynamic organization right down to the minutiae of molecular biology.

For example, using Luria's dynamic method of clinico-anatomical syndrome analysis, it was possible to isolate the white matter of the ventromesial frontal lobes as a fundamental component part of the functional system supporting dreaming. Moreover, it was possible to identify the basic function of this part of the system: psychological analysis of cases of cessation of dreaming with lesions in this area revealed that the fundamental deficit was a *motivational* one. Moving from the neuropsychological level of analysis to the neurophysiological one, it becomes possible to ask the question: *why* does this particular region contribute that particular function? Anatomical methods of study reveal that the white matter implicated in this syndrome is composed essentially of fibre tracts connecting ventral midbrain nuclei with the limbic system (e.g. cingulate gyrus and nucleus accumbens) and frontal cortex. Next, physiological and chemical methods reveal that the fibres in question form part of an ascending dopaminergic system, which—as

we know from clinical and pharmacological methods of study—
forms part of a circuit known as the "curiosity–interest–expect-
ancy" or "seeking" command system of the brain (Panksepp, 1985,
1998): "These systems instigate goal-seeking behaviors and an organism's appetitive interactions with the world" (Panksepp, 1985,
p. 273).

These links can also be used to confirm the theoretical conclusions that we reached by way of neuropsychological methods. For
example, our conclusion to the effect that the cessation of dreaming in cases of damage in the deep ventromesial frontal region is
due to the interruption of a "final common path" that leads to the
initiation of the dream-work proper, and that this component of
the functional system of dreaming should therefore be placed at
the generating rather than the representing end of the dream process, is confirmed by the finding that chemical stimulation of the
dopaminergic "seeking" circuits (by means of L-dopa) results in
states of excessive dreaming and dream-like thinking (very similar
to those described above in the fifth syndrome). This conclusion is
further confirmed by the fact that pharmacological agents that
inhibit activity in this mesocortical–mesolimbic dopamine circuit
(e.g. haloperidol) also inhibit excessive dreaming and dream-like
thinking.

This, in turn, makes it possible to make new theoretical connections between our psychoanalytical understanding of dreaming and the extensive body of psychopharmacological knowledge
that has accumulated in recent years around the role of this dopaminergic circuit in the generation of psychotic symptoms. Freud
always argued that dreaming was akin to psychosis in its functional organization, so it should come as no surprise to learn that
normal dreaming and psychotic illness can also be linked at the
anatomical, physiological, and chemical levels. In this way, it
becomes possible for us to begin to make metapsychological sense
of the vast body of psychopharmacological knowledge that is
now available. These are examples of how the neuropsychological
method of Luria ultimately makes it possible to integrate psychoanalysis with *all* of the neurosciences, and thereby to link
our metapsychological concepts not only with anatomy, but also
with physiology, chemistry, and ultimately even with molecular
biology.

We hope that the point is clear: when we say that Luria's method of syndrome analysis is the appropriate point of contact between psychoanalysis and the neurosciences, we are not saying that other neuroscientific methods cannot be used to obtain knowledge of the physical correlates of psychoanalytic knowledge. All that we are saying is that Luria's method is the appropriate point of *contact*. Once broad correlations have been established at this (clinical, psychological) level—which is the only level at which psychoanalytic concepts can be *operationalized*—it becomes possible thereafter to establish further links, beyond the neuropsychological level, with the full range of methods and concepts currently available in the neurological sciences.

CHAPTER FOUR

The future of psychoanalysis in neuroscience: a methodological proposal

I n the period of thirty years during which Luria applied his method of "dynamic localization" to human mental processes, he elucidated the neurological organization of many complex mental functions. In a book written shortly before his death (Luria, 1973), he summarized his findings under six chapter headings: "Perception", "Movement and Action", "Attention", "Memory", "Speech", and "Thinking". There is much in these chapters that is of interest to the psychoanalyst. However, in the concluding chapter Luria wrote the following:

> Neuropsychology is still a very young science, taking its very first step, and a period of thirty years is not a very long time for the development of any science. That is why some very important chapters, such as motives, complex forms of emotions and the structure of personality are not included in this book. Perhaps they will be added in future editions. [pp. 341–342]

Sadly, Luria did not live to produce future editions.[1] Moreover, after his death (in 1977), neuropsychology developed in a dis-

---

[1] See, however, Luria's famous case study, *The Mind of a Mnemonist* (1968b). This represents his only published attempt to apply the method of

tinctly different direction, and for a period it returned to the narrow localizationist traditions that Luria (and Freud) had always opposed. As a result, neuropsychological methods have generally not been applied to those aspects of mental life that were explored by Freud—that is, to the deep structure of human subjectivity. This trend led Oliver Sacks[2] to remark—in a very apt turn of phrase—that "neuropsychology is admirable, but it excludes the psyche". He elaborated:

> Neuropsychology, like classical neurology, aims to be entirely objective, and its great power, its advances, come from just this. But a living creature, and especially a human being, is first and last ... a subject, not an object. It is precisely the subject, the living "I", which is excluded [from neuropsychology]. [Sacks, 1984, p. 164]

Very recent years have spawned concerted attempts to redress this imbalance, as evidenced by the flurry of neuropsychological studies on the "emotional brain". However, it is difficult to relate the findings of these investigations to the field of psychoanalysis. They were conducted within a conceptual and methodological framework that is completely alien to psychoanalysis. Heilman and Satz (1983, p. 1), for example, in their introduction to the first book in the recent series of works on the neuropsychology of emotion, wrote that psychoanalytic explanations of emotion "do not address the physical state of the brain" and consequently "are not directly relevant to neuropsychology and, therefore, are not discussed in this book". The findings of such research can only be correlated with psychoanalysis by means of indirect translations, akin to those that were employed in the literature mentioned in chapter one (see Panksepp, 1999; Solms & Nersessian, 1999a, 1999b). This raises all the insoluble problems of a speculative methodology.

Clearly, what is required is a neuropsychological method that is capable of accommodating *both* the object of psychoanalytic in-

---

syndrome analysis to the study of personality. (See also *The Man with a Shattered World:* Luria, 1972.)

[2] More than any other modern neurologist, Oliver Sacks has drawn attention to the importance of the subjective experience of the brain-impaired patient, although his writings are generally regarded as popular works rather than scientific studies.

vestigation (namely, human subjectivity) and that of neuroscience (namely, brain structure and function) and is also capable of *corre-lating* these two objects (i.e. observing them both simultaneously) without violating the conceptual premises of either discipline.

A methodological proposal

We will never know how personality, motivation, and complex emotion—the most important and interesting by far of all human mental functions—are represented in the tissues of the brain until we investigate directly the relations between their complex psychological organization and the neurological tissues that support them.

As we saw in chapter one, Freud himself always believed that a correlative study of this sort was feasible in principle (although impossible in practice at that time, given the limitations of the methods available to him). He was well aware that every mental process must *somehow* be represented as a physiological process that occurs in the tissues of the brain, but he also held to the view that it was an error to *localize* complex mental faculties within circumscribed neurological "centres". The reasoning behind this point of view was that mental processes are complex *dynamic* entities, which therefore cannot be correlated isomorphically as static "centres" with the individual structures of cerebral anatomy. He concluded, therefore, that it would not be possible to understand mental phenomena in neurological terms until (1) their dynamic *psychological substructure* had been laid bare and (2) until neuroscience was capable of identifying the physical correlates of such *complex dynamic* entities. Freud himself then devoted his scientific energies to the former (purely psychological) task and deferred the latter, correlative (neuropsychological) task to future investigators—anticipating future methodological advances.

In chapter two, we argued that the required advances have now occurred. Luria's modifications of the clinico-anatomical method (the method that Freud originally rejected) have made possible the correlation of complex, dynamic mental functions with their neuroanatomical "scene of action", in a manner that accommodates both of Freud's major methodological objections. Luria's method of dynamic localization recognizes that the underlying *psychological* structure of a mental process needs to be clarified before it can be localized, and that these complex dynamic processes cannot be correlated isomorphically with individual anatomical structures. The neurological representation of Freud's psychological concepts (the outcome of his research into the functional substructure of human personality, motivation, and complex emotion) is therefore within reach. The methodological proposals for the present study start from this breakthrough.

Luria's method has never been applied to the deeper aspects of mental life which interest us in psychoanalysis, and since those aspects of mental life have some unique attributes, a modification of Luria's method is required before it can be applied to them.

In studying the structure of human personality, motivation, and complex emotion, Freud discovered that the contents of subjective mental life are not easily accessible to the scientific investigator. Powerful forces are at work which strongly oppose the investigator's attempts to lay bare the private contents of an individual's mind. Freud classified these forces—which express themselves clinically as shame, guilt, anxiety, and the like—under the collective heading of "resistance". Due to the existence of this resistance, even the *primary* observational data for a study of human subjectivity are unusually difficult to obtain. These difficulties are compounded by the fact that the inferred *causal determinants* of the primary observational data (i.e. the unconscious mental events that underlie the conscious thought processes) are not conscious by definition. Freud discovered that any attempts to bring these deeper determinants of conscious awareness are opposed by the strongest possible resistances—and yet they are the very processes that are of the greatest interest to the psychoanalytical investigator. He therefore experimented with various techniques for overcoming these resistances (e.g. hypnotism and the "pressure" technique), and on the basis of this experience he gradually developed the definitive psychoanalytic technique of *free association*. Freud's justification for and explanation of this technique are carefully outlined in a number of places (e.g. 1900a, 1904a, 1910a, 1912e, 1913m, 1914d, 1923a, 1924f, 1925d, 1937d).

Both Freud and Luria always insisted that it was not possible to correlate a complex psychological process with its cerebral representation until the internal structure of that process was understood. Accordingly, the first step we have to take in our effort to discover the neurological organization of the human mental apparatus as we understand it in psychoanalysis is *to dissect the internal psychological structure of the various changes in personality, motivation, and complex emotion that occur following damage to different cerebral structures.* Thereafter, *the multiple underlying factors producing these symptoms and syndromes can be identified and each correlated with its anatomical "scene of action".*

However, due to the forces of resistance just described, these factors cannot be revealed by conventional neuropsychological techniques. The psychometric tests and bedside behavioural techniques that neuropsychologists use for assessing the mental status of neurological patients were designed for the investigation of disorders of "surface" cognitive functions (such as speech, calculation, and visual perception), which operate relatively independently of emotional resistances. The technique of free association was specifically developed for the elucidation of the internal structure of functions that *are* obscured by resistances. In order for us to lay bare the underlying psychological structure of the disorders of personality, motivation, and complex emotion that afflict the neurological patient, therefore, *the free-association technique must be introduced into Luria's neuropsychological method.*

This is not a radical departure from Luria's standard approach.[3] However, it is necessary to introduce this modification if we are going to take account of the fact that the internal structure of the mental functions that interest psychoanalysts most is largely inaccessible to conventional neuropsychological techniques. One cannot adequately elucidate the inner psychological structure of a personality change in a neurological patient by simply examining

---

[3] Cf. Mecacci's (1988) remark to the effect that "his approach to patients was purely clinical, closer to the psychoanalytic style than that of the experimentalistic attitude towards behavior. He had no fixed schedule for interviewing and testing a patient, but he employed a free-association technique, selecting the questions and the test trials according to what emerged in the session" (p. 269).

the patient at the bedside, just as one cannot do so with any other kind of patient. To gain access to the inner mental life of any patient, whether or not the patient has a brain lesion, one needs to get to know that patient as a *person*, by providing a reliable human relationship, in a professional setting, within which one can win the patient's confidence by tact and understanding, and by gradually making him or her aware of his or her resistances. Then, having gained relatively free access to the patient's private thoughts, feelings, and memories, one may explore the way in which the *unconscious* determinants of those thoughts, feelings, and memories unfold in the transference relationship, and test the hypotheses that arise in this regard in the form of appropriate interpretations. Only in this way, and by carefully observing the effects that the interpretations have upon the subsequent associative material, can one elucidate the inner structure of the psychological symptoms that are the focus of our interest here.

Every psychoanalyst knows that this is not the easiest way to elucidate a psychological syndrome, but we also know that *it is the best available method when it comes to those deeper aspects of mental life which neuropsychology has left unstudied*, and which have always been of central concern to *us* in psychoanalysis. In fact, the existence of the emotional resistances that conceal the internal structure of personality, motivation, and complex emotion probably explains *why* the neurological organization of these, the most important by far of all mental functions, has still not been systematically explored by neuropsychological methods. This is the scientific contribution that we believe psychoanalysis can now make to neuroscience.

Ironically, we owe the development of a clinical procedure for analysing the deep structure of subjective mental life to the fact that Freud abandoned neuroscientific methods of investigation, when he realized that they were unable to accommodate the dynamic and "virtual" nature of the mental process. Now the time has come for us to re-introduce the fruits of Freud's labours to the neuroscientific field out of which they originally grew. In doing so—although we do not wish to underestimate the enormity of the task before us—we believe that we are now able gradually to rejoin psychoanalysis with neuroscience, on a solid *clinical* basis, in a way that is beneficial to both fields, without ignoring any of the valuable lessons that the pioneers of psychoanalysis fought so long and hard to learn.

What we are recommending, therefore, and what we believe will provide the foundation stones for a lasting integration of psychoanalysis and neuroscience, is a fully *psychoanalytic* investigation of patients with focal neurological lesions. In other words, we are recommending that we chart the neurological organization of the human mental processes that psychoanalysis has laid bare, using a modified version of Luria's method of syndrome analysis, by studying the deep structure of the mental changes in neurological patients that can be discerned within a psychoanalytic setting.

Since valid psychoanalytic investigations can only be conducted in the context of psychoanalytic *treatment*, the investigative method we are recommending has a potential secondary benefit. It remains to be seen whether and to what extent psychoanalytic therapy might contribute to the *rehabilitation* of the various disorders of personality, motivation, and emotion that are associated with focal neurological damage. Hopefully the present study will be able to shed some preliminary light, too, on this very important clinical question.

Sketch of the present study

In the remainder of this book, we report the preliminary results of a study that we began 14 years ago, using precisely this method. We have so far studied the changes that occur in personality, motivation, and emotion following brain damage in 35 neurological cases, by taking them into psychoanalysis or psychoanalytic therapy.

As is well known, a proper application of the psychoanalytic method involves the following basic parameters. The patient is asked to associate freely (i.e. to report candidly whatever comes to mind) in a reliable and confidential setting. This occurs with the patient in a recumbent posture, and the analyst out of view, during regular 50-minute sessions, which take place four or five times weekly. It is an empirical fact that the patient's relationship with the analyst quickly becomes an important focus of the treatment ("transference"). Working in this manner, the analyst aims to discover the underlying (unconscious) functional organization that determines the apparently random and fragmentary manifestations of the patient's personality, motivations, and complex emotions, as they emerge in the transference relationship with the analyst. The analyst applies an evenly suspended attention until he or she is able to form a hypothesis as to what the underlying factors might be that generated the material of a given session (or part of a session). This hypothesis is tested by verbalizing relevant aspects of it to the patient at appropriate moments during the session ("interpretation"), and thereafter the hypothesis is modified in accordance with the patient's responses and other subsequent developments. In this way it is possible, over an extended period, to piece together gradually (in a coherent formulation or "construction") the various underlying factors that determine a given clinical presentation. The reader will recognize in this method the essential features of Luria's "qualification of the symptom" and "syndrome analysis" described in chapter two.

Experience has demonstrated that the elusive and intricate data of human personality, and the powerful resistances that oppose their exploration, can only be mastered by these very laborious means. Any deviation from this technique limits one's understanding of the symptom complex under study and undermines the reliability of one's conclusions. However, since innumerable patients have been studied by this method over the past 100 years, it is also true that the structures of certain typical symptoms and syndromes are now so well established that the essential facts of a clinical presentation can be ascertained in a far shorter time and with considerably less effort than was the case 100 years ago. In this respect, it is necessary to distinguish between the scientific and the therapeutic aims of an individual psychoanalysis.

It follows from the above that the aims of the present investigation should, ideally, involve an application of the following procedure. A wide variety of neurological patients with focal brain lesions that reflect the full range of pathological, anatomical, and clinical presentations should undergo, with appropriate controls, standard clinical neurological and neuropsychological investigations. Thereafter, they should be studied in the context of full five-times-a-week psychoanalysis. The various symptoms and syndromes would thus be observed and qualified in order to expose their internal structure, whereafter the results of each analysis could be correlated with the relevant pathological–anatomical and other clinical findings. This procedure would provide a complete nosology of neurogenic syndromes of personality, motivation, and complex emotion and, thereby, a comprehensive picture of the deep mental structure of those syndromes. This would pave the way for a definitive account of the anatomical representation of the mental processes underlying human personality.

However, considering the time and effort required to conduct and report just one *single* psychoanalysis, it will be apparent to the reader that the actualization of this ideal would require more than the life's work of two individual investigators. For this reason, further modifications were introduced for the purposes of the present study, in order to gain at least a preliminary foothold on this vast field. These methodological modifications consisted mainly in reducing the frequency of sessions (most of our cases were seen less frequently than five times weekly) and limiting the period of analysis (most of our cases were treated for only a few months). The details of these modifications in each case are provided in the clinical reports presented in part II (chapters five through nine).

The findings reported and the hypotheses advanced in the remainder of this book will require substantial confirmation, extension, and revision through further research, with many more patients, treated far more thoroughly than were our own. However, even within the limits of this preliminary study, our investigations produced a great wealth of raw data, the session-by-session reporting of which would make excessive demands on the attention and interest of the reader. We have therefore decided to present in this book only *a broad overview of our findings.*[4]

In chapters five, six, and seven, we report summarized accounts of psychoanalytic therapy in three cases of damage to the

---

[4]Selected cases will be reported in greater detail in monograph form in the near future (Kaplan-Solms & Solms, in press).

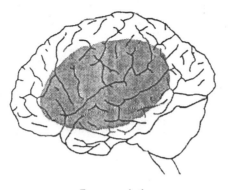

FIGURE 4-1

left perisylvian region of the brain (Fig. 4-1). The aim of these chapters is, first, to provide an initial orientation to the sort of data that is generated by conducting psychoanalytic therapy with neurological patients, and, second, to begin to illustrate how very differently patients present with damage to different parts of the brain. This is especially evident from the three cases that we report in these chapters, because although in these cases the lesions were only a few centimetres apart from each other and on the same side of the brain, they produced radically different clinical syndromes. In chapters eight and nine, we provide summarized reports of two *groups* of patients: in chapter eight, we describe our psychoanalytic findings in five cases with damage to the *right* perisylvian region of the brain (Fig. 4-2), followed in chapter nine by an equivalent

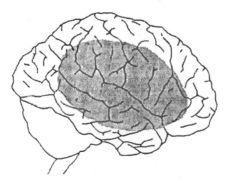

FIGURE 4-2

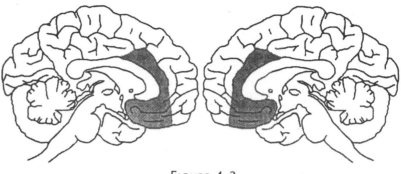

FIGURE 4-3

description of four patients with bilateral damage in the *ventro-mesial frontal* region (Fig. 4-3).

A comparison of these three groups yields many important insights into the neurological organization of the mental apparatus, as we understand it in psychoanalysis, but they represent nothing more than a first *sampling* of the vast field that needs to be explored. As reported in chapter ten, we have begun to extend the data reported in this book into other areas of the nervous system, but for the purposes of this initial presentation of our findings we limit ourselves to the three anatomical areas just mentioned: the left perisylvian region, the right perisylvian region, and the bilateral ventromesial frontal region (Figs. 4-1, 4-2, 4-3). This, we hope, will suffice to convince the reader of the *principle* that it is now possible to discover the neurological correlates of our psychoanalytic understanding of the structure of the human mind, without overwhelming the reader with too much clinical data to digest in one sitting. Finally, in part III we present an overview—based on all the evidence currently available to us—of how the human mental apparatus seems to be represented in the brain.

However, we wish to emphasize again that this initial overview is far from definitive and that it is subject to substantial revision. We have only just begun to investigate this extremely complex field. Many more patients will have to be treated far more thoroughly by far more investigators before we will have a scientifically reliable account of the neurological correlates of the human mental apparatus, as we understand it in psychoanalysis.

At this stage in our attempts to draw a first sketch of how our psychoanalytic model of the mind might be represented in the tissues of the brain, we should not shy away from bold and speculative formulations. We now have a method by means of which we can test these formulations and correct our errors along the way. There is, for this very reason, no shame in being proved wrong in science.

PART II

OBSERVATIONS

CHAPTER FIVE

Psychoanalytic observations on a case of Broca's aphasia: normal mourning

In this chapter, we summarize our analytic findings in a single case: a patient with damage to a specific part of the brain. Our aim in this chapter is to provide the reader with an initial orientation to the sort of data that is generated by analytic work with neurological patients. Our observations on this patient then form the starting point for comparisons with other cases, with damage in other parts of the brain, which we present in the subsequent chapters.[1]

The most striking feature of this patient's case, as the reader will see, is his relative *normality*. Despite the fact that he suffered a significant neurocognitive impairment—namely, loss of the capacity to express himself in language (and a physical loss, too, in the form of right-sided paralysis)—*he did not undergo any dramatic*

This chapter is based on a paper entitled "Psychoanalytic Observations on a Case of Broca's Aphasia" presented by Karen Kaplan-Solms and Mark Solms at the Neuro-Psychoanalysis Center of the New York Psychoanalytic Institute on 5 December 1998.

[1] To protect patient confidentiality, some minor biographical details have been changed in the case reports presented in this book.

changes in personality, motivation, or emotion. He was no different in his essential presentation from any other patient who has experienced a major loss and was therefore engaged in a process of normal mourning (i.e. the process of coming to terms with the loss and making a functional adaptation to it). He did not differ in this respect, for example, from seven paraplegic and quadriplegic patients whom we have treated in psychoanalytic psychotherapy. This, in itself, is an interesting and important scientific finding. We therefore thought it appropriate to begin our series of case reports with a description of this patient, who may serve as a sort of "control" case in comparison with the reports in the subsequent chapters.[2]

With this first report, we wish also to begin to demonstrate to readers that not all "brain-damaged" patients are alike. Some of these patients, despite the fact that they have sustained substantial damage to their brains, which has seriously impaired their motor, perceptual, and cognitive functions, nevertheless retain essentially normal ego (and superego) functions. Other patients, with equivalent degrees of damage *in other parts of the brain*, undergo radical personality changes and present clinically with extremely abnormal emotional and motivational changes (see chapters seven to nine). What determines these major differences is one factor and one factor only: the *location* of the neurological damage. This points to a fundamental fact about neuropsychology: *different parts of the brain serve different mental functions*. This simple fact provides the essential scientific rationale of this study. Our task is to discover and describe—in psychoanalytic terms—the functional contribution that each of the areas that we study makes to the overall functional organization of the human mental apparatus as a whole.

As the reader peruses this first case report, we ask him or her to bear all these points in mind. In the chapters that follow, we present cases with progressively more profound disturbances of mental functioning, as we proceed from the functional surface of the mental apparatus to its unconscious depths.

---

[2] Another reason why we thought it appropriate to begin our series with a report of this case is a historical one: the patient suffered from Broca's aphasia, the very disorder that ushered in the modern neuropsychological era in the first place (see chapter one).

Case J

Mr "J" was a 22-year-old, right-handed male. He was unmarried. He came from a lower-middle-class background, and at the time of his stroke he was employed as a junior officer in the armed forces. He had had 12 years of formal education. He had suffered a stroke (i.e. a thrombosis in the region of the left middle cerebral artery, in the cortical and thalamostriate branches) at the age of 20. This was due to subacute bacterial endocarditis. The resultant infarction of the left inferior frontal and anterior temporal lobes of the brain, and the involvement of the underlying white matter, can be seen in the diagram of his CT scan, reproduced as Figure 5-1.

This stroke left the young Mr J with dense right-sided hemiplegia (i.e. paralysis affecting his face, arm, and leg) and with something even more disabling—a severe, non-fluent aphasia. He returned to work for the army, in a menial capacity (as the supervisor of the cleaning staff). But it soon became obvious that he was

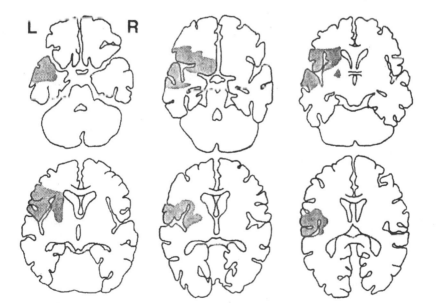

FIGURE 5-1

not going to recover his speech and right-sided motor function sufficiently, and he was therefore given what was euphemistically termed an honourable discharge.

Neuropsychological assessment

Following a period of intensive speech therapy, physiotherapy, and occupational therapy, Mr J was assessed neuropsychologically. The assessment was conducted 20 months after the stroke. At this point, a chronic non-fluent aphasia and a dense right upper-limb paralysis were present. The aphasia conformed to the classical syndrome of Broca's aphasia. Mr J's spontaneous speech was sparse, severely telegraphic, and agrammatical. His repetition of things said to him was only slightly superior to his spontaneous verbal output. Object naming was poor. Examination of writing and reading revealed an aphasic agraphia (his writing, like his speech, was severely non-fluent, telegraphic, and agrammatical) and a literal alexia (i.e. he was unable to read individual letters). However, his writing was slightly superior to his speech, which suggested an oral apraxic (i.e. complex articulatory) component to his speech disorder. This was confirmed on direct examination. Comprehension was essentially preserved, but there were isolated instances of alienated word-meaning (inability to understand occasional words). In addition to these purely aphasiological deficits, there was moderate acalculia (inability to calculate) and a severe limb-kinetic apraxia (i.e. a complex disorder of skilled movements in the non-paralysed hand). Mr J continued to dream normally (in fact, in his dreams, he saw himself as whole again—with normal speech and normal motor functions). There were no other neuropsychological symptoms or signs of note. In particular, there was no evidence of prefrontal, mesial temporal, or parietal-lobe dysfunction.

Following this assessment, Mr J was offered a course of psychoanalytic psychotherapy (with twice-weekly sessions), which he gladly accepted. Unlike most of the patients that we describe in subsequent chapters, he was treated on an out-patient basis. The main features of his sessions are summarized below.

Psychoanalytic observations

It may be surprising to hear that a patient with Broca's aphasia can make use of psychoanalytic psychotherapy at all, since it is, after all, a *talking* cure. We are aware of only a single case of this type having been described before in the psychoanalytic literature (Weitzner, 1987). It was, indeed, impressive to see how readily Mr J took to the psychoanalytic situation (albeit a modified one). He sat next to a small table, with a pen in his left hand, and he used diagrams, complex drawings, and occasional written words—together with abundant gestures and non-speech sounds with rich intonation—in order to make himself understood. This he did with surprising ease, especially considering the complexity and abstract quality of many of the communications that he wanted to convey to his therapist [K.K.-S.]. It is difficult to describe how he did this. Mostly his therapist felt that Mr J was indeed managing to make his thoughts and feelings absolutely clear to her. Of course, there were moments when things were not clear, but then are there not similar moments in every psychotherapy? On such occasions, Mr J sometimes gave up the struggle to communicate, but if his therapist persevered then so did he, until eventually—through one channel or another—he did manage to make himself understood.

What all of this points to, above all, we think, is something that, as we have stated already, was also the main feature of Mr J's clinical presentation in general. We are referring to the striking *integrity* of his ego functioning. He was fully aware of the difficulties that he was having in communicating, and he spared no effort in overcoming these difficulties. Constantly monitoring his therapist's facial expressions and verbal responses for evidence of understanding on her part—or the lack of it—Mr J would either move on to the next topic or persevere with the current one, using now one method of communicating and now another, often deploying considerable ingenuity and creativity in the process, until at last he was able to satisfy himself that the therapist had indeed understood the precise point that he was wishing to convey.

The content of his communications, too, revealed the same intactness of his ego functions. That is to say, the thoughts that Mr J went to such lengths to convey provided abundant evidence of normal underlying intelligence, excellent problem-solving abilities, a high degree of conscious self-awareness, mental agility, and flexibility, a full range of emotions, and so on. Considering the depth and severity of his speech and language deficits, and the central place that we are accustomed to assigning to verbal processing in our conceptualization of the metapsychology of the ego, this high degree of ego integrity in a case of severe Broca's aphasia was indeed remarkable. This fact provides us with a first important clue as to the role that this region of the brain plays in the deep psychological organization of the mental apparatus in general. Whatever this role is, it certainly cannot be too central to what the ego does on the whole. As the reader will see in chapter nine, it was patients with damage to an entirely different part of the brain that presented with the sort of ego deficits that one might have expected (on classical metapsychological grounds) to find in a patient with profound impairment of the "speech apparatus".

Mr J participated actively and deeply in his sessions. With rare exceptions, which were clearly related to periods of inner resistance at specific points in the treatment, he always arrived on time and made full use of the analytic sessions that were available to him. There was an entirely normal therapeutic alliance, disrupted only (once again, as occurs in non-neurological cases) by transference resistances which began to appear after an initial "honeymoon" period.

It was clear from the start that Mr J intended to make use of his treatment as part of a self-motivated programme for recovery. By "recovery", we do not mean that Mr J harboured an unrealistic belief that he would actually overcome his considerable physical handicaps by means of psychoanalytic psychotherapy (although, of course, not surprisingly, this wish was indeed unconsciously present). Rather, what we mean is that he wanted to make use of the opportunity that this form of therapy provided for purposes of learning to adapt to his incapacities, for helping him to *come to terms* with them emotionally, and for assisting him in his efforts to find new and realistic ways of living as normal and as full a life as possible within the tragic circumstances in which he found himself. In other words, Mr J used his treatment to assist him with the process of *normal mourning*. In this respect, as will be seen in chapter eight, he differed radically from the patients with damage to equivalent areas of the *right* cerebral hemisphere—patients who had, if anything, suffered a *lesser* degree of loss.

In his earliest sessions, Mr J spent most of the time telling his therapist about himself, about his life before his stroke, and about his earlier family history. Mr J was the eldest son in a family of three children, each of whom were born two years apart. He said that he and his sister were never close, and also that when he was younger he used to fight constantly with his younger brother. In recent years, however, he and his brother had become emotionally inseparable, and this was especially so since his stroke two years earlier. (Mr J put two fingers together like this,||, to indicate the quality of their present relationship.)

The early family environment had been problematic. The father was a heavy drinker, and he was often violent when drunk. Mr J's mother was the main target of this violence. However, Mr J himself was frequently involved also, especially as he got older, usually in the role of protecting his mother. This was, needless to say, very important to him, and he described with evident masculine pride his determined efforts to protect his mother, and his willingness to stand up physically to his father despite the great disparity between them in terms of strength and size. *Fighting back* seemed to be one of Mr J's main characterological traits, and this was evident in the way in which he tackled the aftermath of his stroke too.

As a result of all the strife at home, when Mr J was 15 years old his parents divorced. Thereafter, he had little contact with his father, and he seems to have gone out of his way to model his own identity as a man on an image that was directly antithetical to the one that he held of his own father (reaction formation). He vowed that he would never be like his father—in particular, that he would never hit a woman, no matter what the circumstances. His choice of profession, too, seemed to arise at least in part from a desire to be a morally "good" man—a man of whom he himself and society at large could be proud. In other words, his ego ideal was the narcissistic antithesis of his father figure.

As soon as he left school, he joined the army and took up a position as a junior officer in the military police, where his main function—at least as he described it—seemed to be to track down and root out undesirable elements in the army's own ranks. As he put it, his main function was to round up young soldiers who went absent without leave, to bring them to book, and to teach them the error of their ways.

An important meaning of the cerebrovascular accident, from Mr J's subjective standpoint, was the way in which it undermined his efforts to build up this adult masculine identity for himself, of which he could feel proud and which distinguished him from what he saw as his good-for-nothing father. In his early sessions he spoke in loving detail about his life in the army, how much he enjoyed it, and, above all, how much he *missed* it. These were very poignant descriptions, saturated with sadness not only by virtue of the warmth of the memories of the life that was and that could have been but was now irrevocably lost, but also for the humiliation that Mr J felt at the way in which he had been dumped by the army—his alternative father. He experienced this as a painful judgement upon his value and usefulness to civil society and therefore upon his own personal definition of what was acceptable in manhood. He spoke movingly of how he now felt that *he* was absent without leave, as it were, and how in phantasy he was constantly at risk of being so judged by an internal equivalent of a military tribunal. Analytic work in this area was readily able to reveal that, for Mr J, the "undesirable elements" in the army, the disciplining and rehabilitation of whom he had been responsible for professionally, unconsciously represented his own bad father. Similarly, it was easy for him to see how he felt that he had become that father himself—that he, too, had become one of life's emotional cripples, an embarrassment in good society, and a burden to all. In this emotional context, it was not difficult to understand what it was that neurological recovery meant for Mr J—it meant, quite simply, the recovery of self-respect.

In our description thus far, it will be apparent to some readers why it is we think that all of those functions that we conceptualize in psychoanalysis under the heading of the ego ideal, the superego, and the like were functionally intact in Mr J's case, notwithstanding his brain damage.

In the context of the early phase of his treatment, Mr J described how he had initially hoped he would be able to return to work for the military police, how he imagined, hoped, and believed that the army—his good internal father—would still want him. He hoped initially that they would make the necessary effort to adapt to his present circumstances and to find an appropriate new role for him. When this did not work out, Mr J shifted his hopes to a relative of his who owned a small farm. He loved the countryside and nature in general, and he was very much hoping that this relative would be sympathetic to his plight and would offer him a job. Mr J remarked in one session, in a particularly moving description, that he felt a close affinity with animals ever since his stroke because they, like him, could not express themselves in words. But despite an invitation to spend an extended period of time on this relative's farm, the wished-for job offer never materialized.

By the time that Mr J came into analytic therapy he was no longer under any illusions as to how difficult it was for someone with his degree of handicap to make his own way in the world, and he was therefore well prepared for the work that he needed to do with his therapist—that is, mourning the loss of the life that he would never have. This process took the form, initially, of a period in which he attempted to prove to his therapist how independent and self-sufficient he was. He emphasized especially the overtly masculine activities that he still participated in, such as billiards and competitive bowling, and even—on one occasion—a bar-room brawl. But as the untenability of this picture of his undiminished manhood gradually became increasingly evident to both patient and therapist (based, as it was, on denial), it was replaced by a period of deeply felt depression.

This period in the treatment began with a series of sessions that seemed to be devoted to the pained question that dominates the thoughts of so many people who have suffered a tragic loss—namely, "Why me?" In these sessions, Mr J vividly portrayed how abandoned by Fate he felt (and how cruelly and unfairly treated he was by the phantasized father that Fate represented). He eventually found it possible to verbalize—or, rather, we should say, to symbolize—the wish that one of his siblings would have suffered the stroke rather than himself. These feelings were brought very much to the forefront by the fortuitous circumstance that his younger sister was soon to be married. The full emotional impact of this event only became apparent to Mr J when he woke up on the morning of the wedding and realized that he had actually forgotten that she was getting married that day. The mood of his sessions around this time was heavy and foggy, almost as if he were in a fugue state. He arrived late for a number of sessions, which was very unusual for him, and he missed one session completely. As he emerged from this fugue-like period, Mr J recognized for the first time how deeply envious he felt towards his sister, and how resentful he was of her normality and happiness.

He spoke thereafter of how he never wanted to marry and have children because he knew that it would end in disappointment and agony for all concerned—just as had happened with his own parents. For him, marriage always started out looking good, but in the end it always broke down. He was not going to make that mistake. It was not fair to the children. The self-destructive aspects of this phantasy were relatively easy to trace back (analytically, that is) to the father identifications which were mentioned earlier, against which Mr J fought so vigorously.

This difficult phase in the treatment culminated in a period of aggressive acting out at home (where Mr J still lived with his mother). His mother bore the brunt of his aggression. He resented bitterly how he had lost his previous status as the oldest male and breadwinner in the family, and how dependent he had since become on his mother in particular. His sister had married, and his brother had also recently left home (to join the armed forces, as he had). Mr J described how he was having to put up with the frustration of being reliant on his mother for help in writing letters to his brother, whom he was missing terribly. His mother, who was having to work longer hours than ever before to meet her new and unexpected responsibilities, had delayed this help for a good few days, despite his repeated requests. The infantile quality of the ensuing outburst at his mother was unmistakable, as was the humiliation that Mr J felt in his diminished role as a renewed dependant of hers.

Following these outbursts, which were forcibly recounted in his sessions over an extended period of time, Mr J was gradually able to begin the long and painful process of mourning his immense loss, and of coming to terms with his tragic situation. The thoroughgoing nature of this process was unmistakable—Mr J acknowledged fully just how much he had lost, just how much he wished this were not the case, and just how much he missed and longed for what he could no longer have. The simple pain of his situation was conveyed most poignantly by just two words, which he uttered repeatedly during this period in the treatment: "I miss." Due to his verbal non-fluency, he could not complete the sentence and give it an object, but somehow his objectless "I miss" seemed for that very reason to convey the essence of his emotional state.

On the basis of this full recognition of what he had lost, Mr J was eventually able to discover a new enthusiasm for life, and a renewed resolve to make good his loss, not by trying to replace what he could no longer have but, rather, by setting himself four specific, realistic, and modest goals: (1) to get a job, (2) to buy a car, (3) to eventually buy a house, and (4), lastly, the most deeply felt wish of all, to have a wife—even if that meant a handicapped wife. We add this last qualification because he was sometimes of the view that he would never be acceptable to any normal and healthy woman. Only somebody who had been through, or was living through, the same sort of ordeal that he had could possibly understand that somebody with a physical handicap could still be a valuable person and a desirable companion in life. For Mr J, normal women would never see beyond his paralysed arm and his lack of normal speech, and they would never find the loving, compassionate, ambitious young man that he knew himself to be. In this, sadly, of course, he was not entirely wrong.

All of this was simultaneously lived out in the transference, as we shall see. Initially, Mr J had indicated his affectionate feelings towards his therapist plainly. He was clearly taking considerable trouble over his appearance, dressing in fashionable clothes, commenting frequently on how nice she looked, how soft her jumper was, how kind and understanding she was, and so on. It was clear that he was developing (perhaps even consciously) hopes that she would become the partner he was looking for; in other words, that his therapy with her would literally end in marriage to her. This was not as concrete or immature a phantasy as it might at first seem to be. He was leading an extremely isolated life, and he had very few opportunities indeed to communicate with people outside his immediate family. It was symptomatic of his healthy ego resources that he saw his developing relationship with his therapist as one of the few chances that he was ever likely to get of forming an emotionally close relationship with a woman. To him, she was clearly exactly what he needed: someone who could see beyond his handicaps and find the real personality that was locked inside him. Unlike most of the girls that he had contact with, his therapist was clearly not repelled by his inability to speak and by his paralysed arm; to her, given her profession, such things were commonplace. It was against this background that he allowed this wishful phantasy to grow in him and gradually to take hold of him. (We are referring to the phantasy that his therapist would indeed fall in love with him and become the answer to all his dreams.)

Needless to say, the subsequent disappointment of this dream posed a serious threat to the treatment alliance, as the positive transference was quickly transformed into a dangerous source of resistance. No longer was his therapist seen as a professional who was reliably available to help him with the difficult emotional and social tasks that he faced. Now she was just like all the rest of them: a self-interested woman who pretended to care for him only for as long as it suited her, which to him seemed to mean for as long as it allowed her to think of him as a needy, dependent little boy; but she quickly clammed up and dropped him as soon as she had to deal with the reality of his being an adult sexual man. For him to continue to work analytically with such a woman was an intolerable humiliation, and the aggression that had previously been directed at his mother pervaded his attitude towards his therapist for some time.

In one particularly difficult session, Mr J told her in an agitated way that he knew how he must look to her, how she could never really believe that he *was* once attractive to women, and that all the things that had now become his greatest aims in life were things that he already had before (or at least that those of them that he did not yet have—namely, a house and a wife—were things that he could take for granted as imminent acquisitions). He said that at the time of his stroke he had a job, a car, a rented apartment of his own, and a beautiful girlfriend of two years' standing. In addition, when he awoke after his stroke and realized that he was paralysed and could not speak, he knew that in one blow he had lost all that he had built up for himself since leaving home and becoming a man in his own right. At that time, he said, he had still allowed himself to hope that he would gradually be able to build it all back up again. His girlfriend had stood by him, but that had not lasted long, and the same experience had been repeated with a succession of subsequent girlfriends, culminating in his present, almost complete social isolation. The extent of the resistance and negativity that characterized this period in the analytic work is perhaps best conveyed by the fact that on one particular occasion Mr J even went so far as to bring his brother's girlfriend along with him to a session, right into the consulting-room. He then proceeded to interrogate the poor unsuspecting girl in front of the therapist— trying to force her to show his therapist how she could never marry a handicapped man.

The fact that Mr J was able to continue working through this difficult period, and find a way of making use of psychotherapy (despite the terrible disappointment of his transference wishes), is a testimony to his sheer determination and strength of character, his typical determination to fight back, and, behind that, the integrity of his ego functions, which we mentioned earlier. A direct consequence of this period of the analytic work was that it became possible for him to tackle directly the central organizing phantasy that had become unconsciously associated with his stroke and consequent handicaps. In a word, the stroke was experienced unconsciously by Mr J as an act of *castration*. Access to this phantasy was provided initially in one particular session during which Mr J— ostensibly speaking about his right paralysed side—did a drawing of *half a man* and then said (with obvious awareness of the figurative meaning of the phrase) "half a man". This was what he himself now was. Through discussion of this image, it became possible to work through the full emotional ramifications (both past and present) of Mr J's damaged and vulnerable situation. It also ultimately emerged through this work that Mr J seemed to have resolved his earlier oedipal struggles in an unusual way: he had reversed the relationship between his father and himself and had equated his good-for-nothing father with the castrated little boy and himself with the powerful father who ends up possessing the mother and becoming the head of the household.

For this reason, when he was forced by virtue of the stroke to relinquish that position, he felt that not only did he have to revert to the inferior position of the little boy without an adequate penis, but simultaneously that he had become the damaged and defeated father whom he so despised. As a result of this ego/superego configuration, what emerged during this final period of the analytic work was that at a deeply unconscious level, Mr J felt somewhat paranoid (since his stroke). He felt as if people despised him absolutely in his damaged state, that they were laughing at him, and that men in particular were constantly wanting to attack him and to beat him up. This, it seems, was the main phantasy underlying the macho, phallic material that he brought in the early period of his treatment. Thus a new phrase was added to the earlier "I miss"—namely, "I scared". The working through of these immensely vulnerable, frightened feelings that his stroke had left him with, and the associated castration phantasies, enabled Mr J to make a far better adaptation to his social environment during the last phase of his treatment.

This improved adaptation was illustrated above all by the fact that he managed to find and then join a social club for disabled people, which seemed to be largely a men's club. After his initial anxiety about attending the first meeting, this club became a source of very great pleasure to him. There he would spend most evenings, mixing with other "guys" in similar situations to himself (they were all handicapped in one way or another), playing billiards, darts, and cards, and so on. He made some very good friends there, too. Eventually, he became one of the stalwarts of this club, not only with respect to organizing its activities, but also in that he seems to have been a very helpful, kind, and caring figure to new members who were struggling to go through the depressions and anxieties that he himself had worked through before.

We are happy to be able to report that, before Mr J's psychotherapy ended, he had achieved the first of the four lifetime goals that he had set himself. That is, through one of the new social contacts he had made at the handicapped people's club, he found a job. By the time that his treatment ended, he was fastidiously saving the money he would need to meet his second and third goals—namely, the acquisition of a car and, eventually, a home of his own.

Discussion

The above are, then, our analytic observations of a case of Broca's aphasia. In subsequent chapters, the reader will see that this case differed enormously from patients with damage *elsewhere* in the brain: in Wernicke's area (chapter six), in the *left* parietal lobe (chapter seven), in the *right* cerebral hemisphere (chapter eight), and in the medial surfaces of the *frontal* lobes (chapter nine). Before we move on to those cases, however, it will be worth while to review very briefly what this case revealed about the contribution that the left inferior lateral frontal region of the brain (Broca's area; Fig. 5-2) makes to the functioning of the human mental apparatus as a whole.

It is often stated in the neuropsychiatric literature that patients with left-hemisphere lesions suffer from depression, whereas patients with right-hemisphere lesions are indifferent to their predicament. It is also said (in that literature) that the "depression" of left-hemisphere patients in comparison to the "indifference" of right-hemisphere patients reflects an underlying functional asymmetry: the left hemisphere is supposed to be dominant for "positive" emotions, whereas the right hemisphere is dominant for "negative" emotions. We have occasion in later chapters to reconsider these widespread assumptions in the light of our psychoanalytic findings. For now, we would like only to point out that Mr J was not, clinically speaking, *depressed*. His reaction was not in any

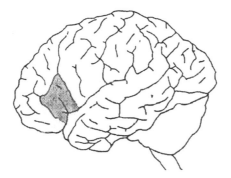

FIGURE 5-2

way *pathological*. Rather, as already stated, the therapeutic process in his case was dominated by the work of *normal mourning*.

Normal mourning is not possible in the absence of a normal ego and of normal superego functions. This points to our primary conclusion in this case: that his ego and superego functioning were essentially *intact*. His ego performed its basic tasks—namely, the mediation between its wishes (the id) and ideals (the superego) on the one hand, and external reality on the other—more than adequately. This was illustrated by the manner in which Mr J negotiated the very difficult process of mourning his loss and of constructing an alternative life for himself on the basis of his new, greatly diminished circumstances.

This fact is very striking, in view of the widespread tendency within psychoanalysis to equate ego functions with verbally mediated thinking. This has its roots in Freud's (1915e) distinction between "word-presentations" and "thing-presentations", which he assigned to the functional domains of the systems preconscious (*Pcs.*) and unconscious (*Ucs.*), respectively. This conventional equation of ego functioning with verbally mediated mental activity is, however, erroneous. It is based on a failure to appreciate that Freud subsumed *both* the system *Pcs.* and most of the *Ucs.* into what he later termed, from 1923 onward, the "ego" (see Freud, 1923b).

We will return to this important issue again later, when we are in a position to compare the analytic presentations of a group of left-hemisphere patients with those of a group of *right*-hemisphere patients. Just as the ego has frequently been conflated with the functional domain of the "word-presentations" in the psychoanalytic literature, so too the systems *Pcs.* and *Ucs.* have frequently been (mistakenly) equated with the asymmetrical functions of the left and right hemispheres, respectively.

But even if "word-presentations" are not co-extensive with the ego, should we not have expected *some* significant impairments of ego and superego functioning in this case? Do word-presentations not perform some extremely important ego and superego functions? Did Freud not say, for example, that words render unconscious thought processes conscious (Freud, 1915e) and that the superego functions primarily on the basis of internalized verbal injunctions (Freud, 1923b)? Why, then, were these fundamental ego and superego functions not disrupted in the case of Mr J, where speech and language abilities (and the cerebral tissues that serve them) were so obviously compromised?

The answer to this questions resides in a fact that Freud had already recognized in 1891—namely, that "the word" is produced by a complex functional system, with a number of component parts, linked (among other things) with the four primary modalities of language: visual, auditory, kinaesthetic, and motor (Freud, 1891b). Each of these primary elements has a different cerebral representation. Broca's area, which is the area that was affected in Mr J's case, is associated primarily with the *motor* element of speech, and only indirectly with the three other elements. And the motor element, according to Freud, was not the component of language that subserved the important ego and superego functions just mentioned:

> Verbal residues are derived primarily from auditory perceptions, so that the system *Pcs.* has, as it were, a special sensory source. The visual components of word-presentations are secondary, acquired through reading, and may to begin with be left on one side; *so may the motor images of words*, which, except with deaf-mutes, play the part of auxiliary indications. In essence a word is after all the mnemic residue of a word *heard*. [Freud, 1923b, pp. 20–21, emphasis added]

The motor aspect of the word, then, and therefore the motor component of the speech apparatus—Broca's area—lies at the sensorimotor *periphery* of ego. It is little more than an output channel for the ego's complex workings; its role in verbal *thinking* is superfluous. When the ego is deprived of this channel of communication with the outside world, its inner workings (and therefore the ego itself) are left fundamentally intact; it can simply make use of alternative components. The functional role of the *auditory* component of the speech apparatus, however, is completely different—as we shall see in the next chapter, which takes us one step deeper into the functional organization of the mind.

CHAPTER SIX

Psychoanalytic observations on a case of Wernicke's aphasia: perforated consciousness

In the previous chapter, we discussed psychoanalytic observations on a case of Broca's (motor) aphasia. The case described in this chapter is that of a patient who was recovering from *Wernicke's* (sensory) aphasia. The outstanding feature of the previous case, from the psychoanalytic viewpoint, was his relative *normality*. Our psychoanalytic observations on him led us to the conclusion that, despite his severe speech and language disorder, and his other physical handicaps, the young man in question was essentially unchanged as a person. This, we felt, was a remarkable observation, considering the central place that has always been assigned in psychoanalytic metapsychology to "words" in the structure and dynamics of mental functioning. That is why at the end of chapter five we reminded the reader that "the word" is a complex neuropsychological entity—comprised of numerous com-

---

This chapter is based on a paper entitled "Psychoanalytic Observations on a Case of Wernicke's Aphasia", presented by Karen Kaplan-Solms and Mark Solms at the Neuro-Psychoanalysis Center of the New York Psychoanalytic Institute on 23 January 1999.

ponent parts—each of which plays a different role in the functional organization of the human mental apparatus. The mental functioning of the patient described in the present chapter was, as will be seen shortly, far from being unaffected by her speech and language disorder.

Case K

Mrs "K" was 67 years old. She had married three times, and was widowed three times, and she had three grown-up children—two sons and a daughter. She was born in a small rural community, to a lower-middle-class family, and although she had, in many ways—as she put it—"bettered" herself, she always had to work hard in order to make ends meet. She had more than her fair share of hardships in life, but she was never defeated by them. She seemed to expect from life nothing more or less than she herself put *into* it; as a result, despite her many troubles, she had lived a full, vigorous and joyful life.

One anecdote will, we hope, suffice to convey the essence of her indomitable, adventurous—and, indeed, mischievous—premorbid personality. After the death of her third husband, from cancer, she found herself in a difficult financial predicament, as a result of which she was compelled to take on two jobs simultaneously. She was employed as a secretarial clerk by day and as a waitress by night; thus she worked a full 16 hours, six days a week, every week. After doing this for more than a year, she reached a point of emotional and physical exhaustion, where she felt that she simply could not carry on any longer. On the verge of collapse, she resigned her waitressing job—and checked into a luxurious hotel, which was certainly way beyond her means. She rested there for almost a month; that is, she slept late, took long baths, watched television, ate four-course meals, and so on. In the meanwhile, as she was a very sociable person, she befriended the reception staff, the kitchen staff, and even one of the duty managers. By the time she checked out, therefore, she knew almost everyone in the hotel and almost everything there was to know about all of their private lives—and they hers. As a result, when she considered herself to be sufficiently rested, and when it was time for her to face up to her pressing responsibilities once more, she simply made an appointment with the duty manager, and applied for a job at the hotel! (She had learned from the kitchen staff that a position was vacant.) So she transferred directly from being a valued guest to being a much-loved employee, and she worked there (as a kitchen supervisor) first in a temporary and then in a permanent capacity.

By the time that she was admitted to our neuro-rehabilitation unit, she was semi-retired, living in a modest residential hotel, and working for a charity (selling raffle tickets for a small commission). Nobody knows for certain what the origin of her brain injury was; however, she had failed to turn up for breakfast one day and was subsequently found, the day after, lying unconscious in her room, with a large gash over the left parietal region of her head. There was blood all over the floor, and her raffle-ticket money and the few other valuable items that she possessed were missing.

She was admitted through the Accident & Emergency department of the hospital to which our neuro-rehabilitation unit was attached. A CT scan demonstrated an acute left fronto-parietal subdural haematoma (with slight midline shift) and a left temporo-parietal intracerebral haemorrhage. She was transferred immediately to our neurosurgical unit, for evacuation of the haematoma. Intra-operative observation revealed a substantial haemorrhagic lesion in the mid-temporal area, extending posteriorly to include the supramarginal gyrus. After the operation, a follow-up scan demonstrated an extensive area of low density in the left temporal lobe. Figure 6-1 provides some indication of the location and extent of this residual lesion.

Neuropsychological assessment

Mrs K did not regain consciousness fully until three weeks after the initial trauma, which is when she first began to respond to verbal commands. At that point, however, she displayed very little comprehension, and her speech—although it was fluent—was almost completely nonsensical. This is called "jargonaphasia". (Her subjective experience of what was going on during that acute period was very interesting, as will be seen.) She recovered very

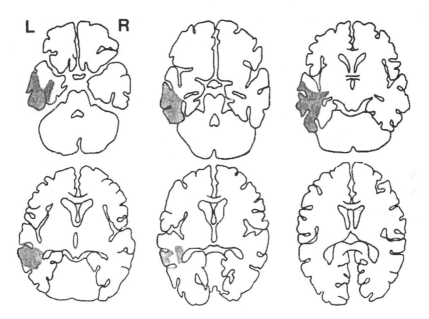

FIGURE 6-1

rapidly, however, and by the time that we first saw her, five weeks after the trauma, her language was characterized by fluent "empty speech" (i.e. a stream of connected discourse that lacks substantives) with abundant verbal paraphasias (i.e. misuse of words). At the time of this assessment, Mrs K (unlike Mr J) reported that she had stopped dreaming completely since the assault (cf. chapter three, "first syndrome").

The psychoanalytic therapy began one month later. By that time, the Wernicke's aphasia had resolved further, into what is perhaps best described as a severe *amnestic* aphasia—or into what Luria (1947) called "acoustico-mnestic aphasia". The essential features of this disorder, as will soon become apparent, are due to an *inability to retain audioverbal material in working memory* (i.e. in consciousness). At that point, her speech was still fluent, but it had become more circumlocutory than empty. Mrs K was also reading with ease, but with limited comprehension, and her writing was—like her spoken language—fluent but paraphasic (and also marred by the fact that she kept forgetting what it was that she was intending to write).

Mrs K complained constantly of what she described as an "inability to think", which—as we shall see—was the main way in which she experienced her aphasia subjectively. However, formal neuropsychological assessment showed that she was able to solve simple calculations with ease (as long as they were written down). There were, in fact, no definitive signs of parietal-lobe dysfunction. Right–left orientation, finger gnosis, constructional praxis, and graphaesthesis, in addition to calculation, were all intact. (With left parietal-lobe damage, these functions are normally impaired.) Visuospatial memory, too, was completely intact, as were her visuospatial *perceptual* functions, apart from a right upper quadrantanopia (i.e. blindness in the top right corner of the visual field). There was no sign of right-hemisphere dysfunction, and the various executive functions associated with the frontal lobes, too, appeared to be entirely preserved. In summary, Mrs K presented clinically with a right upper quadrantanopia, a fluent aphasic disorder, and an audioverbal material-specific working-memory disorder that was, in a profound sense, indistinguishable from her aphasia.

Psychoanalytic observations

Mrs K's psychoanalytic therapy lasted for a few months only, so our psychoanalytic understanding of her is limited. The material that we are going to present is somewhat fragmentary, but, as will be seen, this is a reflection of the essential nature of her difficulties. We are not suggesting that Mrs K was fragmented and disconnected in general (as were the ventromesial frontal patients described in chapter nine). Far from it. In fact, it is fair to say that Mrs K's pre-morbid personality was more or less intact. In this respect, she was no different from the case of Broca's aphasia that we discussed in chapter five. She was still the same old indefatigable spirit, with the same sense of fun, and the same sense of proud independence, and so on, that she had always been.

We do not intend to enter into a detailed analysis of her personality. In her case, this would not convey what is scientifically interesting. Rather, we would like briefly to summarize two or three striking features of her clinical presentation, which seem to capture the essence of what her brain lesion had done to her mental life. These features appeared to be two aspects of a single underlying abnormality. This abnormality attached itself to what was essentially, in all other respects, as we have said, a normal personality.

Our presentation of this case takes the form of a series of short extracts from the clinical material, which illustrate the main features that we are focusing on. We start with Mrs K's subjective experience of emerging from her coma.

She described that experience as follows (no attempt is made to represent her paraphasias and other dysphasic errors here):

"I didn't know where I was at first—I first thought I was in *heaven*, and, because I couldn't understand what people were saying, I thought they must speak another language in heaven, which I would have to learn." [*laughs*] "I thought, this is how people live and dress in heaven. But then I began to think that maybe I was outside heaven—in the place where you sit and wait to hear whether or not you can get into heaven, or must go to hell. You know, they say that even if you commit one *tiny* sin on earth, you go to hell. So I've been trying to make sure that I don't do anything bad at all, so I can go to heaven. I am sure I have done some bad things in my life, but I don't know exactly what they are!" [*laughs again*]

In response to a question from her therapist [K.K.-S.], she said that the first time she realized that she was actually alive and on earth was when her children came to visit her: "When they came, in the very first instant I thought I was still in heaven and they were there with me. But then I realized they couldn't all have died as well, and that I must be wrong."

The reader will learn in chapter nine that one of the ventromesial frontal cases, too, when he regained consciousness after his stroke, believed that he had died and gone to heaven. In fact, the delusion of being dead is common enough to have a technical name of its own: *Cotard's syndrome*. It seems that when consciousness is suddenly lost for an extended period such as this, and the patient's continuity of being is interrupted so dramatically, the sense of *personal identity* can be disturbed. This disturbance is no doubt reinforced by the fact that these patients' worlds appear radically changed, by virtue of the fact that their brains no longer work normally and therefore no longer represent reality in the way that they used to. In Mrs K's case, for example, due to her Wernicke's aphasia, everybody seemed to her to be speaking a foreign language when she first emerged from her coma. And there were other important changes in her consciousness, too, which are described below. The phantasy of having died, then, was her initial way of making sense of what had happened to her. But that explanation was quickly abandoned, as she began to integrate the bits and pieces of the emerging evidence in a rational way.

In fact, the question of what had happened to her was a major preoccupation of hers, and her struggle to answer it was the main purpose for which she used her psychotherapeutic sessions. She seemed to have great difficulty reconciling her subjective experience of what had happened (i.e. that nothing at all had happened, simply a blank period and a discontinuity in her sense of being) with the objective evidence (i.e. that really a great deal had happened, and that these events of which she knew nothing had changed her forever). She asked her therapist repeatedly, for example, if she had *really* been unconscious for a whole three weeks, and she wanted to know the precise date of her injury, the date of her operation, and so on. Then she would recount, over and again, what she believed must have happened during the intervening period, and in this way she tried to shore up the gaping hole in her continuous experience of her life, and to fill that hole with a plausible account of what might have happened.

These reconstructions always started with her last conscious recollection of what she was doing before the trauma. That is, she remembered sitting in front of the mirror, brushing her hair. At this point in her story, she would almost always emphasize that she used to have long, flowing black hair, and contrast it with her current, semi-shaven state, from which she seemed to want to dissociate herself. She did not know what happened next. She knew only—from what others had told her—that she was found the next day, on her bed, with her walking-stick lying beside her. She believed that her assailant must have used the walking-stick as a weapon, and cleaned it afterwards, as there was blood on the floor but no blood on the stick, although the stick was dented and was not standing in the place where she normally kept it. Perhaps the assailant had come back sometime after the crime, she speculated, cleaned the stick, and then placed her on the bed. And so it went on. There were endless variations on this theme.

Equally uncertain was the identity of the assailant—although Mrs K. had some definite ideas on this subject. Her suspicions focused primarily on a handyman, who, as she always emphasized, was rude and common. The other main suspect was a cleaning lady, whom she evidently had always mistrusted. In one version of her story, the handyman had assaulted her, possibly for some reason other than robbery, and then the cleaning lady had found her the next morning, had shifted her onto the bed, and had taken the opportunity to steal all the valuables in the room. That would explain why she had not reported the crime. There was even a hint that the handyman might have had an unreciprocated sexual interest in her, and that that was what lay behind the assault in the first place.

In any event, whatever really happened, all the different permutations were equally plausible. What mattered most to Mrs K was that the disturbing gap in her continuity of being should be *somehow* filled—if not by conscious memories, then at least by a plausible reconstruction that was capable of accommodating all the available facts. Nevertheless, the slightly compulsive quality of this gap-filling process was noteworthy. What was also interesting was that none of her various reconstructions really satisfied her (as she seemed constantly disturbed by the possibility that none of them actually bore any relationship to reality at all). In this sense, she sometimes spoke about the different versions as though they were dreams—the kind of dreams that one sometimes has that haunt one throughout the day and leave one feeling unsure as to whether or not they really happened. To deal with this dream-like sense of doubt, Mrs K would usually ask her therapist what *she* thought, often with some embarrassment, but sometimes also with a hint of desperation. Did *she* think that what Mrs K was saying made any sense—could that *really* be what happened to her, or did her theories all seem crazy?

This need to fill in the gaps was undoubtedly the overriding feature of Mrs K's presentation. This leads to the main aspect of it, which Mrs K described as an *"inability to think"*. The gaps in Mrs

K's consciousness were not confined to the three-week period of her coma. She was still experiencing gaps in her consciousness, even as she spoke, in the sense that her ongoing awareness of her own self and thoughts *kept disappearing*. Her mind kept slipping through the fingers of her consciousness, as it were. This difficulty was inextricable from her aphasia and, in fact, seemed to be the crux of her subjective experience of it.

She described the problem as follows, in her first session. After entering the consulting-room, which she did rather apprehensively, she asked the therapist to remind her of her (the therapist's) name—explaining that she kept forgetting people's names. No sooner had this been done than she asked again, this time looking a little flustered and embarrassed. She explained that she knew she had met her before, but was not sure where. Had she been present at the police interview the day before? The therapist answered that she had not, and she explained that she had met Mrs K during the neuropsychological assessment, and also that she had been present at some of the ward rounds. This seemed to orientate Mrs K to who the therapist was, and she seemed genuinely to recognize her.

Then she spoke about the assault, but as she did so she constantly lost her place and forgot what it was that she was trying to say. Eventually, she stopped, took a deep breath, and started all over again; she said for the second or third time that the last thing she remembered was sitting in front of the mirror and brushing her hair. She added that the man whom she suspected of being the attacker was common. (She seemed to want to emphasize, by implication, that she herself was not common.) She explained that *someone* must have assaulted her; if not him, then someone else, as the doctors and the police had told her that she had sustained multiple blows to the head. "He must have been trying to *kill* me!", she reflected, with evident alarm. She speculated that he or somebody else must have shifted her body onto the bed, the following day. She had probably been left lying on the floor all night, she added, with strong emotion. Then, after a moment of reflective silence, she said that she used to be very independent, and that she did all sorts of things on her own; but now, as a result of this experience, she had become too scared to go anywhere without someone accompanying her—she would not even go for a walk during the daytime in the hospital grounds. (At this point, the therapist recalled how apprehensive she had looked when she first entered the consulting-room.)

This led her on to the main point. She said, "and sometimes I also don't know if I myself won't have a crazy spell". The therapist asked her what she meant. She replied: "Well, look at me. I was always clever and I spoke very well. Now I *can't think*. I don't know what's going on—even simple things such as names of animals, which I knew very well because I grew up on a farm. For example, I went to the school . . . I mean zoo . . . I went to the zoo yesterday, and . . . *what* are those *very big* animals?" The therapist asked her if she was referring to elephants. She responded: "It's too terrible—I can't remember the simplest things—it's *just not me!*" She repeated this a few times. "I just can't understand what's happened to me". Since the therapist was unsure how much she actually knew at that point about the concrete facts of what had happened to her, she explained that the part of her brain that controlled speech—*her memory for words*—had been damaged. But Mrs K quickly interrupted and said, "but here is another example of how silly I've become! You know, I just *can't* understand what you're saying. I know it's English, but I don't know what it *means*. What do you *mean*?" So the therapist repeated herself, as succinctly as she could, using much shorter sentences and phrases, trying to circumvent the apparent acoustico-mnestic deficit. Mrs K listened intently to the explanation, looking very surprised. When it was over, after a short silence, she exclaimed: "*Oh!* I must be in the right place then!" However, it was still not clear how much she had taken in of what the therapist said.

Then she said, yet again, that she could not remember the simplest things. She continued, "I never know what's going to happen. If I go out, maybe I'll have to talk to someone or deal with something, and I can't . . . not like this . . . I don't talk to everyone I'd like to, except for person . . . people here at the hospital. I won't even see my friends like this. And I'm too nervous to be alone anywhere." She continued: "And I want to work and be independent like I always was. I used to work, and go dancing, but it's all so *different* now. I had a job selling pictures . . . I mean tickets . . . books of tickets, till recently. . . ." At this juncture, she struggled for a long time to find the name of her employers, and to explain what it was that she did for them. She then moved on to the subject of her physical appearance, which is something we will return to later, although, as can be seen, this association was obviously related to the "inability to think" that she was describing—with the connecting link being her *sense of estrangement from herself.*

We want first of all to provide a fuller impression of what she meant by her "inability to think". This was, as we have said, the central feature of her presentation. The following extract is from the second week of her treatment. As usual, Mrs K entered the consulting-room hesitantly. In fact, the nurses said that she was reluctant to leave her bed at the best of times, and that she always seemed rather nervous; but she was especially reluctant to leave her bed to attend her psychotherapy sessions. Also, whenever she did summon up the courage to leave, she always asked the nurses if she could smoke there.

Initially, on entering the consulting-room, cigarettes and ashtray in hand, as usual, she did not seem to recognize the room right away, and she looked at her therapist quite nervously and suspiciously. It was as if she was not sure what this was all about, even though her visual recent memory was certainly intact. She later explained that what usually happened was that within a few minutes of the session starting, her conscious recollection of the previous sessions suddenly came flooding back into her mind, and then she felt much safer about being there. She explained that she knew intellectually that she had been there before, but that it did not *feel* familiar to her; it was only once she had started conversing that she consciously remembered what had previously transpired between them. Then all of a sudden the sense of familiarity—and of safety—would return.

Also noteworthy in this connection was the fact that her subjective sense of the passage of time was abnormal. Typically, the interludes between the sessions felt very much longer to her than the couple of days that they actually were (she was seen three times a week).

In one particular session, she began—as usual—by sitting down, and after an initial period of hesitation she launched into her abundant associations. She said: "I am *so* mixed up. Sometimes I remember things and sometimes they are *gone* . . . or mixed up. And often they are things that I know very well, or did before . . . like the names of my children, and my grandchildren, and friends and so on. I even mix my sons' names up, and call the one by the other's name." While she was saying this, she got stuck for a word. Then she said: "*Look* at this—I used to be so fluent . . . at least I could think. And it's not working any more . . . often I can't even remember what I was trying to say, and then I just drop the whole thing and forget about it." She then exclaimed, with a characteristic expression of bewilderment, "I just don't know how I could get like this!"

Next she complained that she developed headaches when she tried to think, but she usually failed so would give up trying. She could not even remember clearly the places that she had always visited on holiday. "For example, in Florida I used to love the. . . ." And then she stopped, and just sat there looking at the therapist blankly, with bewilderment. The therapist reminded her that she was talking about Florida. "Yes", she said, "that's what happens. Yes, there were those dolphins. I used to love the dolphin place." The therapist supplied the word "aquarium", and Mrs K continued to say that she loved it, though the rest of her family hated it. The therapist said that she appeared a moment earlier to have lost track of her self and the world. Mrs K misunderstood this, and thought that she was speaking about international travel. The therapist explained that by "world" she was referring to Mrs K's experience of what was going on around her. Then Mrs K said, "Oh, yes, I am in bits and pieces. I am in bits and pieces through my mind", pointing at her head. "Often I just want to sit down on my own so I don't have to talk, because I can't remember things. And this is not like me, because I'm a very good-natured person and there is no one in the world I do not like to talk to." Then she went on to speak about her appearance again, thus underlining the link, mentioned earlier, between her experience of her appearance and her experience of her mind. We describe later how she experienced her appearance, but first we provide some further examples of what she meant by her "inability to think".

She began one session by saying that she could not speak properly, and that she never used to be like that. She used to speak quickly and easily, but she was finding that she forgot single words as well as what she wanted to say in general, and then—as she put it—"then it *all* goes". She described a conversation she had had the previous day, in which someone had asked her a direct question and no answer had occurred to her, and she realized that "there was *nothing* there". She elaborated: "And when there's nothing there, I can't say or do anything! It feels so terrible!" She kept saying, with apologetic disbelief: "I have never ever been like this, ever before, and I used to be so speakable . . . oh no—speakable!— what that? . . . I mean . . . I mean so fluent. I've never been like this in my life, and now I don't want to talk too much—like to the people in this hotel . . . oh, listen to me . . . I mean hospital. It is so terrible that I ask that Indian man . . . what's his name? . . . to help me when I can't remember. When these things go, everything goes." The therapist asked her to clarify what she meant by "everything goes". Did she mean that when the words go, *all* her thoughts, verbal and non-verbal, go with them. Mrs K replied, "Yes, *everything* goes. Well, first, everything goes, and then at those times I go and lie on my house . . . I mean bed, because what else can you do? And I don't want to see anyone. But it doesn't all come back to me, not everything. Some of it comes back but not other things. Then I'll suddenly remember the things when I'm not try-ing to. Like the other day, I gave my name and I was giving my address and suddenly it was gone . . . my *own* address! And some-times I can't even think of my own name. Can you believe it—my *own name*! I know it now, today, but sometimes I don't." She then said that she had been called by a few names during her life, various nicknames and so on, but all the names were equally liable to disappear.

Hopefully, it is clear from these examples that what Mrs K was experiencing were constant *gaps in her consciousness* or *disruptions in the continuity of her stream of consciousness*. This sets her in sharp contrast to the case of *Broca's* aphasia that we discussed in chapter five. It matches much more closely what we might have expected (metapsychologically) would occur following damage to the cere-bral substrate of language, which plays such a central role in our psychoanalytic conceptualization of the mental apparatus. We dis-cuss these issues a little later. First we provide one more extract.

In a session in the third month of her treatment, Mrs K was saying how relieved she was to know that she was not the only person in the world with such strange deficits. She had noticed that other aphasic patients in the unit had difficulties similar to her own. She went on to say that she never used to have any social problems, but since her trauma she sometimes preferred to stay on her own because she could not talk. She continued: "Sometimes I'm okay and sometimes I'm not. There are times when my mind goes entirely blank—there are *no* words. Then I just lie on my bed and my mind is empty, and I look at the table across from me, and wait for the words to come back." Again the therapist asked her to clarify whether it was only words that disappeared, or everything. Mrs K replied emphatically that at times there was nothing in her mind—in other words, her mind went completely *blank*, and she had no control over it; all she could do was sit and wait for it to come back again, which it did in bits and pieces, in a muddled-up sort of way. A characteristic look of puzzlement appeared on her face. She then went on once more to talk about her appearance.

Thus far we have left the issue of her appearance in abeyance, because we wanted to describe the primary disorder of consciousness first. But, as we mentioned, she very frequently associated from her difficulties with words, and with her thinking, to her feelings about her appearance. The story about her appearance always took a similar form. She would say how the last thing that she remembered was herself sitting in front of the mirror, brushing her hair. Then the next thing she could remember was that she woke up in what seemed to be heaven, where everybody spoke a foreign language, including the members of her own family. Then she remembered walking up to a mirror and looking at her reflection and thinking, "but *that* isn't *me*". She would see the bandages over her hair, and her swollen face, and so on, and she would be genuinely unable to believe that the person she was looking at was her*self*.

Here is an example:

I [the therapist] said to Mrs K that it seemed she could no longer take her mind for granted. She exclaimed: "*Yes!*—I can't any more—I *never* know what is going to happen. If I go out, maybe I'll have to talk to someone or deal with something I can't . . . not like this . . . I don't talk to anyone I'd like to . . . I mean everyone, not anyone. And I'm so nervous. I don't know what I can do with my brain like this. How can I know what to do if it is like this? It's just not *me* any more. And what's another thing . . . look at my hair. I can't curl it or change the style, and it looks terrible like this. Do *you* think I look terrible? I *feel* so terrible. I don't want anyone to see me like this." She showed [the therapist] a picture of herself, which was apparently taken a good few years earlier as she looked significantly younger. "Its a few years ago and my hair was dark because I tinted it, but I can't do anything like that now. I can't even wear plaster . . . oh, listen to me . . . I mean mascara." She kept saying that she knew she was not pretty, but that she had always been very presentable, very well turned out. She went on: "I've never had my hair like this. It just isn't me. I've never had it this length. I want it longer, like yours. So I can't even cut the normal side off. I always look awful without a fringe around my face." While she was speaking she kept losing her thoughts. She explained: "I know what I want to say but I can't find the words; they just aren't there. And then, before I can find the words, the *thought* is gone. I just can't *think* anymore. You see, my mind isn't working, and I was always so well-spoken." She kept saying, "It's not me . . . it's not me!"

She continued: "And when I first looked in the mirror, it was *not me* that I saw. I was completely shocked. I looked completely different. When I looked in that mirror, I saw someone else there. I suppose it must be because I had bandages on; and that looked even worse than this, with half my head shaved. Also, my face was very swollen. I turned away from the mirror because I couldn't cope with the shock. Then I saw the two dots . . . I mean moles . . . the two moles on my right cheek, in order to remind myself that I was still the same person. Also, I'm not talking like myself. I used to be so *fluent*. I cannot believe that I don't know all these words that I've always known. It's just not me . . . I'm not myself." And so she went on.

Clearly she kept associating from feeling that she was not herself, due to her inability to find words and to think, to her inability to recognize her own reflection in the mirror. Subjectively, they seemed to be two aspects of the same thing. But there was a deeper unity to this disturbance of personal identity, which was also hinted at by her simultaneous inability to remember her own name and address. It seemed as if Mrs K sometimes really did not feel as if she *was* herself. This touches on the very important metapsychological question of *the relationship between words and things*.

To illustrate this further, we quote from a session that took place four months into her treatment. She had been talking about how her mind sometimes went completely blank. Then she went on to say that, despite this, she was aware of how much progress she had made during the months since her injury: "My brother and relatives told me how bad I was. They came to visit me in the neurosurgery ward, and there were sounds coming out of my mouth, but they could not understand them at all. It was as if I was talking Chinese. Actually, at first I couldn't speak at all; I said nothing. Then by the time I came to this unit I was still talking a lot, but not making sense; but I couldn't *hear* that I was not making sense. Also, in the neurosurgery ward my face was so swollen that my family could not recognize me at all. And I couldn't recognize myself in the mirror either."

Then Mrs K continued in a confessional tone: "Actually, it's not just my speaking, or finding words that I know but can't find . . . I am also confused in what I *know*. For example, the other day my sons came to visit . . . and only my older son looks like my husband; not my younger son. But the whole time that they were here I thought that my younger son *was actually* my husband. It was only a few hours after he left that I realized that I had made a mistake! An unbelievable mistake!" She went on to say that this kind of confusion was happening regularly, though less often than it did initially. However, she was unable to provide further specific examples. She then went on to speak once more about how she sometimes forgot her sons' names and even her own name and address, and how embarrassed this made her feel, because she was sure that her friends and family had never come across this sort of thing before.

On a subsequent occasion, she said that she was going to visit some friends of hers in another ward of the hospital, only to realize later that these were friends who lived together with her in her residential hotel—they were not living in this hospital. This reduplicative error was especially interesting, because it seemed to concretize an aphasic error that she frequently made, in which she confused the words "hospital" and "hotel" (paraphasia). So here, too, it was apparent that the missing *words* and the confusions about *words* in her mind generalized (in certain ways) to the underlying *things* that those words represented.

We wish to emphasize that, for the most part, Mrs K came across as fundamentally reality-oriented. She always noticed her errors, with embarrassment, and corrected them, and she was always trying to improve her grasp of what was going on around her, in time and space. In this respect, as we have said already, despite all her confusions, she was radically different to the ventromesial frontal patients described in chapter nine, who seemed totally immersed in their confusions and quite unable to gain a grip on reality at all. Thus, for example, even when her mind was completely blank, as she experienced it, Mrs K would behave in a sensible way, putting herself to bed and waiting for her thoughts to return.

Indeed, she was even sufficiently *compos mentis* to be acutely aware of how *embarrassing* her situation was, and she was always very concerned about how she might appear to others. She also went to considerable lengths, over and again, to assure her therapist that she had not always been like this—that she used to be witty and articulate and presentable, that she was always well spoken and intelligent, and so on. In fact, this was a major theme of the transference, such as it was. She was anxious that her therapist should know that this was not the *real* Mrs K, that she was really another person, whom the therapist had never met—the person in the photograph. Apart from anything else, this embarrassment and sense of shame speaks volumes for the integrity not only of her ego, but also of her ego ideal and other underlying superego structures and functions.

The other major transference theme was a sisterly one, in which Mrs K joined the therapist in a huddle and confided in her—that is, told her her private thoughts, and her innermost fears and secrets, as an adolescent may have done with a close and trusted friend. For the rest, Mrs K simply used her therapist to help her to orientate herself to what had happened to her—to help her to fill in the gaps in her conscious recall, and to reassure her that she was not silly, crazy, or a moron—that she was not the only person in the world like this, and so on, as we described earlier. In these respects, then, her therapist was used mainly as an auxiliary ego (cf. chapter nine).

Towards the end of her brief period of treatment, she used the time mainly to express her considerable anxiety about how she was going to cope in the outside world again, in future, after she was discharged; and she went over and over the practical arrangements that had been made for her by her sons and the social workers. Here, once again, what emerged most clearly was how solidly in touch with reality she was—despite the great unreliability of her speech and her consciousness in general, and despite all her fleeting confusions. She was still fundamentally the same person—a survivor, who had her feet solidly on the ground after her brain injury no less than she always did, despite the fact that the ground seemed to keep disappearing from under her.

By the time the treatment ended, she had, furthermore, made considerable progress. As her speech and language recovered, so too did her "thinking" in general, and she became far more integrated in her reflexive sense of her self. She realized that she could not return to her previous level of independence. In this way, as she recovered, she became less agitated about her predicament, and she related to her therapist more deeply and more openly, and—in a sense—with greater sadness. In this respect, therefore, as with the case described in chapter five, the therapeutic process was ultimately used also for the normal work of *mourning* (cf. chapter eight).

So, in summary, this was a case of recovering Wernicke's aphasia, with what can in colloquial terms be described—as indeed it was in the first, classical case descriptions—as a "loss of memory for words". This loss presented externally as a word-finding difficulty and paraphasia, and as an inability to understand some of what was said to her; however, internally it was experienced as a perforation of her consciousness, and therefore of the very fabric of her being. As a result of this "loss of memory for words", Mrs K experienced herself as being "unable to think". This change in her consciousness (coupled with the change in her appearance, and exacerbated by the large gap in her continuous recall due to a three-week period of unconsciousness) combined to radically undermine her sense of personal identity. At times, this seemed to reach the very foundations of her being, and her loss of memory for words became a loss of memory for things, and her confusions between words became a confusion between things. However, *Mrs*

K was always fully able to reflect rationally on these strange and deeply disturbing experiences: she could describe them to her therapist, and she could use all the available information to reassure herself that she was not going crazy, that she did indeed still exist, and that the world, and the place that she occupied in it, despite all appearances, was still the same world that it had always been.

Discussion

This patient's language disorder was experienced subjectively as what she called an "inability to think". However, as the reader can clearly see, she was far from being truly unable to *think*. Rather, we would like to suggest, she suffered from an inability to *attach words to her thoughts*, resulting in an inability to *bring her thoughts to consciousness* (and to *keep* them there). This immediately evokes our metapsychological understanding of *the relationship between words and things*.

One of the most basic assumptions of psychoanalysis states that "mental processes are in themselves unconscious" (Freud, 1915e, p. 171). This assumption raises an obvious question: how, then, do we become conscious of our mental processes? Freud's proposal was the following:

> Conscious processes occur on the periphery of the ego and everything else in the ego is unconscious. Such would be the simplest state of affairs that we might picture and such may in fact be the state of affairs in animals. But in man there is an added complication through which internal processes in the ego may also acquire the quality of consciousness. This is the work of the function of speech, which brings material in the ego into a firm connection with mnemic residues of visual, but more particularly of auditory, perceptions. Thenceforward the perceptual periphery of the cortical layer can be excited to a much greater extent from inside as well. Internal events such as passages of ideas and thought processes can become conscious. [1940a (1938), p. 162]

It seems reasonable to suggest, then, that *this* was the function that was defective in the case of Mrs K: the capacity to bring material in the ego into a firm connection with mnemic residues of auditory perceptions. It was not that she did not have *thoughts,* but rather that she was unable to *attach words* to her thoughts and, therefore, was unable to render her thoughts *conscious.*

It is worth reminding readers at this juncture that Freud conceived of consciousness as being comprised of at least two component systems, which he denoted by the abbreviations *Pcpt.* (perceptual system) and *Cs.* (consciousness system). The *Pcpt.* system was excited by external stimuli, which only became conscious once these stimuli attracted an additional, attentional cathexis from the system *Cs.* The system *Cs.*, for its part, could also be excited by internal processes (such as thoughts), but these could only become conscious by being brought into associative contact with mnemic traces of *Pcpt.* excitations.

> It [thus] dawns upon us like a new discovery that only something which has once been a perception can become conscious, and that anything arising from within (apart from feelings) that seeks to become conscious must try to transform itself into external perception. [1923b, p. 20]

The case of Mrs K presents confirmatory evidence for this analysis of the substructure of consciousness. Mrs K was perfectly capable of registering new external perceptions (the *Pcpt.* system was essentially intact), but she had great difficulty in attaching consciousness to mental processes arising from *within* her mind (her *Cs.* system was defective). (Even her aphasia could be understood in these terms: she *heard* what was said to her, but she could not determine what it *meant.*) Here we begin to see the scientific usefulness of a neuro-psychoanalytic approach to metapsychology. It is hard to imagine how this particular topographical hypothesis of Freud's could be tested against purely psychopathological material; however, in focal neurological cases (such as Mrs K) it is relatively easy to demonstrate functional dissociations of this order. Moreover, once a metapsychological concept such as this has been dynamically localized in this way, it becomes possible to probe its functional properties in further detail (i.e. to define more precisely the functions that may be allocated to the *Pcpt.* and *Cs.* systems, respectively). For example, Luria (1947) suggested that the fundamental deficit in cases of this type is an inability to stabilize audioverbal traces (i.e. to retain a reverberating firing pattern in left mid-temporal neurons)—a function that we would nowadays suggest is supervised from the left dorsolateral prefrontal convexity. This begins to draw possible parallels between the systems *Cs.* and *Pcpt.* on the one hand, and the dorsolateral prefrontal convexity and the mid-temporal region on the other, and it begins to link the classical Freudian metapsychology with the functional architecture of the "working-memory" system, which is attracting so much attention in contemporary cognitive science. However, we do not propose to pursue such detailed theoretical questions at this stage. For now, we want only to make the point that basic metapsychological mechanisms such as this one *can*, in principle, be dynamically localized within the tissues of the brain, using the methods that we are recommending.

In psychoanalytic metapsychology, great importance is attached to the particular mechanism in question here. This is due not only to the fact that psychoanalytic therapy revolves centrally around the process of rendering unconscious thought processes conscious (hence the "talking cure"), but also because Freud argued, in his first topographical model of the mind, that *repression* itself could be understood as a simple reversal of this process. That is, Freud (1915e) proposed that repression simply involved a withdrawal of the associative links that the system *Cs.* is capable of establishing between internal (*Ucs.*) mental processes and audioverbal (*Pcpt.*) traces. Once this link is withdrawn, the thought processes at issue are no longer capable of becoming conscious—that is, they are *repressed*.

However, repression involves more than a mere absence of consciousness; it implies a loss of *executive control* over the thought processes in question. Freud eventually recognized that these two processes (consciousness and executive control), too, can dissociate. For this and other reasons, he realized (1923b) that the system *Cs.* is not the executive agency of the mind. It is not the withdrawal of *word* associations (i.e. consciousness) that constitutes repression, but rather the withdrawal of executive (i.e. ego) control—something that is independent of the property of consciousness.

The validity of this functional dissociation, too, is demonstrated by the case of Mrs K: despite her inability to attach consciousness to her thoughts, she nevertheless continued to behave in an essentially reasonable way (some exceptions to this are discussed below). That is, her ego and superego functions remained essentially intact; she continued to function as an essentially rational and reality-oriented agent, and she continued to experience shame and guilt, etc., as she tried to come to grips with what had happened to her. In this respect, she was identical to Mr J. She retained executive control over her *behaviour*; all that she lost was control over her *consciousness* (and it is only in this respect that she differed from Mr J). This confirms Freud's revised (1923b) topographical proposals, to the effect that consciousness is not the executive agency of the mind, and that even the ego itself is fundamentally unconscious.

Why, then, *did* Mrs K and Mr J differ in relation to the specific function of reflexive consciousness? According to Freudian metapsychology, once more, this difference is accounted for by the componential substructure of the function of speech. We have said that the deficit of consciousness in Mrs K's case was attributable to her damaged word-presentations. But did not Mr J, too, have damaged word-presentations? The solution to this apparent contradiction is to be found—as we discussed at the end of chapter five—in the fact that *different components* of the complex functional system that is designated by the simple term "word-presentations" were damaged in each of these two cases. In Mr J's case it was the *motor* component of speech that was damaged, whereas in Mrs K's case, it was the *auditory* component. Even in Freud's day, neurologists knew that "words" did not have a simple neuropsychological structure. As early as 1891, Freud emphasized that words are complicated things, that they have a complex, distributed representation within multiple sensorimotor analysers. He never forgot this insight, and when he later developed his psychoanalytic metapsychology, he took pains to emphasize more than once that it was only the *auditory* component of language that had a special relationship with consciousness. This continuity between Freud's aphasiological and his psychoanalytical theorizing is demonstrated by the following quotation, which we have already quoted once before, from *The Ego and the Id* (1923b):

> Verbal residues are derived primarily from auditory perceptions, so that the system *Pcs.* has, as it were, a special sensory source. The visual components of word-presentations are sec-

ventromesial frontal patient to be described in chapter nine truly *believed* that he was dead (and he applied this belief like a patch over a rent in his contact with reality). By contrast, Mrs K *tested* her phantasy of being dead against the perceptual evidence that attested to the fact that she was actually still alive, thereby exposing the *mutual contradictions* between her phantasy and her perception, and accordingly—on the basis of an act of *judgement*—she rejected the phantasy (psychic reality) in favour of external reality.

All of this implies that the basic inhibitory functions of the ego—which underpin the whole of the secondary process and the reality principle—which were radically undermined (as we shall see in chapter nine) in cases of ventromesial frontal damage, were basically intact in this case of left temporal convexity damage (Mrs K), just as they were in the case of left frontal convexity damage (Mr J). These functions were *less stable* in the case of Mrs K than they were in Mr J's case. This suggests that the auditory component of the word-presentation does participate in some way in the executive functioning of the ego, but that this contribution is not fundamental to the integrity of that agency. In chapter nine, we consider what it is that *does* fundamentally underpin these functions of the ego. For now, we can say only that it is *not* the word-presentations—and this applies to both their motor and their sensory components. Although the audioverbal component of language is a basic ingredient of the fabric of *consciousness*, the fabric of the *ego* itself is provided by something other than sensorimotor speech presentations. Therefore, the limited ego deficits that were evident in the present case reveal nothing more than the limited contribution that consciousness makes to the executive functioning of the ego as a whole. Real as that contribution may be—affecting, as it does, the sense of self (of personal identity) and the like, as can be seen from the case of Mrs K—it is far from being fundamental to the basic reflexive and other executive operations of the ego as a whole. These functions, as this case vividly demonstrates, do not depend on consciousness and language. And this is what Freud, too, concluded, after 20 years of considering the evidence available to him from purely psychopathological material:

> The inside of the ego, which comprises above all the thought processes, has the quality of being preconscious. This is characteristic of the ego and belongs to it alone. It would not be

correct however to think that connection with the mnemic residues of speech is a necessary precondition for the preconscious state. On the contrary, that state is independent of a connection with them, though the presence of that connection makes it safe to infer the preconscious nature of the process. [1940a [1938], p. 162].

There is one further feature of this case that we would like to re-emphasize briefly, before we move on to the next case and proceed deeper into the functional organization of the mental apparatus. That feature is the fact that, with her intact ego and superego functioning, Mrs K (like Mr J in chapter five) made use of the therapeutic process for the purposes of *normal mourning*. There is nothing especially striking about this. It is illustrated, for example, by the way in which she gradually had to relinquish her image of her premorbid self (an image represented by the younger, independent-spirited, dark-haired woman in the photograph of herself that she carried around with her). By the end of the therapeutic work, this image was replaced by a new, updated image of her now-damaged, older, and more dependent self, with all of the losses, resignation, and sad feelings that that necessarily implied. All of this, and the underlying ego and superego functions that are necessary for the normal process of mourning (resting as it does, fundamentally, on the function of reality-testing), were strikingly absent in cases with equivalent damage to the cases of Mr J and Mrs K, but on the *right*-hand side of the brain (see chapter eight).

An analysis of the psychological mechanisms that distinguish between these different groups of cases enables us to gradually identify the neural correlates of the basic metapsychological functions that comprise the human mental apparatus as a whole. Hopefully, the differences between the cases of Mr J and Mrs K are beginning to demonstrate that this can be done, and *how* it can be done. Now, before we move on to a consideration of the ventromesial frontal and right-hemisphere cases with which we have been contrasting the cases of Mr J and Mrs K, we wish to describe, in the next chapter, one further case of left perisylvian damage—a case that seems to occupy an intermediate position between the superficial disturbances of the previous two cases and the far deeper disturbances to come.

CHAPTER SEVEN

Psychoanalytic observations on a case of left parietal damage: a man with a shattered world

Case L

Mr "L" was a research chemist. He was 26 years old and unmarried. Five months prior to his admission to our neurological rehabilitation unit, he had sustained a focal head injury in a motor-vehicle accident. He was initially admitted to the high-care unit of another hospital. On admission, his level of consciousness on the Glasgow Coma Scale was 7/15. A right-sided hemiparesis was noted. A CT scan of his brain showed left parietal haemorrhagic contusion. He recovered well initially (and began to move both arms spontaneously). However, he subsequently developed respiratory failure, and he required ventilation for 25 days. Thereafter, it was apparent that he had developed a spastic right hemiplegia. When he began responding to verbal commands and

This chapter is based on a paper entitled "Psychoanalytic Observations on a Man with a Shattered World", presented by Karen Kaplan-Solms and Mark Solms at the Neuro-Psychoanalysis Center of the New York Psychoanalytic Institute on June 5, 1999.

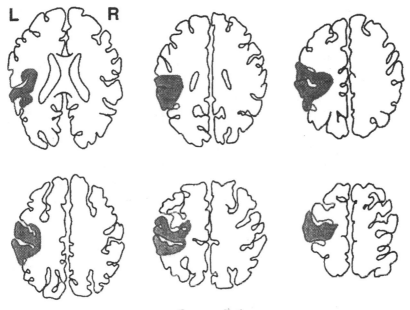

FIGURE 7-1

attempting to speak, 39 days after the accident, he was considered to be globally aphasic.

A follow-up CT scan demonstrated a discrete area of damage in the left parietal lobe of the brain, localized mainly to the supramarginal gyrus, but also extending anteriorly to include the primary sensorimotor cortex (Fig. 7-1). Following a three-month period of intensive speech therapy and physiotherapy at another hospital, he was transferred to our neurological rehabilitation unit, with a final diagnosis of mixed transcortical aphasia. At this point he was still hemiplegic. The hemiplegia affected both limbs on the right, but primarily his arm. He was wheelchair-bound.

Neuropsychological assessment

The neuropsychological assessment was conducted 21 weeks after the accident. The language disorder dominated Mr L's clinical presentation. His spontaneous verbal output was nonfluent, telegraphic, and paraphasic. The paraphasias were both literal and verbal (i.e. he both mispronounced and misused words) and included some neologisms. Repetition (i.e. copying of the examiner's speech) was fluent by contrast. Confrontation naming (i.e. naming of objects to command) was very poor. Audioverbal comprehension was intact, but this broke down with complex logico-grammatical material. This pattern of deficits is consistent with the diagnosis he had been given—namely, mixed transcortical aphasia. Writing was severely impaired (and took the form of an apraxic agraphia). Oral reading was more difficult for individual letters and words than for sentences. Semantic paralexias were common (e.g. he read "thermometer" as "gauge", and "spirit" as "whiskey"). Further cognitive testing confirmed the presence of deep dyslexia.

As regards other functions, severe ideomotor and oral apraxia were demonstrated, and he was unable to identify parts of his own body to verbal command. It later transpired that his *image* of his body was abnormal too. This included finger agnosia (i.e. misidentification of fingers). In addition, he was severely acalculic, he frequently confused right and left, he was unable to orientate a compass correctly, and he could not identify the time on a watchface. In other words, in addition to the transcortical aphasic syndrome and the deep dyslexia, Mr L suffered a full Gerstmann syndrome.

Constructional tasks were affected only by right-sided inattention. This tendency to neglect the right-hand side of space was confirmed on formal tests of hemispatial attention, but it quickly recovered over the next fortnight. Mr L also suffered a total cessation of dreaming following his accident (cf. chapter three, "first syndrome"). Prefrontal, right-hemispheric, and occipital-lobe functions were considered to be entirely normal.

Shortly after his admission to the rehabilitation unit, Mr L was referred for psychotherapy, as he was thought to be severely depressed and had apparently expressed suicidal wishes. His various therapists (speech, occupational, physical) all felt that he had greater residual function than he was using, and that his "depression" might be preventing him from progressing as much as he could.

Before we describe his presentation in the psychotherapeutic situation, we would like to say a word or two about Mr L's personal history.

Personal history

His father was Malaysian-Chinese and a devout Muslim. However, following his immigration to Europe, he had married a Catholic Englishwoman (who converted to Islam). Mr L had an older brother, Conrad, the first-born, and two sisters, one on either side of him in age, Doris and Roxy. Mr L's father was a successful although uneducated man. When he first came to England he was a manual labourer, working for a frozen-fish packaging company, but by the time of his death at the age of 57, he was the manager of an entire factory. He seems to have been the proverbial head of the household, and a strict disciplinarian. He valued family togetherness and educational achievement above all else. He gained some fame at one stage, when he won the national Karate championships. Mr L's mother did not work until his father's death. Thereafter, she is said to have found her real vocation in life—looking after children with cerebral palsy in a residential care setting. Conrad was an engineer in the nuclear industry, and he was a difficult character. He took over his father's role as family patriarch. Doris was a secretary in a legal firm. At the time of Mr L's accident, Roxy, the youngest, was studying in Germany to become a music therapist in the Rudolph Steiner movement. Her intention was ultimately to do work similar to her mother's.

Mr L's premorbid personality was described by his sisters as follows. He was always the "middle man", always mediating and negotiating and making peace between estranged and warring parties. He was described as easy-going, outgoing, friendly, and popular. He had an excellent sense of humour. However, he also went through occasional periods of self-doubt and mild depression. In his matriculation year, he was elected head prefect of his school. After leaving school, he went through a two-year period of vacillation over his choice of occupation, before he finally settled down to studying for a degree in inorganic chemistry at a university in Scotland. By the time he had his accident, he had completed his studies, with flying colours, and held a junior lectureship at a well-regarded institute of technology.

It was never entirely clear what had caused the accident. Apparently Mr L was driving. He was taking two friends of his, a colleague and a graduate student, on a weekend holiday to the countryside. According to the "official" version of the story (as told to Mr L by his family), a tyre burst on a straight road and the car hit a tree. According to another version, Mr L fell asleep at the wheel. In the official version, the two passengers had both escaped completely unscathed; in the other version, the front-seat passenger was killed outright. At the time that Mr L was seen for psychoanalytic psychotherapy, his therapist [K.K.-S.] had only heard the official version and had no inkling of the version that the family conspired to keep from him.

We now describe Mr L's presentation in the psychotherapeutic situation. This was complicated by the fact that he was seen during a period of rapid recovery. His treatment therefore fell into two relatively distinct phases.

Psychoanalytic observations: first phase

This first phase was characterized, above all, by severe *restriction of all ego activity*. In fact, at times, there seemed to be an *absence* of any mental activity. We have seldom been confronted by a patient who was less suited to the technique of free association than Mr L. The early sessions were excruciating. Mr L conveyed a sense of extreme—really extreme—panic and anxiety, but at the same time it was as if he were lost in a thick, impenetrable fog of lethargy and psychic blankness. It is difficult to convey this combination of factors in his presentation. He just said *nothing* and looked at his therapist in a bewildered, awkward, and at times pleading way; along with this, he appeared to be totally devitalized and half asleep. There seemed to be a real *absence* of constructive thought or even simply of active associations. There was no *elaboration* whatsoever—and no abstraction. There was just a terrible, concrete presence.

It was soon clear that conventional analytic techniques would yield nothing. The therapist felt that it would have been cruel in the extreme to leave Mr L in that state; she also felt a strong need to try to make some sort of contact with him, to throw him a life-line, and to try to ignite a spark within him. She felt compelled to fill the void with something—almost anything. And when she did so, for brief moments Mr L would latch on to the ideas that had been implanted in his mind, and there would be a momentary flickering of inner life, before—all too quickly—his associations came to a grinding halt once more, and he would return to the excruciating, lethargic fog of unbearable anxiety and tension.

We wish to emphasize that Mr L's therapist was never in any doubt that this was a tragedy for him. He was not deliberately withholding, nor narcissistically withdrawn, nor angrily uncoop-erative. He appeared simply crushed. His mood was that of some-one whose world was entirely devastated, a man with a totally shattered world. The sense of *loss* was palpable and quite over-whelming.

In this respect (although, as will be seen shortly, depressive ideation was certainly evident on occasion), Mr L's presentation was nothing like the classic presentation of narcissistic melancholia that we saw in *right* perisylvian cases (reported in chapter eight). There were no endless monologues of self-accusation and self-denigration and so on, which place these patients at the very centre of their delusional worlds, in which all their minor failings are noticed and commented upon. There was nothing egocentric about this patient, and nothing so *active*.

We will try to convey a direct impression of what he was like by citing a brief vignette from one of the sessions in this first phase of his treatment. The following passage is extracted from the notes that his therapist took after one of the early sessions:

I had arranged with Mr L that I would fetch him from the ward at 8:00 am, as usual. But when I arrived I was surprised to find that he had left breakfast early. The nursing staff reported that when all the patients returned to the ward, Mr L had disap-peared, although his glasses were on his bed. We all searched for him, and eventually a nurse found him sitting in his wheelchair in one of the bathrooms, doing nothing in particular. It was extremely difficult to communicate with him, so nobody asked what had happened and what he was doing in the bathroom.

When we got to the consulting-room, Mr L appeared withdrawn and said nothing. After a very long silence, I commented on how difficult talking about one's feelings could be. He nodded in agreement but was still completely silent and looked tense and terrified. After a further long silence, I tried to put him more at ease and asked how things were going. He pointed at his leg and said, "Better". After another very long silence, he said, as if continuing the previous thought, "Working hard". I realized with a slight shock that he had probably been leading up to saying those two words for the whole of the last five or ten minutes. He now looked at me as if we were in the middle of a conversation, but then I seemed to lose him again.

After another interminable silence, I said that one of the nursing staff had told me that he had told her that he had had a dream. Suddenly, Mr L's face lit up and he said emphatically, as if it were a new discovery, "Yes!". This was his first dream in months—the first since his accident. He looked at me expectantly. I tried to keep the conversation going. "What did you dream?", I asked. He looked puzzled, then crest-fallen. I wondered if he couldn't remember. "Can you remember it?", I asked. "No", he confirmed glumly, and sank back into silence. His face was riddled with pain. After another long silence I realized that he was drooping in his chair, and he looked very sleepy. "I am not sure whether you are feeling sleepy or feeling low?", I asked. This question reverberated in the room for a good few minutes. Then, after an inordinate length of time, as if from nowhere, an answer came back: "No." Then after a further silence, he continued: "Sometimes low, sometimes better." Then, after another very long silence, I asked what he was thinking about. "Nothing", came back the reply, and I felt he really meant it. He was flat, lifeless, introverted, devitalized.

After another excruciating, sleepy silence, I tried again. I asked if Mr L had been visited by any of his friends from the institute. He had not. I tried to keep the conversation going, and Mr L told me, haltingly, that the two passengers in the accident were entirely unhurt. He seemed upset by this. "I feel", he said, and then completed the sentence after a very long delay ". . . why *me*?". I tried to get him to elaborate this idea, which seemed to be the most important thing he had said, but he appeared to have difficulty understanding me, and after a while he fell back into his earlier lethargic state.

At the end of the session, Mr L wheeled himself towards his physiotherapy session. When he had covered some distance, he stopped, removed his glasses, and rubbed his eyes. Then he just sat there, with his head in one hand, for about five minutes. Thereafter he continued to wheel himself along. It was difficult to assess whether he was upset or not, and what the meaning or purpose of the long pause might have been.

One could recount almost any one of the sessions from the first few months of his treatment—they were all alike. We will now try to summarize the main themes from the rest of that period.

There was fleeting evidence of depressive ideation, but much more pervasively and for longer periods he seemed to be experiencing extreme anxiety. Above all, there was blank sleepiness. Whenever his therapist managed to get through the fog, she was surprised to find that he was not *altogether* absent, and that at times he actually seemed to be working very, very hard; it was just that all this work did not seem to be achieving any results. He seemed to be searching for thoughts, or waiting for them to occur to him, or trying to put those that did occur to him into some sort of meaningful order. And then there was the problem of trying to put the thoughts that did finally crystallize into words. When he did manage to communicate, it was clear that Mr L's ego activities, such as they were, were well anchored in a sense of reality. They seemed rational enough, and appropriate enough, but they were extremely impoverished, restricted, and concrete. There seemed to be no *elaboration* of anything. Just scattered islands of ideas in nothingness. Thus, although he was fundamentally aroused and alert, he was mentally blank, save for these fragmentary islands which he tried desperately to join together, usually without success.

It gradually emerged, considering as a whole all of the fragments that he did communicate, that Mr L was intensely preoccu-

pied by a limited number of concrete problems. These all revolved
directly around the practical question of his potential for recovery.
He reported on and asked questions about his various disabilities,
and what could be done and what was being done about them; but
he displayed little capacity for elaborating any of these concrete
concerns along constructive or productive lines of thought. There
were, in short, no *associations* to anything; just the stark awareness
of his deficits and of his worries about his progress and the lack of
it. Although we are summarizing all this in just a few sentences,
we wish to emphasize that these practical concerns about recovery
were his all-consuming preoccupation for session after session.

What then became clear was that Mr L was unable to coun-
tenance the possibility of a life with permanent disability. He displayed an all-or-nothing attitude to his recovery and rehabilitation.
During this phase, the mental subtleties associated with mourning
and working through, and the need to find new solutions in a
different kind of life, seemed impossible for him. He experienced
only the pain of his incapacities, the bewildering shock of them,
coupled with a sense of panic, as he realized gradually that this
nightmare might become permanent. In short, his entire mental life
seemed for a long while to oscillate between only these two concrete ideas—"recovery" and "no recovery".

We must re-emphasize that he seemed to be unable to *do* anything with these preoccupations—he just *had* them. He was, as it
were, fixated on them, and simultaneously he was quite overcome
by the anxiety that they induced. It was not possible during this
first phase of his treatment to explore his feelings about his situation, nor the meaning to him of his predicament; nor could he *link*
this predicament with past events such as other losses, and so on.
He seemed to be almost totally devoid of a representational and
associative internal world, save for these few concrete preoccupations.

The therapist felt that she was expending enormous and unre-
warded effort, with a restriction of her own ability to communicate
and to think. She felt as if she had to vitalize Mr L physically, by
implanting topics for thought and discussion in his mind. When
she succeeded in doing so, he was momentarily alive within the
narrow confines of the theme that she had introduced. But despite

great effort on her part to extend these themes, or to connect them with something else, he always reverted quickly to his previous empty state. The therapist's overriding impression was that *he had lost some essential component of the ego apparatus which elaborates and links ideas, and which therefore serves symbolic and abstract ideation.*

Interestingly, in retrospect, Mr L himself later recalled this phase as a period in which he had felt "bored and lost". That description captured his therapist's experience of those sessions, too. She did not feel that Mr L was depressed; rather, she gained the impression of a far more basic, far more terrible *stasis* and *emptiness,* coupled with a monumental struggle to haul himself out, which was almost always unsuccessful.

What then became apparent was that, alongside this extremely impoverished and restricted range of ego activities, Mr L had an essentially intact, and indeed quite a harsh, superego. As a picture of his inner world became, over time, more accessible, so it became possible to see that his anxiety-ridden preoccupations were linked, above all (and surprising as this may seem), with a deep sense of *shame.* This presented clinically as a severe social awkwardness. The only escape for Mr L from this relentless self consciousness was a return to the highly developed work-ethic that had been inculcated in him by his father. In this way, he avoided all human contact (including with his psychotherapist), and he focused almost exclusively on the practicalities of his various physical therapies, with the single-minded aim of regaining the skills that were required in order for him to return to work. The purpose behind this goal, it also gradually became clear, was not so much a practical matter as a moral one: he needed to work in order to repay an unspecified emotional debt to his brother and sister. It was not possible to clarify what this internal sense of indebtedness was all about. It was only apparent that what little ego activity he had seemed to be almost entirely driven by superego demands of this kind.

Hereafter, still deeper anxieties began to emerge. These related primarily to issues surrounding *bodily unity and integrity.* For example, Mr L suddenly asked his psychotherapist one day if she was *sure* that all of his physical problems were due to his brain injury. It transpired that he was concerned that his right arm might fall out of its socket, and on one occasion that it *had* in fact fallen out of its socket; he worried that his symptoms were getting worse and that something else—that is, something other than brain injury—might be wrong with his body; he was sure that he would die in his sleep; and so on. He also began to notice cognitive symptoms that he had had all along, albeit without awareness of them; and he reported these to his therapist with blind panic. For example, one day at the start of a session he told her, with terror in his voice, that he had noticed that when he heard words he sometimes had no idea what they *meant*. He knew they were words, but they didn't bring anything else to mind, they did not seem to mean anything. It appeared that this gradual process of discovering the full extent of his deficits was one source of his worry that he was getting worse. It later emerged that his bodily anxieties were caused by strange sensations that he was experiencing—that is, sensations of not being able to find the different parts of his body, or of feeling that they were located in the wrong places.

In this respect, Mr L used his therapist as a reassuring and orientating figure. She connected him to his environment and to the people in it. She explained his symptoms, drew diagrams of his brain for him, contextualized his condition in relation to that of other patients, and so on, and all of these reassurances and explanations brought him intense relief. This, in turn, seemed to usher in the second phase of his treatment, as well as his transition towards recovery, which we now describe.

Psychoanalytic observations: second phase

The second phase was heralded above all by the recovery of his ability to walk. This development was a definite watershed. It was followed in quick succession by a number of interconnected psychological developments.

First, Mr L *remembered* the essential details of his accident for the first time. He told his therapist with astonishment—in the middle of a session—that he remembered driving along a flat, open road, when he heard a loud bang and the car swerved out of control, towards the left. This island of recall had, in fact, returned to him a few days earlier, but he had forgotten it again, and now it had reappeared in the middle of his session. From then onward, he gradually began to piece together the fragments of his memory into a continuous account of what had happened during the period immediately preceding and following his accident. Simultaneously, he began to experience explicit, continuous memories of his life as a student and, beyond that, of his school-days and his childhood. It was not that he had *forgotten* all this before; it was as if all these memories had existed in bits and pieces, and now for the first time they were being connected again in a coherent narrative.

Then he started to *dream* again. During the first phase of his treatment, he had had only one dream (over a period of six months) and could not remember it. Now he was having dreams at the rate of about one or two per week. These dreams were impoverished and difficult to interpret, as he was completely unable to associate to them, but they were dreams nonetheless and he could remember them. Most of them seemed to be related to the theme of social encounters in the outside world, and they seemed to have to do with his anticipation of returning to the world beyond the hospital after his long stay in the rehabilitation unit.

We describe two examples of these dreams. The first was one that he remembered he had had while he was visiting his sister Doris for the weekend. He had asked his sister to write it down so that he could show it to his therapist. This is what she wrote:

> *I am walking down the street from my apartment in Soho when I meet three Chinese people—an adult and three children. I walk a little bit further and meet the mother and a friend of the same family that I have just seen.*

Mr L had no associations to this short dream, and he said that he did not recognize anyone in it. The people did not remind him of anyone he knew. The only spontaneous thought that occurred to him was that he noticed that he dreamt of himself as a normal person—that is, that he was able to walk and talk normally in the dream.

In the subsequent session, Mr L returned to this dream. It was obviously very important to him that he had begun to dream

again; to him the dream was a vital sign of inner life and of psychological recovery. He asked his therapist what she thought of his
dream. When she said that it was impossible to say what it might
mean without having his associations to it, he tried again to relate
it to some other thoughts or memories, but he simply could not.

He reported the next dream one week later. In this dream,

> he went back to his old high-school, but he went as an adult, in
> the paralysed and aphasic state that he was actually now in,
> following his accident. He saw an old teacher with whom he
> used to be on very good terms. Then he went to see two other
> boys, who had been a year below him at school. He went back
> to the school to talk to these pupils and to the old teacher about
> himself, and about how he was after the accident.

He tried to remember the name of one of the boys, but he couldn't.
He knew that the name started with the letter "S", but all he could
think of was "Sean", which was not the correct name. He repeatedly drew the letter "S" on his leg and searched his memory for
about five minutes, but the name did not come. He kept saying
"Sean" followed by the exclamation, "no!". He was obviously very
frustrated. He persisted for an inordinately long period of time
but eventually had to abandon it. He looked upset and disturbed.
Again, he could not associate to the dream. The therapist asked if
the name Sean meant anything to him, but he said that it did not.
He was obviously distressed by his inability to produce associations, so the therapist did not pursue the matter any further.

To return to his progress: the first two things that changed were
that he began to recover his memory of the accident and the period
immediately surrounding it and of his earlier life, and he began to
dream regularly again and to remember the dreams. Another
thing that changed, simultaneously, was that he began to *communicate propositionally* in grammatical sentences. Until this point, he
had spoken in single words or couplets only, usually linked with
non-verbal gestures; now he began to string series of three or more
words together into short sentences. The effect was almost miracu-
lous. Within the space of a day or two, he had moved from uttering
his first connected sentences to embarking on discussions with his

therapist about abstract and symbolic concerns, such as the meaning of life and the question as to whether or not God exists! The
transformation in his thinking was astonishing.

Finally, at around the same time, he started displaying an *interest in the external world*, and especially in *the well-being of the other
patients around him in the rehabilitation unit*. In this way, for the first
time he built up a social identity for himself in the ward. He also
revealed a healthy capacity for mourning his own losses and for
successfully sublimating his wish to recover and his anxiety about
his lack of recovery into a desire to help others and a concern for
their physical and emotional well-being. He simultaneously began
to display intense interest and pleasure in the development of his
young niece (Doris's daughter), who was just at that time beginning to master written language and to take her own first (symbolic) steps in the wider world, which Mr L himself was beginning
to re-enter. He did not seem to be aware of the rather obvious
associative connection between himself and his niece; however,
the mere fact that symbolic connections of any kind (conscious or
not) were beginning to appear in the associative material of his
sessions was an enormous breakthrough, and an enormous relief.
It seemed as if, all of a sudden, *things in his mind were beginning to
link up with one another*. With this, the whole mood of his sessions
changed, and the intense claustrophobic preoccupation with one
or two concrete, panic-stricken concerns gave way to a vast inner
space which could be explored at leisure. The feeling of such extreme effort and hard work disappeared at the same time.

All of these developments occurred more or less simultaneously, which suggested that the recovery of a single underlying
function was involved. In essence, our impression was that *the
recovery of symbolic thinking seemed to coincide with an internal capacity to move freely and independently between mental objects, and thereby
to restore the links between them.* That is, a parallel development
seemed to occur between the recovery in the *external world* on the
one hand (of his capacity to move physically and to interact and
communicate socially), and in the *internal world* on the other (of his
capacity to manoeuvre between ideas and connect them up with
one another symbolically by means of words). This parallel development coincided with the recovery of verbal (logico-grammati-

cal) thought, which was unconsciously linked in the patient's mind with the developmental acquisition of these functions in his little niece.

With all of these developments, a significantly different Mr L emerged. He was transformed in the space of a few weeks into a patient whose personality was remarkable only for its strength, tenacity, and perseverance—and even good humour—in the face of considerable physical and social obstacles.

We now quote an extract from the therapist's notes, from a session in this second phase of his treatment, to provide a direct impression of how dramatically Mr L had changed.

I made coffee for myself and went to my office for 20 minutes while the patients had their breakfast. To my surprise, when I opened my door I saw that Mr L was standing outside my consulting-room waiting for me, without his stick or his wheelchair. He had arrived early for his session. I invited him to come in, which he did with very great effort. He struggled to walk inside, to fetch a chair, and to place it with one hand on a spot that he had selected. Once he had done so, he sat down. He was quiet and relaxed, and I expressed pleasure and surprise at his walking so independently.

He smiled and seemed eager to talk. His words tumbled out, albeit nonfluently and with paraphasias. He said, with a mischievous expression, that one of the other patients had taken his chair away and given it to someone else on the ward. He (Mr L) now had to stay out of it *permanently*. But in fact another patient who was also supposed to discard his chair had since offered to share his chair with Mr L. (There was a new and positive interaction between him and the other patients.) I remarked that he seemed to have been liberated by his progress and that he was obviously very happy. He smiled silently. Then he said that he had not really had physiotherapy that week, because the whole department was busy moving to another floor. The physiotherapy department would be next to the occupational-therapy department in future. Then he said "OT, but okay, is fine" (conveying that his occupational therapy was continuing uninterruptedly, as it had moved the week before). He was making a toy wooden duck there, for his niece, which he was copying from a picture.

He had been waiting to ask me a question. [This was one characteristic way in which he had begun to make and try to keep contact with me.] As he asked his question, his non-verbal communication demonstrated that the issue at stake was difficult for him to conceptualize or verbalize. He wanted to know if I was *sure* that the problem with his arm and leg was definitely caused by an underlying problem with his *brain*, and not something else. [Only later did it become apparent that he was experiencing abnormal body-image sensations and ideas.] I drew a brain for him and carefully revised everything that I had told him previously. When I discussed his neuropsychological problems, he listened intently, lifting his glasses and rubbing his eyes, as he usually did when he was depressed or upset about himself. At these moments, both his muscle tone and his emotional vivacity decreased dramatically. Then he spoke of others in the ward, expressing great concern and sympathy for them, although he still found it very difficult to relate to them directly.

For a while he sat in silence and looked thoughtful. Then he said, gesturing to me that he would like to ask me a personal question: "Is okay?" When I said that it was, he asked me if I believed in God. I said I was not sure what he wanted to know—was he asking whether I believed there was a God who was aware of our suffering and distress and able to comfort us? He nodded, but added that he did not believe in God any more. If there was a God, this would never have happened to him. He could not find any gain in his situation for anyone. He saw only the loss of his life and his faculties, and he felt only despair. I said that his loss was all the greater if he felt also that God was no longer there to guide and protect him, as his father had. He nodded firmly. Then, after a while, he said that his brother Conrad was devoutly religious, and that Doris was too, but slightly less so. Then he was silent again.

It was time to end, and I linked these thoughts with the earlier part of the session. I emphasized that as he was recovering, so he was becoming more fully aware of what he had lost and of what he might never recover. This insight was a source of pain, but it was also a source of hope in the sense that he could use it to build his new life in future.

When we stood up, he indicated to me that I had not finished my coffee. When I told him I had had sufficient coffee, he asked me to give him the cup and saucer. Then, with the greatest effort, adding to his struggle in barely having mastered the capacity to walk again, he carried these to the kitchen for me. In this moment, he once again conveyed that he felt he had a relationship with me as a person, which was positive and in which he felt more equal.

Within about three months of this session, Mr L was discharged from our unit. He continued his treatments on an outpatient basis. At the same time, he enrolled in a college for disabled people. There he took a diploma in computer studies. One year later, about 30 months after his accident, we received the following note from one of the therapists who was still working with him, a cognitive psychologist who had helped him to learn to read and write again:

I am sure you will be pleased to hear that Mr L is making incredible progress (mostly without my help). He seems to be recovering a lot of skills and the clinical picture is still in constant flux. He is definitely moving and progressing and he can no longer be diagnosed as "deep dyslexic". His picture is more that of a phonological dyslexia now, and the prognosis is accordingly far better. He is able to read (although slowly and haltingly) for meaning in a passage. I am concentrating on his working memory, as this is where I think the main problem still lies at present. At times he gets a bit depressed and despondent, and sometimes we speak about this a bit, but I think it is healthy. His speech has improved and he is starting to be able to connect sentences together more fluently. Overall, I think, great improvement.

Six months later, she wrote again. This was the last time we had news of him:

He can now read and write slowly but adequately, and is concentrating on working on computers so that he can find a job in
that field. I am seeing him in April for his final follow-up. He
really is his own person and has a strong sense of what does and
does not suit him . . . he even looks good and has quite a bit of
confidence. I think, all things considered, that he is one of neuropsychology's success stories.

Summary

So, in summary, this was a man who presented initially with a
near-total loss of associative thought. His mental life was dominated by what seemed, from the outside, to be a torpor. It is hard
to know what he experienced from the inside. Later he said that he
felt bored and empty, but it was also clear that at times he was
engaged in a titanic struggle with his own thought processes—that
he was trying desperately to make sense of the isolated, fragmentary thoughts that did occur to him. These were almost exclusively
of a concrete, practical nature and were linked directly to his physical and mental handicaps and to the prospects for his recovery.
These restricted, stereotyped preoccupations were, it seems, associated with extreme anxieties and moments of unmitigated panic,
in which he was brought face to face with problems about which
he could do absolutely nothing, other than simply *experience*
them—he was not even able to *think* about them. As his inner
world expanded, his therapist became aware of two other components of his thinking. First, he experienced confusions and extreme
anxieties about his body and about the nature of his illness. Second, he felt intense shame and self-consciousness and an overwhelming feeling of indebtedness. Only thoughts of *work*, and
concrete physical *effort*, brought him any sense of escape from the
shame, and relief from the sense of being in debt. Then, suddenly,
over a period of a few weeks, he underwent a dramatic transformation. This was heralded by a recovery of the capacity to walk.
As soon as Mr L regained this capacity, it was as if he were simultaneously able to move around freely in the inner space of his

mind again for the first time since his accident. More correctly, it was as if his mind had acquired a dimension of *inner space* once more. This manifested in various ways: he recovered continuous autobiographical *memory*, he recovered the ability to *dream*, and he also recovered the ability to *speak* in connected, logico-grammatical discourse. Thereafter, Mr L rapidly became connected with the social world once more, and he began the long process of mourning his losses and working through the implications of his limited gains. He also sublimated his unfulfilled hopes and unbearable disappointments by caring for people in distress around him and by taking a keen interest in the developmental progress of a much-loved little niece.

Supplement: Luria's "man with a shattered world"

It is difficult to know what to make of the first phase of Mr L's treatment. At that time, due to the nature of his aphasia and other neuropsychological deficits, he was almost completely unable to obey the "fundamental rule" of psychoanalysis; he remained essentially inaccessible. As a result, we have only indirect evidence as to what he was actually experiencing, subjectively, during that period of his recovery. Since this means that we have almost no access to the material that normally provides the raw data for a psychoanalytic investigation of a mental state, we would like to *supplement* what we were able to learn directly from Mr L, with some extracts from Luria's (1972) famous case of *The Man with a Shattered World*. This patient of Luria's—L. Zasetsky—suffered a very similar wound to our patient, with strikingly similar clinical consequences. (Zasetsky was shot in the left parieto-occipital region, during the Second World War.) Over a period of 26 years, with monumental effort, Zasetsky set about recording—one word at a time—*what it is like* to be without a left parietal lobe as a result of traumatic damage to that part of the brain (Fig. 7-2). Zasetsky's experiences give us more direct information as to what Mr L is likely to have been going through.

We will start with Zasetsky's description of the extended period of "blankness" that he, like Mr L, experienced immediately

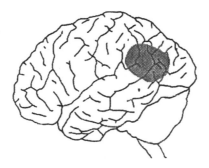

FIGURE 7-2

after his accident and acute post-operative period. Zasetsky described his subjective state during this period as follows:

My head was a complete blank then. I just slept, woke, but simply couldn't think, concentrate or remember a thing. My memory—like my life—hardly seemed to exist.

At first I couldn't recognize myself, or what had happened to me, and for a long time (days on end) didn't even know where I'd been hit. My head wound seemed to have transformed me into some terrible baby.

I'd hear a doctor talking to someone. But since I couldn't see him, I'd pay no attention to him. [At this point, Zasetsky's eyes were bandaged shut.] Suddenly he'd approach me, reach out and touch me, and ask: "How goes it, Comrade Zasetsky?" I wouldn't answer, just begin to wonder why he was asking me that. After he'd repeated my name several times, I'd finally remember that "Zasetsky" was my name. Only then would it occur to me to say: "Okay".

Immediately after I was wounded, I seemed to be some newborn creature that just looked, listened, observed, repeated, but still had no mind of its own. That's what I was like in the beginning. Afterwards, when I'd had a chance to hear words that people use again and again in conversation or thinking, various clusters of "memory fragments" developed, and from these I began to make some sense out of the life around me and remember what words meant. [. . .]

Because of my injury I'd forgotten everything I ever learnt or knew . . . everything . . . and had to start from scratch to develop again—at least up to a certain point. After that, my development suddenly stopped, and I've been that way ever since. Mostly, it's because of my memory that I have so much trouble understanding things. You see, I'd forgotten absolutely everything and had to start all over again trying to identify, recall and understand things with the kind of memory a child has.

Because of that head wound I'd become an abnormal person—except that I wasn't insane. Not at all. I was abnormal because I had a huge amount of amnesia and for a long time didn't have any trace of memories.

My mind was a complete muddle and confusion all the time, my brain seemed so limited and feeble. Before, I used to operate so differently. [. . .]

I'm in a kind of fog all the time, like a heavy half-sleep. My memory's a blank. I can't think of a single word. All that flashes through my mind are some images, hazy visions that suddenly appear and just as suddenly disappear, giving way to fresh images. But I simply can't understand or remember what these mean.

Whatever I do remember is scattered, broken down into disconnected bits and pieces. That's why I react so abnormally to every word and idea, every attempt to understand the meaning of words. [Luria, 1972, pp. 23–25]

This vivid account immediately evokes the matter of the connection between "words" and "things", which we discussed at the end of chapter six in relation to another patient who experienced (for different reasons) an "inability to think". This is how Zasetsky described his deficit in this regard:

In part, words have lost meaning for me or have a meaning that's incomplete or unformed. This is true mostly of the objective characteristics of things like *table, sun, wind, sky*, etc. I've lost track both of these words and their meaning. Mostly, I can't think of or imagine a lot of the words that have to do with things I studied.

Because of the trauma that my skull and brain suffered, my visual and auditory memories have become detached. I'll see a letter or number but won't be able to think of the word for it right away, or hear a letter or number mentioned and not be able to visualize what either one looks like. I've often thought that's why my speaking and memory have become so bad—

sometimes it takes me an entire day to think of a word for something I've seen and be able to say it. And vice-versa: I'll hear a word (or say a particular number) but not be able to visualize it right away or form any image of it. It may even take a long while for me to remember what it means. [. . .]

Every word I hear seems vaguely familiar (after all, I'd once learnt to get through three years at a polytechnic institute). As far as my memory's concerned, I know a particular word exists, except that it has lost meaning. I don't understand it as I did before I was wounded. This means that if I hear the word *table* I can't work out what it is right away, what it is related to. I just have a feeling the word is somewhat familiar, but that's all.

So I have to limit myself to words that "feel" familiar to me, that have some definite meaning for me. These are the only ones I bother with when I try to think or talk to people. For some time (after my injury) I began to fight to recover my memory and speaking ability, to understand the meaning of words. I'm still doing this, since my memory is so limited that there always seems to be a gap between a word and its meaning. These two are always disconnected and I have to yoke them together somehow. But I can't keep them yoked together for any length of time; they come loose and just vanish into thin air.

Sometimes when I take a walk in the field or the woods, I test myself to see what I can remember. It turns out I've completely forgotten the names of the trees there. True, I can remember the words *oak, pine, aspen, maple, birch* and others sometimes (when they happen to come to mind). But when I look at a particular tree, I don't know whether it's an aspen or some other kind, even though the tree looks familiar to me. If someone points out some mushrooms, I can't remember what they're called and how they're used, though I remember the names of different kinds of mushrooms—orange cap, white or brown "edible" types. But I can't tell whether a particular mushroom is a brown edible type or some other variety, despite the fact that I must have been able to identify them before I was wounded.

I've even forgotten what a dandelion is, a flower I knew when I was a child. When it becomes faded, I remember what it is, but until then I just can't imagine, I have absolutely no idea what flower it is.

Out of habit I tend to see things in my environment in much the same way as I did earlier. But when I'm faced with objects, I don't really recognize or remember them. I don't understand how plants grow, what nourishes them, or how you grow a new plant by cutting off a leaf and putting it in water. I don't understand the essential things about the plants and animals I see, because I can't remember the names for them or what they mean. [pp. 89, 91–93]

It is not surprising to learn, in the light of the above, that—as in the case of Mr L—the recovery of Zasetsky's *memory* was linked directly with the recovery of his *language*.

For the time being I put together a vocabulary mostly out of visual images and tried to remember words better and make my memory more flexible. I had to start from scratch and learn to recognize objects and try to associate them with words. I myself wasn't aware of how these words happened to come back to me, but little by little some things about my environment managed to register in my memory—the sort of memory and understanding I have now.

Towards the end of the first month or early in the second after I was injured, more and more often I'd remember things about my mother, brother and my two sisters. I didn't recall all these things immediately, but only bit by bit. Some memory of my mother, brother, or one of my sisters would come to mind at different times. These details would occur to me suddenly, not when I myself wanted to remember them—they'd just come to me. Towards the end of the second month one of the fellows in the hospital took an interest in me and started to jot down my family's address—bit by bit, as it came to me. I'd suddenly remember the name of the region I was from; the next day or perhaps a day later, the name of the settlement I lived in; then I'd think of my sister's name. And each time he'd write these down. Finally, my friend took it upon himself to write my family a letter, though he didn't have the exact address, since I couldn't remember my apartment or building number on the street I lived on. Naturally, I still couldn't think of my mother's and younger sister's last name (and that of my mother's second husband).

Sometimes I'd remember the name of a city, but in a minute or even less, I'd forget it. At times I'd recall the address of the

region I lived in, but quickly forget that too and couldn't remember it for a long time.

I heard everything people around me were saying, and little by little my head was crammed with songs, stories and bits
of conversations I'd picked up. As I began to remember words
and use them in thinking, my vocabulary became more flexible. [pp. 81–2]

It is important to recognize also the impact that these language/
memory deficits had on his *semantic* capacities in general:

I remember nothing, absolutely nothing! Just separate bits of
information that I sense have to do with one field or another.
But that's all! I have no real knowledge of any subject. My past
has just been wiped out!

Before my injury I understood everything people said and
had no trouble learning any of the sciences. Afterwards I forgot everything I learnt about science. All my education was
gone.

I knew that I went to elementary school, graduated with
honours from the middle school, completed three years of
courses at the Tula Polytechnic Institute, did advanced work in
chemistry and, before the war, finished all these requirements
ahead of time. I remember that I was on the western front, was
wounded in the head in 1943 when we tried to break through
the Germans' defence in Smolensk, and that I've never been
able to put my life together again. But I can't remember what I
did or studied, the sciences I learnt, subjects I took. I've forgotten everything. Although I studied German for six years, I
can't remember a word of it, can't recognize a single letter. I
also remember that I studied English for three solid years at
the institute. But I don't know a word of that either now. I've
forgotten these languages so completely I might just as well
have never learnt them. Words like *trigonometry, solid geometry,
chemistry, algebra*, etc., come to mind, but I have no idea what
they mean.

All I remember from my years at secondary school are some
words (like signboards, names of subjects): *physics, chemistry,
astronomy, trigonometry, German, English, agriculture, music*, etc.,
which don't mean anything to me now. I just sense that somehow they're familiar.

When I hear words like *verb, pronoun, adverb*, they also seem
familiar, though I can't understand them. Naturally, I knew

these words before I was wounded, even though I can't understand them now. For example, I'll hear a word like *stop!* I know this word has to do with grammar—that it's a verb. But that's all I know. A minute later, I'm likely even to forget the word *verb*—it just disappears. I still can't remember or understand grammar or geometry because my memory's gone, part of my brain removed.

Sometimes I'll pick up a textbook on geometry, physics or grammar but get disgusted and toss it aside, since I can't make any sense out of textbooks, even those from the middle school. What's more, my head aches so badly from trying to understand them, that one look is enough to make me nervous and irritable. An unbearable kind of fatigue and loathing for it all comes over me. [pp. 116–117]

The same applied even to *skilled movement* (ideational and ideomotor praxis):

The instructor gave me a needle, spool of thread, some material with a pattern on it, and asked me to try to stitch the pattern. Then he went off to attend to other patients—people who'd had their arms or legs amputated after being wounded, or half their bodies paralysed. Meanwhile, I just sat there with the needle, thread and material in my hands wondering why I'd been given these; I sat for a long time and just did nothing. Suddenly the instructor came over and asked: "Why are you just sitting there? Go ahead and thread the needle!" I took the thread in one hand, the needle in the other, but couldn't understand what to do with them. How was I to thread the needle? I twisted it back and forth but hadn't the slightest idea what to do with any of these things.

When I first looked at these objects, but hadn't yet picked them up, they seemed perfectly familiar—there was no reason to think about them. But as soon as I had them in my hands, I was at a loss as to how to work out what they were for. I'd lapse into a kind stupor and wouldn't be able to associate these two objects in my hand—it was as though I'd forgotten why they existed. I twisted the needle and thread in my hands but couldn't understand how to connect the two—how to fit the thread in the needle.

And then another annoying thing happened. By then I'd already learnt what a needle, thread, thimble and material were for and had some vague idea of how to use them. But I couldn't for the life of me think of the names of these or other objects people pointed out to me. I'd sit there stitching the material with the needle, completely unable to remember what the very things I was using were called. [p. 51]

The effect on his conception of *space* was no less remarkable:

When I came out of the bathroom, I forgot which way I had to turn to get back to my room. So I just started walking, dragging myself along. Suddenly I banged my right side against the door—something I had never done before. I was amazed that this had happened. Probably it was because I had forgotten the way back and was confused. I tried to work out where my room was, looked around everywhere, but couldn't get the layout of things and decide which way to go.

I turned in the other direction and fell, because I got confused again and didn't know which way to walk. Suddenly the words *right, left, back, forward, up* and *down* occurred to me, but they weren't any help since I didn't really know what they meant. A minute later I also remembered the words *south, north, east* and *west*. But when I tried to work out what the relationship was between any of these words, I was lost. I didn't understand whether *north* and *south* meant areas that were side by side or just the reverse. I even forgot what direction *north* or *south* indicated. But just then someone called me. At first I wasn't aware I was being called, but when the fellow repeated my name a few times I looked around to see who it was. Finally, I saw a patient approaching and beckoning to me.

When I went for a walk the same thing happened. I forgot where our building was, what direction I should walk to go back. I looked at the sun but couldn't remember where it was supposed to be at that time of day—whether to the left or the right of me. I had already forgotten how I'd got to this place and what direction to take to get back, even though I had only gone a short distance from the building. The hospital was hemmed in by enormous evergreens, a little way off there was a lake, and after that—nothing but dense forest. What was I going to do? How was I going to manage? [p. 55]

Lastly, the following excerpt from Zasetsky's notes provides an account of the subjective experience of *body-image* distortion of the kind experienced by our patient Mr L:

Often I fall into a kind of stupor and don't understand what's going on around me; I have no sense of objects. One minute I stand there thinking about something, the next I lapse into forgetfulness. But suddenly I'll come to, look to the right of me, and be horrified to discover half of my body is gone. I'm terrified; I try to work out what's become of my right arm and leg, the entire right side of my body. [...]

Sometimes when I'm sitting down I suddenly feel as though my head is the size of the table—every bit as big— while my hands, feet and torso become very small. When I remember this, I myself think it's comical, but also very weird. These are the kinds of things I call "bodily peculiarities". When I close my eyes, I'm not even sure where my right leg is; for some reason I used to think (even sensed) it was somewhere above my shoulder, even above my head. And I could never recognize or understand that leg (the part of my foot to my knee).

Another annoying thing that happens (it's a minor problem, and I have some control over it) is that sometimes when I'm sitting on a chair, I suddenly become very tall, but my torso becomes terribly short and my head very, very tiny—no bigger than a chicken's head. You can't imagine what that's like even if you try—it just has to "happen" to you. [...]

Often I even forget where my forearm and buttocks are and have to think of what these two words refer to. I know what the word *shoulder* means and that the word *forearm* is closely related to it. But I always forget where my forearm is located. Is it near my neck or my hands? The same thing happens with the word *buttocks*. I forget where this is, too, and get confused. Is it in my leg muscles or above my knees? My pelvic muscles? The same sort of thing happens with other parts of my body. I've also forgotten a good number of other words for parts of my body. [...]

When the doctor says: "Hands on your hips!" I stand there wondering what this means. Or if he says "Hands at your sides ... your sides ... hands at your sides ..." What does that mean? [pp. 47–49]

Discussion

We are beginning to gain a more articulated picture of the psychological functions of the left perisylvian convexity (Fig. 7-3).

In our case of Broca's aphasia, Mr J, discussed in chapter five, we witnessed a process of *normal mourning*: someone coming to terms with a terrible loss and attempting to make a functional adaptation to it. We found that this patient did not present differently, as a personality, than other patients who have experienced a similar degree of loss without sustaining a brain injury (patients with spinal cord lesions, for example). We concluded that the motor component of speech and language play only a limited role in the functional organization of personality, complex emotion, and motivation. We therefore ascribed this functional component of language to the very *periphery* of the ego's organization.

In our case of Wernicke's aphasia, Mrs K, discussed in chapter six, we once again witnessed a process of normal mourning, but in this case the process was accompanied by a striking disorder of *reflexive consciousness*. The patient experienced an "inability to think", which (we suggested) actually consisted of an inability to *attach audioverbal images to thoughts* and thereby to render them conscious. The importance of this observation related to the fact that becoming aware of one's thoughts is the central mechanism of the "talking cure", insofar as it reverses the process of repression (as that process was understood in the early years of psychoanalysis). However, our patient's ego and superego functions remained

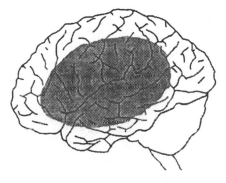

FIGURE 7-3

fundamentally intact. Although she did display fleeting abnormalities of cognition, she always retained a firm connection to
reality. (In this respect, as we shall see in the next two chapters, she
behaved very differently from the patients with right-hemisphere
and ventromesial frontal-lobe damage.) Our observations in this
case therefore confirmed the conclusion that Freud (1923b) reached
towards the end of his analytic career—namely, that *consciousness
is not the executive agency of the mind*.

In the present chapter, we have described a case of transcortical
aphasia, and we have supplemented our description with extracts
from an autobiographical account of another case of a very similar
type. Our observations on these two cases take us a little deeper
into the fabric of the ego and shed further light on the important
role that language plays in its functional organization.

Mr L was truly (at least initially) a man with a shattered world.
His "inability to think" extended far beyond the mere inability
to bring thoughts to consciousness which affected Mrs K. The
early phase of his treatment was apparently characterized by a
near-absence of any mental (ego) activity at all. He was in a foglike,
stuporous state; he was adynamic and lethargic, bordering on the
akinetic and mute. In his case, in short, it appeared to be not merely
consciousness of thought but, rather, *thinking itself* that was affected
by the brain damage.

The autobiographical reflections of Luria's case provide us
with valuable information as to what this state feels like from
the *inside*. Zasetsky's observations suggest that, in this state, in
addition to a pervasive feeling of "blankness", the patient experiences isolated, fragmentary thoughts *without being in possession of
an (ego) apparatus to think them with*. In other words, the thoughts (or
thought-fragments) just "happened" to him. He could not *do* anything with them; he could not *connect* them with other thoughts in
such a way as to generate a coherent store of knowledge and skills.

What might the functional basis of this mindless state be?
Whatever it is, it is obviously quite fundamental to what the ego
does. For in its absence there is an almost total shut-down of functional ego activity. Luria (1973, 1980) suggested that the inferior
parietal region of the left cerebral hemisphere is a region in which
information derived from the various sensory modalities *converges*.
This convergence, he thought, was the functional prerequisite for

the conversion of concrete sensory facts about the world into higher-order *abstractions* and logico-grammatical *concepts*. These latter operations, he thought, which were greatly facilitated by the function of language, operated as a tool for such fundamental intellectual activities as classification, categorization, and storage and retrieval of information.

> The tertiary zone of the posterior cortical region is . . . essential, not only for the successful integration of information reaching man through his visual system [and other unimodal perceptual systems], but also for the transition from direct, visually represented syntheses to the level of symbolic processes—or operations with word meanings, with complex grammatical and logical structures, with systems of numbers and abstract relationships. It is because of this that the tertiary zones of the posterior cortical region play an essential role in *the conversion of concrete perception into abstract thinking*, which always proceeds in the form of internal schemes, and for the memorizing of organized experience or, in other words, not only for the reception and coding of information, but also for its storage. [Luria, 1973, p. 74, emphasis altered]

Recently neuropsychologists have begun to question whether these processes actually depend on a concrete "convergence" of unimodal information cascades, and they have cast doubt on the implication that multimodal abstractions are actually "stored" in the parietal regions. Mesulam (1998), for example, has suggested that the transmodal region in question functions not as a zone of converging information but, rather, as a system of *directories* that serve to *bind together* meaningful constellations of information. This enables the ego to "look up" and *create links between* the concrete mnemonic facts of past perceptual experience.

> The role of transmodal nodes is not only to support convergent multimodal synthesis but also, predominantly, to create directories (or address codes, maps, look-up tables) for *binding distributed modality-specific fragments into coherent experiences, memories and thoughts*. This . . . process can be likened to obtaining green by superimposing a blue and a yellow lens, which can be separated from each other to yield back the original uncontaminated colours. Transmodal areas allow multidimensional integration through two interactive processes: (i) the

establishment, by local neuronal groups, of convergent cross-modal associations related to a target event; and (ii) the formation of a directory pointing to the distributed sources of the related information. Transmodal areas can thus enable the binding of modality-specific information into multimodal representations that have distributed as well as convergent components.

Transmodal areas are not necessarily centres where convergent knowledge *resides*, but critical gateways (or hubs, sluices, nexuses) for accessing the relevant distributed information. (Mesulam, 1994). Paradoxically, they also provide "neural bottlenecks" in the sense that they constitute regions of maximum vulnerability for lesion-induced deficits in the pertinent cognitive domain. [Mesulam, 1998, p. 1024, emphasis added]

It is clear that the function that Mesulam describes would be essential for any associative mental activity. It would simply not be possible to establish links between perceptions and ideas without such a function. Small wonder, then, that the ego's functions virtually shut down in the absence of this all-important capacity. (It should also be clear why *words* are ideally suited to serve as such "directories" that link disparate facts together into coherent networks or arrangements.)

Kosslyn (1994) evidently had something similar in mind when he recently assigned the function of *associative memory* to the left parietal region. He described this function as "a subsystem at a relatively late stage of processing that receives input from multiple sensory modalities and stores associations among facts about objects" (p. 216). He added that:

the contents of associative memory are more abstract than those of the modality-specific pattern activation subsystems; associative memory not only stores associations among individual perceptual representations, but also organizes "conceptual" information that may not be directly derived from the senses (e.g. mathematical truths, meanings of abstract terms, and so on). [p. 215]

How might we conceptualize this process *metapsychologically*? It appears that the process in question is nothing other than the fundamental mental mechanism that we have long designated by the conventional term "association" (as in "association of ideas"). This, it appears, was the mechanism that was lost in the case of Mr L, and this is what deprived him of the capacity to "think". It seems reasonably clear that the associative *linking* function in question also forms the essential basis for the process of *symbolization* (the process whereby one idea *stands for* another in an associative chain, or by means of which the properties of one idea are *transferred* onto those of another; cf. Jones, 1916). This process, too, is fundamental to everything that the ego does. It is, in a sense, the crux of its *representational* function. All of Mr L's mental deficits can be understood on this basis, as can the nature and sequence of his recovery.

Mesulam's (1998) account of the "directory" function of the left parietal region provides us with the beginnings of an insight into the neurophysiological mechanisms of these absolutely fundamental mental processes. However, it seems inappropriate on the basis of the limited data available to us to attempt a detailed analysis of these processes here. We will have achieved enough at this stage if we are merely able to demonstrate that the method we are recommending is capable *in principle* of paving the way for such correlations, in future, between abstract metapsychological concepts and concrete neurophysiological mechanisms.

CHAPTER EIGHT

Psychoanalytic observations on five cases of right perisylvian damage: failure of mourning

In the previous three chapters, we considered psychoanalytic observations on patients who sustained damage to different parts of the left perisylvian region of the brain. In this chapter, we summarize the very different presentations of patients who sustained equivalent damage on the opposite side of the brain: in the perisylvian region of the *right* cerebral hemisphere (Fig. 8-1). In all of the cases to be described in this chapter, the damage in question was caused by cerebrovascular accidents in the distribution of the right middle cerebral artery.

In analysing these cases, we will proceed somewhat deeper beneath the surface of conscious awareness than was necessary

This chapter is based on papers presented by Mark Solms (which summarized earlier clinical presentations by Karen Kaplan-Solms and Mark Solms) at the Neuro-Psychoanalysis Center of the New York Psychoanalytic Society (6 June 1998), a Research Forum of the British Psycho-Analytical Society (20 October 1998), and the Neurosciences Study Group of the Vienna Psychoanalytical Society (21 November 1998). A version of this chapter appeared in Solms (1999b).

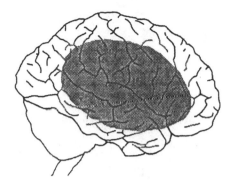

FIGURE 8-1

in our analyses of the previous three cases (chapters five, six, and seven). This is because, as the reader will soon see, damage to the right perisylvian region of the brain produces far more profound disturbances of personality, emotion, and motivation than does equivalent damage on the left-hand side of the brain. This, in turn, reveals that the metapsychological functions of the right perisylvian convexity involve somewhat deeper levels of ego organization than did those of the equivalent region of the *left* hemisphere.

We hope in this chapter to begin to demonstrate how the method that we are recommending in this book can be used, not only to gain an understanding of the neural correlates of our psychoanalytic model of the mind, but also to make *a psychoanalytic contribution to contemporary neuropsychology*. If the fundamental mental mechanisms that underlie the surface phenomenology of human personality, motivation, and emotion are indeed inaccessible to simple behavioural observation due to the dynamic resistances that Freud described, then it certainly follows that these mechanisms cannot be adequately characterized and understood by conventional neuropsychological research techniques, which do not take account of the mental processes that occur beneath those resistances.

The right-hemisphere syndrome:
some basic facts and theories

We will preface our psychoanalytic observations on the right-hemisphere cases by summarizing very briefly what is generally accepted nowadays about the neuropsychology of the right perisylvian convexity. Thereafter, we outline what we believe our psychoanalytic perspective is able to add to this existing knowledge.

The cognitive and emotional symptoms that are associated with damage to this part of the brain are conventionally grouped together under the loose nosological heading of the "right-hemisphere syndrome". These symptoms fall into three categories.

The first category goes by the name of *anosognosia*—that is, *unawareness of deficit*. In its extreme form, this symptom presents as a near-delusional disavowal of illness, even in the face of the most obvious contradictory evidence—such as in Babinski's (1914) seminal collection of cases in which densely hemiplegic patients insisted that they could walk without difficulty, or in Anton's (1899) classical study in which cortically blind patients insisted that they could see normally.

In less extreme cases, this symptom takes a more subtle form known as *anosodiaphoria*, in which patients do not actually *deny* that they are disabled, and are even prepared to concede the point in an intellectual sense, but they assume an *emotionally indifferent attitude* to their disabilities. Although they recognize and acknowledge intellectually that they are significantly disabled, they do not appear to feel concerned about that fact; it does not really seem to bother them.

Not uncommonly, florid anosognosia in the acute phase of right perisylvian disease resolves into a persistent anosodiaphoria in the chronic phase.

The second major category of right-hemisphere symptoms is described under the heading of *neglect*. Patients with neglect tend to ignore the left-hand side of space, including the portion of space that is occupied and represented by their own bodies, even though they are quite capable at a purely sensory level of perceiving it. They even neglect the left-hand side of the imaginary space that is generated in their mental imagery. There is also a motor form of neglect, known as hemiakinesia, in which the patient fails to use the left arm even though it is capable of movement at an instrumental level.

In acute cases, this symptom is every bit as bizarre as anosognosia; it is also not uncommon for these patients, when their own paralysed left arm (for example) is presented to them in such a way that they are *forced* to acknowledge its existence, to insist that it does not belong to them. They are more willing to accept that it belongs to the examiner—even though this would imply that the examiner has three arms—than they are prepared to accept that the impaired limb is attached to their own bodies. It is easy to see how this symptom overlaps with the symptom of anosognosia. Some authors refer to this combined form of neglect and anosognosia under the heading of "somatoparaphrenic delusions".

To illustrate the sort of phenomenon we are talking about, we quote briefly from an interview that V. S. Ramachandran (1994, p. 319) recorded with such a patient, a woman by the name of Mrs M. This patient suffered dense hemineglect and profound anosognosia, following a right parieto-occipital stroke which extended subcortically to the level of the thalamus and head of caudate. She was completely hemiplegic on the left, with particularly severe involvement of the arm, but she persistently denied the paralysis. We cite a short extract from Ramachandran's interview with her, to provide a direct impression of her condition:

Dr R: Mrs M, when were you admitted to hospital?

Mrs M: I was admitted on April 7th because my daughter felt there was something wrong with me.

Q: Mrs M, can you use your arms?

A: Yes.

Q: Can you use both hands?

A: Yes, of course.

Q: Can you use your right hand?

A: Yes.

Q: Can you use your left hand?

A: Yes.

Q: Are both hands equally strong?

A: Yes, they are equally strong.

Q: Mrs M, point to my student with your right hand.

A: [Patient points.]

Q: Mrs M, point to my student with your left hand.

A: [Patient remains silent.]

Q: Mrs M, why are you not pointing?

A: Because I didn't want to.

Later, the patient denied that the paralysed hand belonged to her. Ramachandran therefore asked her, pointing to her left hand: "Whose hand do you think it is?"

A: Well, it certainly isn't yours!

Q: Then whose is it?

A: It isn't mine either.

Q: Whose hand do you think it is?

A: It is my son's hand, Doctor.

This is an example of a somatoparaphrenic delusion, which is quite common in severe cases of neglect. However, as we said, these florid presentations usually settle following the acute phase of the underlying illness.

In milder presentations of neglect, and typically in chronic cases, there is merely a tendency to overlook the left-hand side—a persistent, lopsided failure of attention and concern.

Of special interest is the fact that patients with neglect have been reported who feel a curious sense of *disgust* when they are compelled to attend (e.g. using mirrors) to the left-hand side of their bodies. Sometimes this sense of repulsion is organized into a near-psychotic *hatred* of the left arm or leg—a condition known as *misoplegia*. This is, therefore, a paradoxical form of neglect, in which patients become *obsessed* by the left-hand side of their bodies, rather than ignoring it. This variation on neglect has not been adequately integrated into contemporary neuropsychological models of the mechanisms underlying the syndrome, or into models of the normal psychological functions of the right cerebral hemisphere. We shall have occasion to return to this point later, in the light of our psychoanalytic observations on such patients.

The third category of symptoms that comprises the so-called right-hemisphere syndrome goes under the heading of *disorders of spatial perception and cognition*. These take various forms. One of the most common is known as constructional apraxia—that is, an inability to appropriately arrange objects in space, or to arrange lines on a page, despite adequate primary perceptual and motor capacities. A closely related disorder is dressing apraxia—that is, loss of the ability to appropriately arrange one's clothing about one's limbs and torso. Other symptoms of this type include topographical amnesia—that is, an inability to represent or remember spatial relationships between topographically distributed elements, like buildings, streets, and other landmarks, or like the internal layout of a building. This results in route-finding difficulties. Other commonly observed disorders of spatial perception and cognition are defective face recognition, imperception of facial emotion, inadequate judgement of line orientation, and the like.

This last category of symptoms has provided the basis for the classical neuropsychological conceptualization of the *normal* psychological functions of the right hemisphere. It is now almost universally accepted that the right hemisphere of the brain is specialized for *spatial perception and cognition*. This lateral specialization of spatial functions is usually conceptualized as a literal localization within the tissues of the right hemisphere of the engrams for allocentric topographical relationships, and for the orientation of one's own body in extrapersonal space. Sometimes these inferred spatial functions of the right cerebral hemisphere are embedded within broader theories of right-hemisphere specialization, in which it is claimed that the right hemisphere is dominant for concrete as opposed to symbolic functions, or for perceptual as opposed to linguistic functions, or even for holistic–gestalt functions as opposed to logical–analytic ones. Some of these theories are also meant to account for the other aspects of the right-hemisphere syndrome which we described earlier. For example, it has been suggested that patients with anosognosia and neglect fail to situate perceptual information concerning their paralysed limbs in an appropriate gestalt context; they fail to integrate the parts into a whole, and therefore they cannot draw correct conclusions about their physical condition.

More recently, three additional theories of normal right-hemi-sphere functioning have been proposed to account specifically for the symptoms of anosognosia, anosodiaphoria, and neglect, which were not adequately explained by the purely spatial theories.

The first and most important of these newer theories is that the right cerebral hemisphere is dominant for *attention arousal*. Accord-ing to this theory—which is associated above all with the names of Heilman (Heilman & van den Abell, 1980) and Mesulam (1981)—the right perisylvian region is an integral part of an attention-arousal loop, which also includes right frontal, anterior limbic, thalamic, and core brainstem structures. This loop privileges the right cerebral hemisphere with regard to the arousal and spatial distribution of attention, with the result that both spatial hemi-fields are under the purview of the right hemisphere, whereas the left hemisphere attends only to the right-hand side of space. Con-sequently, when the left hemisphere is damaged, the right hemi-sphere is still capable of maintaining a full attentional focus in both spatial fields, whereas when the right hemisphere is damaged, attention is restricted to the right hemispatial field of the intact left hemisphere.

This accounts for the cardinal features of neglect, and for some major aspects of anosognosia. However, as we shall see, it cannot account for some of the more complex psychological phenomena that one readily observes in the psychoanalytic setting.

The second theory is just as well known and equally widely accepted as the attention-arousal theory, although the two theories have not to our knowledge been properly integrated. This theory states simply that the right cerebral hemisphere is domi-nant for *negative emotions*, whereas the left hemisphere is dominant for positive emotions. This is meant to explain the frequent occur-rence of anosognosia and anosodiaphoria with right-hemisphere lesions, in the following way: when this hemisphere is damaged, patients only have access to the intact positive emotions of the left hemisphere, and therefore they feel inappropriately positive about their condition. Conversely, patients with left-hemisphere lesions are supposed to be prone to "depression", since these patients have access only to the negative emotions generated by the intact right hemisphere. (Hopefully the reader will agree that the psychoanalytic observations reported in chapters five, six, and seven suggest that the "depression" left patients suffer is not a *pathological* reaction to their loss; the typical reaction is one of "mourning" rather than "melancholia"; cf. Freud, 1917e [1915]).

Despite its almost absurd simplicity, we must emphasize that the notion that the right cerebral hemisphere is a repository for negative emotions is a very serious and respectable theory in contemporary neuropsychiatry, and much experimental evidence has been gathered in support of it (by Flor-Henry, for example).

The third theory we wanted to mention is associated with the name of Damasio (1994). This theory has two components. The first is a modified version of the James–Lange theory of emotion, which states that emotions are perceptions of the current state of one's own body—of one's own visceral state. Damasio accepts the James–Lange theory but adds that the brain also contains mnemic representations of previous visceral states, with the result that what Damasio calls "as if" emotions can be generated when current perceptions activate somatic memory dispositions, thereby bypassing the current state of the body. Second, Damasio suggests that the right cerebral hemisphere is dominant for the perceptual representation of the body, and therefore for monitoring the current somatic and visceral state. He concludes that damage to the right cerebral hemisphere will result in an inordinate reliance on "as if" emotions, based on the *premorbid* state of the body. This mechanism is meant to account for the symptoms of anosognosia and anosodiaphoria, and presumably it also produces an impoverishment of emotionality in general. The latter is a feature of the right-hemisphere syndrome that is frequently remarked upon and has led to the view in some quarters that the right hemisphere is not only dominant for *negative* emotions, but in fact for *all* emotions—that it is, in short, the "emotional" hemisphere.

These are the prevailing theories of normal right-hemisphere functioning in contemporary neuropsychology and neuropsychiatry. As can be seen, these theories do not go very far beyond the directly observable data. Right-hemisphere lesions disproportionately produce disorders of spatial perception and cognition; therefore it is claimed that the normal right hemisphere must be dominant for normal spatial perception and cognition. Right-hemisphere lesions produce unilateral disorders of attention; therefore it is claimed that the normal right hemisphere must be responsible for the bilateral distribution of attention. Right-hemisphere lesions are associated with an inappropriate degree of emotional indifference and unconcern; therefore it is claimed that the right hemisphere must be normally dominant for negative emotions. Right-hemisphere lesions result in impoverished emotionality and defective somatic awareness; therefore it is claimed that the right hemisphere must be responsible for monitoring the somatic basis of normal emotionality.

There is nothing wrong in principle with simple theories that stay close to the observable phenomena; indeed, such theories—being directly testable—are highly valued in science. But those of us who are trained in the psychoanalytic method have reason to be cautious in this regard, for there are two things that we have learnt time and again when investigating the psychological mechanisms of mental disorders: first, the disorders themselves are almost invariably far more complex than they initially appear to be; second, the fundamental mechanisms underlying these disorders are *not* manifest in the directly observable phenomena—and not infrequently, once we expose the underlying mechanism, we find that the psychological basis of the disorder is the *very opposite* of what it appears to be. This obscurity of the underlying mechanism is due to a function that we describe loosely as "repression", a function that manifests itself clinically in the form of what we call "resistance"—that is, a motivated diverting of consciousness away from certain thoughts and perceptions, which are usually of a distressing nature. We are aware that even these basic discoveries of psychoanalysis, which barely add to folk psychological knowledge, are disputed in some quarters.

In order, therefore, to demonstrate these facts empirically, and by way of a further preface to the clinical psychoanalytic findings that we shall present, we would like at this point to inform the reader about the results of an experiment that Ramachandran performed on Mrs M, the right-hemisphere patient with the somatoparaphrenic delusion whom we introduced a little earlier.

Experimental demonstration of "repression" in a case of right perisylvian damage

In this experiment, Ramachandran (1994, p. 323) aimed to confirm an observation that was first reported by Bisiach, Rusconi, and Vallar (1991)—namely, that if one simply pours cold water into the left ear of a patient with neglect, the neglect disappears completely, until the effects of the caloric stimulation have worn off, at which point the neglect reappears again. This is interpreted as a temporary, artificial correction of the attentional imbalance between the hemispheres. In this experiment, a short while after the interview that we cited above, Ramachandran administered 10 ml of ice-cold water to Mrs M's left ear and waited until nystagmus appeared. Then he asked her: "Do you feel okay?"

A: My ear is very cold but other than that I am fine.

Q: Can you use your hands?

A: I can use my right arm but not my left arm. I want to move it but it doesn't move.

Q: [holding the arm in front of the patient] Whose arm is this?

A: It is my hand, of course.

Q: Can you use it?

A: No, it is paralysed.

Q: Mrs M, how long has your arm been paralysed? Did it start now or earlier?

A: It has been paralysed continuously for several days now.

The reader will notice that Mrs M is now not only acknowledging her paralysis, she is also acknowledging that she has been paralysed *all along*, even at the point when she had previously denied this. Eight hours after the caloric effect had worn off completely, a colleague of Ramachandran's again asked Mrs M: "Mrs M, can you walk?"

A: Yes.

Q: Can you use both your arms?

A: Yes.

Q: Can you use your left arm?

A: Yes.

Q: This morning two doctors did something to you. Do you remember?

A: Yes. They put water in my ear; it was very cold.

Q: Do you remember they asked some questions about your arms,
and you gave them an answer? Do you remember what you
said?

A: No, what did I say?

Q: What do you think you said? Try to remember.

A: I said my arms were okay.

So, as can be seen, not only did the anosognosia reappear, but
the patient also revised her *memory* of the distressing fact that she
had previously consciously acknowledged under the influence of
the caloric stimulation—namely, that her left arm was indeed paralysed. She did not forget the entire episode, just the part about
her handicap. The reader will notice, also, how she seemed to be
positively avoiding this acknowledgement, and skirted around the
issue. This is quite characteristic of these patients, and it is highly
reminiscent of what in psychoanalysis is called "resistance". We
should therefore not be entirely surprised to learn that Ramachandran drew the following conclusions from his remarkable experimental observations:

> They allow us to draw certain important new inferences about
> denial [of illness] and memory repression. Specifically, her [Mrs
> M's] admission that she had been paralysed for *several days* sug-
> gests that even though she had been continuously denying her
> paralysis, *the information about the paralysis was being continuously
> laid down* in her brain, i.e., the denial did not prevent memory . . .
> we may conclude that *at some deeper level she does indeed have
> knowledge about the paralysis.* . . . [However] when tested eight
> hours [after she was made aware of this knowledge by means of
> caloric stimulation], she not only reverted to the denial, but also
> "repressed" the admission of paralysis that she had made dur-
> ing her stimulation. The remarkable theoretical implication of
> these observations is that memories can indeed be selectively
> repressed. . . . Seeing [this patient] convinced me, for the first
> time, of the reality of the repression phenomena that form the
> cornerstone of classical psychoanalytical theory. [p. 324, empha-
> sis added]

So, in short, Ramachandran (who, incidentally, knew next to nothing about psychoanalysis at that time) was led to the conclusion that the mechanism of repression underlies—or at least contributes to—the manifest clinical symptoms of anosognosia. If this is true, it casts considerable doubt on the prevailing neurocognitive theories of this disorder, which we enumerated a few moments ago. If these patients are indeed continuously encoding information about their paralyses, as Ramachandran suggests they are—and if it is true, therefore, as Ramachandran says, that at some deeper level they do indeed have knowledge about their paralysed limbs, but that this knowledge is selectively repressed—then we cannot accept Damasio's theory to the effect that these patients lack perceptual information about the current state of their bodies, or that they are relying exclusively on memories of the premorbid states of their bodies. This theory is incompatible with Ramachandran's observations. We also cannot accept Heilman's and Mesulam's theories to the effect that these patients are unable to direct their attention to the left-hand side of their bodies. Or, rather, we would have to say that these neurobehavioural theories apply only to the *conscious* aspect of the perceptual, mnestic, and attentional functions of these patients. We would have to say that *unconsciously* they *do* perceive, attend to, and remember that they are paralysed.

We take it that it is now generally accepted that human perceptual and memory functions are largely unconscious. It is, however, more questionable whether there is such a thing as unconscious attention. Many people—Freud included—would say that it is precisely the function of attention which renders unconscious mental processing conscious, that it is attention that raises perceptions and memories above the threshold of awareness. Be that as it may, the important point is that Ramachandran's experiment demonstrates that unconsciously these patients do perceive and remember that they are paralysed, notwithstanding the fact that they are unable to direct their conscious attention to these facts.

If this *is* the case, the question arises: why should it be so? What is it that prevents them from becoming consciously aware of what they know unconsciously about their deficits? Ramachandran suggests that it is the function of *repression* that prevents them. And we would agree with him, although we can see that this is not the only explanation that fits the empirical facts. It is also possible, for example, that somatic perception and memory are divided into conscious and unconscious aspects, and that the two aspects are functionally disconnected by right-hemisphere lesions for reasons other than the dynamic factor of repression—which implies a whole theory of *motivated* unawareness. We recognize this qualification, but we do not accept it, on grounds that will shortly become evident. The clinical psychoanalytic findings, which we are going to report now, suggest that these patients are indeed positively *avoiding* their unconscious knowledge of the paralysed state of their bodies, because this knowledge is a source of intolerable distress to them. And this is precisely how we in psychoanalysis understand the mechanism of repression.

We turn now to the psychoanalytic case material. Unfortunately, we do not have space to describe the full histories of these fascinating cases. We limit ourselves here to the essential facts upon which we have based our conclusion to the effect that the function of repression does indeed play a prominent role in the neuropsychology of anosognosia, anosodiaphoria, and neglect. We also hope to show that the specific variety of repression at issue enables us to understand the relationship between these emotional and attentional symptoms and the purely *spatial* symptoms of the right-hemisphere syndrome—and also to understand the relationship between these negative symptoms as a whole and the positive symptoms of the right-hemisphere syndrome, such as misoplegia, and the paradoxical form of neglect that we mentioned earlier.

Case C: narcissistic withdrawal

Mr "C" was a 59-year-old civil engineer who underwent an endartorectomy of the right common carotid artery following a transient ischaemic attack, which had presented as left-sided hemiparesis. A pre-operative angiogram had induced complete hemiplegia, and the endartorectomy was therefore performed as an emergency procedure. After the operation, however, a dense left hemiplegia persisted, together with an equally dense hemianopia on the left side, and a mild somatosensory defect. An MRI (magnetic resonance

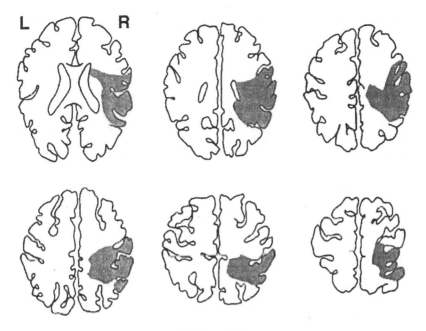

FIGURE 8-2

imaging) scan demonstrated a large area of infarction in the right temporo-parietal region, which was interpreted as a thrombosis of the inferior branch of the right mid-cerebral artery (Fig. 8-2).

Neuropsychological assessment

The neuropsychological assessment, conducted five weeks post-insult, demonstrated a severe right-hemisphere syndrome. Mr C made no attempt to compensate for his hemianopia (in other words, he *neglected* it), and he was inattentive to stimuli arising from the left-hand side in the other sensory modalities too. He even ignored all questions that were asked of him when the examiner sat on his left-hand side. In addition, he was moderately *anosognosic*, or at least *anosodiaphoric*. Although he did not openly deny that his left arm was paralysed, he tended to ignore, minimize, and rationalize the paralysis, saying, for example, that "it *was* like a dead piece of meat, but *now* it's just a little bit lame and lazy". In addition, his visuospatial judgement was very poor, which was a serious deficit considering the fact that, as a civil engineer, his livelihood depended largely on this skill. He retained an abstract knowledge of topographical relationships, but his constructional performances were extremely apraxic, and he displayed the "closing-in phenomenon", often seen in right parietal patients, in which the whole construction seems to collapse in on itself. He was also moderately disorientated in concrete space. This was complicated by his neglect. Furthermore, there was a moderately severe acalculia (of the spatial type). This deficit, too, was a severe blow to his capacity to function as an engineer. He reported a complete cessation of dreaming, but his visual imagery (or revisualization) seemed to be intact (cf. chapter three). Memory was essentially normal. Formal spoken and written language skills were preserved, but speech was severely aprosodic (i.e. monotonous or lacking in expressive intonation) and was punctuated by inappropriate pauses. All higher motor functions were preserved in the non-paralysed limb. Verbal regulation of executive performances, too, was intact. Complex logical problems were solved with ease.

Shortly after this neuropsychological assessment, Mr C began his rehabilitation programme. However, he was soon referred to us by the physical therapists, who reported that he was completely unwilling to cooperate with them. This problem occurs quite often in anosognosic right-hemisphere patients in rehabilitation settings. They do not cooperate with the therapists, because they fail to see why they should; they believe that they are quite well enough and therefore have no need for rehabilitation.

Psychoanalytic observations

In the psychoanalytic setting, Mr C presented in an aloof, imperious, and egocentric fashion. He seemed almost oblivious to the world around him, except insofar as it affected his own well-being and needs, and he appeared quite unable to see things from another person's point of view. This included an eschewing of social convention. For example, he openly picked his nose during his sessions and wiped the products on the knee of his trousers.

He frequently sat blankly staring into space for long periods of time, seldom taking any social initiative, except when he wished to express a complaint or a need or an urgent request. He also responded to direct questions with a minimum of effort, in clipped monosyllabic tones, and not infrequently with manifest irritation. He took nothing in, and he never expressed any gratitude. It was as if he had withdrawn into a cocoon of self-sufficiency, and yet he was simultaneously very needy and demanding.

Despite his tendency to minimize and rationalize his major deficits, such as his hemiplegia and hemianopia, he was frankly hypochondriacal with regard to minor ailments, such as a sore back and a difficulty in sleeping. He was also extremely intolerant of frustrations of any kind. This was expressed most clearly in relation to the nursing staff, whom he treated as if they were all combined into one big mother whose only function it was to meet his personal needs—and, moreover, to do so immediately. His intolerance of frustration and delay was also expressed in relation to the inevitable limitations that were imposed on him by his physical and mental handicaps, by the hospital milieu, and by the demands of his rehabilitation regime. Most important of all, he expected—indeed demanded—to make an immediate and total recovery, so that he could return to work forthwith, as well as to his previous respected position in society. He seemed to harbour an intense need to regress, to be looked after and cared for, and yet he consciously abhorred dependence and vulnerability of any kind and wanted to be treated as if he were the chairman of a public company. Thus, while he made constant, whining demands of the staff, he simultaneously insisted on doing everything for himself. All in all, he closely resembled the proverbial "His Majesty, the baby". He was, in a word, *narcissistic*.

This patient's attitude to his own deficits, as it was revealed in the psychoanalytic situation, was extremely interesting. He treated the left side of his body in just the same way as he did the nursing staff, as if it were merely another piece of external reality that was refusing to do his bidding. It was therefore a source of irritation and annoyance to him, but also something that he did not feel any great interest in or concern about. It was as if it had nothing to do with him personally. From the emotional viewpoint, it appeared that he had single-handedly redrawn the boundaries of his physical self, so that he now only recognized his torso and his right-sided limbs as *truly* belonging to him. The left-hand side was there to serve him, but it was not making a terribly good job of it, and he did not really want to be associated with it. Accordingly, he experienced his deficits as if they were impingements that emanated from the outside world, rather than from his own beloved self. For example, he spoke of his left hand as something that "offended" him or "inconvenienced" him, as one might speak of a rude guest or an unwelcome visitor. On another occasion, he described his hand as "not obeying the orders that I am sending it". It was like an inefficient servant or a disobedient employee, whose behaviour he was not prepared to tolerate for much longer, but with whom he also did not want to become too personally involved. Nevertheless, despite this apparent detachment from his deficits, he was forever clutching at straws of improvement and drawing our attention to them.

We shall have a lot more to say later about this tendency to withdraw from the external world, and for the boundaries of the self to retreat from the left-hand side of the body. For now, we hope only that the reader will agree with us that when one fleshes out the general emotional context within which this patient's anosognosia was embedded (which is something that the psychoanalytic method enables us to do), it becomes apparent that his emotional symptomatology is actually rather complex, and that his anosodiaphoria is not really separable from his post-stroke personality as a whole.

There is, however, little in the picture that we have painted so far which supports the hypothesis that this patient's anosodiaphoria was a product of repression. At this point, we would like to focus on something very specific about his presentation, which we have held back until now, but which we think *does* support this hypothesis rather strongly. In general, as we have said, Mr C presented in a detached, aloof, even imperious fashion. Nevertheless, every now and then, and for no apparent reason, his face would suddenly crumple, and he would either burst into tears for a brief moment, or he would look as if he were about to burst into tears, before rapidly finding his composure again. The whole episode would be over in a flash, forming a curiously incongruous contrast

with his more pervasive attitude of invulnerable, narcissistic supe-
riority.

We assure the reader that if one gave this patient an MMPI or
Beck Depression Inventory, or some other standardized psychometric test, one would obtain no indication of the existence of these
episodes. Mr C was only too happy to overlook them. Standardized psychological testing (which is the form of assessment that is
used in most conventional neuropsychological research in this
area) would therefore produce a somewhat misleading picture of
his emotional state. But in the analytic situation it was impossible
to overlook these episodes. There, his psychotherapist [K.K.-S.]
explored the immediate precipitants of these momentary attacks of
tearfulness or pre-tearfulness, and, in doing so, it became evident
to her that they were directly associated with thoughts and feelings
of the kind that were most conspicuously absent in his more typical, anosodiaphoric state. We have space to illustrate this by means
of just one example, and we hope the reader will take our word for
it that all of these episodes followed a similar basic pattern.

The *physio*therapist reported that she had been trying to teach
Mr C to walk again, but she had made little headway for the
reason that Mr C seemed totally indifferent to the errors that he
was making, and he simply ignored her when she pointed them
out to him. This was a typically anosognosic response, and the
physiotherapist interpreted it as such. Yet, on the following day, in
the privacy of the analytic situation, Mr C described to his psychotherapist what had happened, clearly indicating that he *was* aware
(to some extent at least) of the deficits that the physiotherapist had
tried in vain to point out to him the day before. The session proceeded as follows:

At first he sat silently, in his typical detached state. After a
few minutes, I asked what he was thinking about. He said that
the physiotherapists were teaching him to walk, and he added
in a confessional tone (looking a bit ashamed) that the physiotherapist had told him that he had made a few mistakes. (Here
he was apparently attributing to the physiotherapist his *own*
perception of his mistakes, which he was simultaneously minimizing, as he was very far indeed from being able to walk
normally.) Then he said (with the same confessional, embar-

rassed tone) that the occupational therapist had also assigned a task to him, which involved the use of blocks, and he hadn't managed it. I, in reply, said that it was difficult for him to acknowledge the problems that his stroke had left him with, but it seemed that he was now more able to see them. Mr C carried on as if I had not spoken. He said that his physiotherapy was "okay", but that his arm had not progressed to the degree that he required. Then, at this point, he suddenly withdrew from conversing with me and began to *exercise* his left hand and arm with his right one. I commented that it seemed as if he could not bear the wait, and he wanted his arm to be completely better immediately. "No", he said, momentarily reverting to his rationalizations. "I just don't want my left arm to get weak from non-use." I replied that it was perhaps too painful for him to acknowledge what he was on the verge of recognizing a moment earlier—namely, that his arm really was completely paralysed—and that the question of whether it would recover or not was largely beyond his control. This comment provoked an instantaneous crumpling of his face and a burst of painful emotion accompanied by pre-tearfulness. Turning to me, he said in desperation: "But *look* at my arm [pointing to his left arm]—what am I going to *do* if it doesn't recover?" (This was his most reflective comment to date, which involved a full recognition of his plight—a truly defenceless moment.) Then Mr C was silent for a long while, whereafter he reverted to his usual, apparently indifferent state.

This vignette, which—as we say—was typical of these episodes, illustrates that the sudden moments of tearfulness and pre-tearfulness in this case were easily understood within their emotional context. They represented breakthroughs of suppressed feelings about the deficits that he had previously denied, and, in this instance, this applied to deficits that he had been minimizing and rationalizing away just moments before the suppressed anxiety and concern broke through. In short, the therapist's carefully timed and tactfully worded interventions in the analytic situation had the same effect as Ramachandran's caloric stimulation had in the experimental situation we described earlier. They momentarily overcame the patient's resistances and enabled him to face squarely the facts that he had up until then been strongly disinclined to acknowledge. This begins to suggest that Mr C's whole aloof, detached, narcissistic persona served—at least in part—to divert his attention (and ours) away from the painful underlying facts of his newly dependent and vulnerable position. Perhaps the reader can see now what we meant when we said that psychoanalysis sometimes reveals that the *underlying* emotional basis of a mental disorder—the component that lies *behind* the resistances—is the very opposite of what it appears to be.

If we have not yet convinced the reader of this, then at least, at this stage, we hope the reader will agree that the clinical evidence casts doubt on the simple claim that these patients lack negative emotions, or that they are unaware of the current state of their bodies, or that they are unable to attend to their deficits on the left-hand side. It shows, as Ramachandran's experiment showed, that the underlying psychological situation is more complex than that. These patients are indeed continuously encoding information about their defective bodies, and at some deeper level they do indeed have knowledge about their handicaps and the emotional implications thereof. All that they lack is the capacity—or, as we are suggesting, the *inclination*—to attend to this knowledge, to permit it to enter conscious awareness.

In case the reader thinks that the phenomena we have just described were idiosyncratic to this one case, and that they cannot be demonstrated in other cases of anosognosia or anosodiaphoria, we briefly describe a second case.

Case B: brittle narcissism

Mrs "B" was a 55-year-old woman who had suffered a stroke 18 years earlier, in the final trimester of her third pregnancy. Clinical investigations at the time revealed that there had been a thrombosis of the right middle cerebral artery, affecting primarily the posterior cortical region and underlying white matter. Mrs B was left with a dense left hemiplegia, affecting her face, arm, and leg. A CT

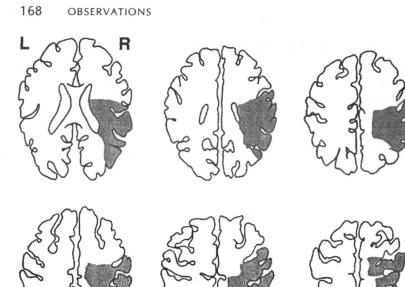

FIGURE 8-3

scan taken six years after the stroke confirmed this diagnosis and localization and revealed a large area of low density in the right parietal lobe, extending subcortically into the internal capsule (Fig. 8-3). The medical notes state only that she was anosodiaphoric and "aloof" at the time of her stroke, and that she had been completely anosognosic in the acute post-stroke period; however, it appears that no formal neuropsychological assessment was conducted. Eighteen years later, when she was referred to one of us [K.K.-S.] for psychotherapy, she was still significantly hemiparetic, but she walked with the aid of a stick and was even able to drive a modified car. By this time, there were no manifest cognitive deficits.

Premorbid personality

In evaluating Mrs B's personality, we are in the extremely fortunate position of being able to compare our own clinical observations with detailed *premorbid* observations, which were recorded by a psychoanalytic psychotherapist who had treated her for two years immediately prior to her stroke. We cannot go into all the details here; we would like to emphasize only that there was no evidence in the premorbid notes of depressive illness or episodes, and certainly no mention at all of the curious symptom that we observed: namely, the fact that Mrs B—just like Mr C—was prone to sudden breakthroughs of tearfulness, in the context of an otherwise rather distant, brittle, and affectless presentation. In sharp contrast to these moments of really quite uncontrollable tearfulness, Mrs B described herself as a "coper" and as someone who "never wore her heart on her sleeve".

Psychoanalytic observations

Mrs B herself described the episodes of tearfulness as involving sad feelings, in relation to which she felt considerable distance, and yet she was simultaneously unable to inhibit them. When asked what the sad feelings were about, she said that she did not know. Yet when describing these episodes, it was immediately apparent to the external observer that they were intimately related to the physical handicaps that had marred her life after her stroke. For example, in her first session, Mrs B reported an episode involving a 29-year-old man who had recently joined the Stroke Aid Society (a voluntary support group for stroke patients). The young man was describing his experience of his handicaps and weeping, when Mrs B, too, began to cry uncontrollably. At this point in the session, the therapist made the rather obvious remark that Mrs B was crying in *identification* with the young man, about her *own* handicaps. However, surprisingly, Mrs B did not agree with this remark. She said that she was a "coper", whom others turned to for help. When the therapist suggested that she might be coping on the outside but sad on the inside, Mrs B again totally rejected the notion and insisted that she really was coping, and she reminded the therapist that her stroke had happened a long time ago and repeated that she had fully come to terms with it.

Here is a second episode. Mrs B commented that she was more emotional than she used to be before her stroke, although, as we have already described, she also felt as if her emotions were not really her own any more. She then elaborated:

> She had noticed that these uncontrollable feelings—notably, weeping that she *couldn't* stop—were always set off by a specific external event. For example, they erupted when she saw *Fiddler on the Roof* [this patient was Jewish, and of Eastern European descent]. Then she corrected herself: "No", she said, "there are times that I am continually tearful, regardless of the external context. The tearfulness seems to come from nowhere." She went on to describe an example of her lack of resistance to crying. She said that the other day she had read *one* sentence in a book, and she immediately started crying uncontrollably. I asked what the sentence was about, but she couldn't remember it. She knew that it involved a husband and wife and a court case, about which they were talking, but that was all. [She did remember the sentence in a subsequent session, as the reader will see in a moment.] She agreed that she might have had personal associations that she was not aware of. Once again, she described vividly how cut off from, and yet simultaneously overwhelmed by, her feelings she had become since her stroke.

One week later, Mrs B returned to this issue:

> She said that she had looked up the "forgotten" sentence, in the book which had made her cry. She described the episode again, this time making it clear how severe the crying was; she said that she had been unable to stop sobbing for over an hour. The sentence referred to *a court case surrounding a thalidomide child.* She said that this episode was typical of how she would start crying and would then be unable to stop until the overwhelming feeling had spent itself naturally. I asked her what the image of a thalidomide child made her think of. She said she had first heard of thalidomide children about six years after her stroke. Her associations were to practical issues; for example, she was preoccupied with how a victim of the drug would grow up and cope in life, without limbs. She thought that physiotherapy might help, as it had always helped her, and still

did. Then she fell silent. I said that it seemed likely that she identified herself with the thalidomide children, and that her overwhelming feelings in response to reading about them showed that she was still holding back powerful feelings about her own physical disability. In response to this comment, Mrs B became defensive and subtly changed the subject. First she said that she and her whole family had always been open about physical matters, including her disability. Then she said that her family of origin, too, had always been very liberal about "those matters"—there was no excessive modesty around bath-times, and so on.

Hopefully the point is clear: this anosodiaphoric patient with a right perisylvian stroke, just like Mr C, was actively suppressing distressing feelings associated with her physical handicaps. She consciously denied or avoided or rationalized these feelings away, but unconsciously they were deeply felt, and under favourable dynamic circumstances the underlying, repressed feelings broke through into consciousness, in the form of uncontrollable tearful-ness. It should be equally clear that the feelings in question were *depressive* in nature and were directly related to the painful losses that this patient had suffered as a result of her stroke. Psychoana-lytic investigation of her defences against these feelings showed that their primary function was to shore up her very fragile and damaged self-esteem—in other words, to shore up what in psycho-analysis would be called her narcissism.

We do not know how prevalent these eruptions of tearfulness and pre-tearfulness are in the anosognosic and anosodiaphoric population in general. No doubt there are cases—again, we do not know how many—in which there are no such episodes. However, the fact that a subgroup does exist in which depressive affects break through in this way suggests, in our view, that even in the cases where negative emotions are more pervasively absent, this may be due to repression; that is, depressive affects may be totally absent in those other cases because in them they are *successfully* kept away from consciousness, not because they are truly absent in the sense implied by the theory that claims that the right cerebral hemisphere is a repository for negative emotions. By simi-lar reasoning, the existence of these cases suggests that even in those cases where such breakthroughs of emotional awareness do not occur, the patients might be unaware of or unconcerned about their deficits not because they *cannot* direct attention to them, in the sense that the attention-arousal theory implies, but, rather, because their attention is actively *diverted away* from them. The same applies, we suggest, to the somatic monitoring theory of Damasio (1994). The case of Mr C, in particular, showed—just as Ramachandran's experiment did—that these patients are unconsciously aware of the damaged state of their bodies. They know perfectly well what has happened to their bodies, but they do not *want* to know.

So, we are suggesting that a fundamental mechanism underlying the inattentional, hypoemotional, and somatoparaphrenic symptoms of the right-hemisphere syndrome is the mechanism of repression. This raises numerous further questions, and most specifically this one: why do right perisylvian patients *in particular* suffer from repressions, whereas other patients—*left* perisylvian patients, for example (see chapters five, six, and seven)—do not? In other words, what is it about the functions of the right perisylvian region that makes patients with lesions there so intolerant of depressive emotions and the associated thoughts about loss and dependency? We shall attempt to address this question in due course. But first we want to describe some further cases with right perisylvian lesions who responded in different ways to Mr C and Mrs B.

The latter two cases were examples of the defences underlying anosodiaphoria breaking down momentarily, and then regrouping. But there also are right-hemisphere cases in which the defence against depression fails more or less *completely*.

Case A: melancholia

Mrs "A" was a 61-year-old Austrian woman who was treated psychoanalytically ten months after she suffered massive damage in the right perisylvian region of her brain as the result of a middle cerebral artery subarachnoid haemorrhage. Her lesion predominantly affected the right temporo-parietal region, but it also

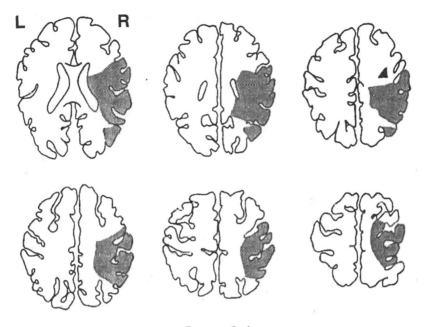

FIGURE 8-4

extended anteriorly into the frontal convexity, and medially down to the depth of the thalamus (Fig. 8-4). This stroke left her with a dense left hemiplegia and hemianopia, and she was wheel-chair-bound. Neuropsychologically, she presented with a severe right-hemisphere syndrome, characterized by dense left *hemi-neglect, anosognosia* for her hemiplegia and hemianopia, *constructional apraxia, topographical amnesia*, and other gross impairments of visuospatial behaviour and cognition, including cessation of dreaming (cf. chapter three). In other words, she was severely impaired, both motorically and visuospatially, but she was consciously *unaware* of most of these impairments.

This was the first case of right-hemisphere syndrome that we studied psychoanalytically, so we were very interested to see what we could learn about the depth psychology of neglect and anosognosia, and we were keen to begin to take our initial bearings for an understanding of the deep psychological functions of the right perisylvian region. However, in one crucial respect Mrs A was an atypical case of this syndrome, because, notwithstanding

her anosognosia and neglect (that is to say, her apparent unawareness of the physical consequences of her stroke), she was *clinically
depressed*. Indeed, that is why she was referred to us in the first
place.

Premorbid personality

According to two letters we received, including one from her GP
(who was a compatriot and a life-long friend), Mrs A had never
suffered from depressions premorbidly. However, one of the most
conspicuous symptoms of her stroke was a severe mood disorder,
which presented with all the clinical hallmarks of a full-blown
melancholia. She was almost constantly in tears, she believed that
she was an enormous burden to the world, and that everybody
hated her, and she had twice attempted to kill herself—once by
trying to jump out of a window and once by throwing herself down
a flight of stairs. The only reason why she did not succeed in these
attempts was because she was too motorically and spatially impaired to manage the physical logistics of what she wanted to do.

Psychoanalytic observations

We are going to describe the inner workings of this patient's mind
in somewhat more psychoanalytic detail than we did the previous
two cases. We know that in doing so we run the risk of losing
the attention, or comprehension, or even the sympathy, of some
readers. It is, however, not absolutely necessary to follow all these
details. The important point is that here we have a patient with a
massive right perisylvian lesion, with apparently normal lateral-
ization, and a full-blown right-hemisphere syndrome, who was
simultaneously severely depressed. This fact alone demonstrates
the main point we are wanting to make, which is simply that these
patients are indeed capable of experiencing profoundly negative
emotions. This is difficult to reconcile with the idea that the usual
hypoemotionality of these cases is due to a literal deficiency of
negative affect. It is, however, entirely compatible with the alternative theory that their hypoemotionality is only *apparent*—that

negative emotions are not *absent* in these cases but, rather, dynamically suppressed.

The reason why we have to go more deeply into the psychoanalysis of this patient is that it would not be possible for us otherwise to explain the paradoxical coexistence in her case of dense anosognosia on the one hand, and profound depression on the other. For, as the reader will see, this strange combination of denial of a loss with a simultaneous depressive reaction to that same loss only becomes comprehensible once we reveal what lies *behind* the repression barrier in her case.

We have up until now been using the term "repression" in a very loose sense, more or less synonymously with the broader term "defence". In fact, psychoanalysis distinguishes between many different varieties of defence. Although all defences serve the same fundamental purpose—namely, keeping distressing thoughts, feelings, or perceptions away from consciousness—they do this in many different ways. In Mrs A's case, as the reader will presently see, the form of defence that she used is known as *introjection*. It is no coincidence that this mechanism, like the defences used by Mr C and Mrs B, is a *narcissistic* form of defence.

We are going to skip over all the details of Mrs A's interesting personal history. We will only mention in passing that she recounted her life story in rather "official" tones, speaking in a somewhat distant way, as if she were sketching the anamnesis of a patient to a colleague. At one moment during this quasi-clinical monologue, however, her distant, professional tone faltered, and she began to cry quietly. This was at the point when she mentioned that her father had died when she was still a child. Her psychotherapist [M.S.] drew her attention to this, and he said that the memory of the loss of her father was still very painful for her. She responded by saying that she was feeling upset at the thought of her *loss of independence* since her stroke. She then quickly pulled herself together and continued with her earlier, official-sounding presentation of her history.

This patient was seen five times a week. In one of her very first analytic sessions, she explained that the reason why she was so depressed was simple: it was because the staff all hated her, especially the cleaning and kitchen staff, and because she kept on losing things—or, rather, because people kept stealing things from her. With this explanation, she burst into tears and said that she would never be able to repay the rehabilitation team for everything that we were doing for her. She sobbed deeply for a good few minutes. Between sobs, she repeated her complaint about being hated, adding that not only did the staff all hate her, her fellow patients hated her too.

So this was *her* explanation of her depression: "I keep losing things" and "everybody hates me".

In line with everything that we have learned in psychoanalysis about melancholic illness in general, her therapist was quite ready to believe that these two facts—or at least the unconscious facts that they reflected—did indeed account for her melancholia, and for her wish to kill herself. Mrs A *had* lost a great deal, and her melancholia—like so many others—was the immediate reaction to that profound loss. Also, she *was* hated—by herself. That is, her melancholia—like all melancholias—was synonymous with a violent, *self*-directed hatred (Freud, 1916–17). As the reader will see, and as is usually the case with melancholic reactions, this self-directed hatred arose as a direct *consequence* of the loss.

An analytic understanding of Mrs A's symptoms might therefore profitably start from the question of what it was, precisely, that she had lost. To the non-analytic observer, this is a silly question. It is obvious what Mrs A had lost: she had lost the ability to walk, she had lost the use of her left hand and her arm, and she had lost the left half of her vision and the bulk of her spatial reasoning. She had lost, in short, a good portion of her life. Mrs A appeared, at least at first sight, to agree with this common-sense explanation. She said, time and again, bursting into tears each time, that she had "lost her independence". This seems reasonable enough. But what, precisely, did she *mean* by this? And why do *other* patients (with left hemisphere lesions, for example) manage to lose their independence without falling into melancholic depressions. Why do *they* manage to mourn the losses that Mrs A found so unbearable?

This leads us to the main question. How could it be that Mrs A was suicidally depressed about the loss of her independence (as she called it) and yet, simultaneously, *consciously unaware* of the immediate physical basis of that loss? Let us not forget that although it seems self-evident to *us* what she meant when she said that she had lost her independence, *Mrs A herself was completely unaware of the fact that she was hemiplegic, and hemianopic, and so forth.* We are thus faced with a paradoxical situation in which Mrs A was depressed about the very events that she simultaneously denied had ever happened in the first place.

Here, as was the case for the other patients we have discussed, including Ramachandran's case, the concept of unconscious knowledge is indispensable to us. This concept allows us to say that Mrs A's depression was a reaction to a loss of which she was *unconsciously* aware; it was a reaction to *knowledge that she was defending herself against.* This loss, which was the immediate cause of her depression, could—because her knowledge of it was unconscious—only be experienced *indirectly,* by way of conscious derivatives of her disavowed knowledge. Thus, whenever her therapist attempted to explore analytically what it was that Mrs A had in mind (i.e. in consciousness) when she complained about what she had lost, she responded by telling him about all manner of *minor losses,* which seemed totally out of proportion to her depth of feeling. For example, she frequently said in this connection that she had lost her spectacles, or that somebody had stolen her cigarettes, and then she would burst into tears. (Incidentally, the reason why she kept losing these things was because she was hemianopic and topographically amnesic.)

So these were the sorts of losses that she was *consciously* referring to when she said that she was depressed because she kept losing things. At other times in her sessions, Mrs A would associate freely from the theme of losing things and things being stolen from her to memories of other, more serious losses that had occurred in the past, such as the loss of her father and of her uterus in an early hysterectomy. She was eventually able to say that "I was never able to mourn the loss of my father" and to recognize that her intense reactions in the present to the loss of trivial objects on the ward was somehow related to these more serious losses in her past.

It is now possible to see something that every psychoanalyst will know from other cases of melancholic depression: namely, that Mrs A's profound emotional response to the minor losses of daily life reflected not only the fact that these were displaced representatives of the repressed loss, but also that it was the fact that this loss was repressed that made it impossible for her to mourn the loss in a healthy way. If you cannot admit that you have lost something, how can you undertake the painful process of gradually detaching yourself from it?

So this is what had happened to Mrs A's neglected body-half, and this was the emotional basis of her anosognosia. She could not mourn the loss of her independence because she could not consciously admit the full horror of what had occurred.

But this global mechanism of defence is only a part of the solution to this case; it does not explain the full clinical picture. It is apparent how the defensive denial of a loss can result in neglect and anosognosia—the *negative* symptoms in this case—but why should this result in the *positive*, melancholic symptomatology? Why, for example, should it result in self-directed hatred and culminate in the wish to kill oneself? And why did Mrs A feel that everybody hated her?

Those who have worked analytically with depressed patients will see what we are leading up to. Mrs A's melancholic reaction to the loss of her bodily integrity was a product of the fact that she had denied that loss in a very particular way. This is something that we are very familiar with from our general psychoanalytic knowledge of melancholia. These patients feel that everybody hates them because *they hate themselves*. That much is obvious. And it was obvious in Mrs A's case too. She positively despised herself—or, at least, she positively despised herself as she was *now*, all crippled and dependent, following her stroke. *But this was precisely the image of herself that she was defending herself against.*

This reveals the *specific* mechanism of defence that Mrs A had used to suppress that image of herself. She had suppressed it by means of an *introjection*. This defence mechanism is absolutely typical of melancholia. These patients cannot bear to acknowledge the loss of a loved object, so they deny that loss by introjecting the lost object—by taking it into themselves and making it a part of themselves. They thereby retain the lost object inside themselves, in the form of an unconscious introject.

This casts new light on the manifest symptoms of neglect and anosognosia in Mrs A's case. She ignored the paralysed left arm that was attached to her real *external* body because, for her, *the original, intact arm was still preserved safely inside her,* in the unconscious part of her ego; thereby, the paralysed arm was neglected and the disability was denied. So this was the emotional basis of her neglect and anosognosia.

But what about the self-directed hatred? It seems that this was directed towards another, very different image of herself, of which she *also* had unconscious knowledge. This is where our existing psychoanalytic knowledge of the unconscious structure of melancholia guides the way.

The analysis of innumerable cases of melancholia has taught us that the defensive mechanism of introjection always comes at a price. This is because it is only a very particular type of object relationship that *can* be introjected. We describe that type of object relationship as a *narcissistic* one. What we mean by this is that the separate, independent existence of the object had never been fully recognized in the first place. The object was always treated as if it were a part of our own beloved selves and, therefore, as if it were under our own omnipotent control. That is why the loss of such an object is so especially intolerable. It shatters our infantile sense of omnipotence, forces us to recognize our real dependence on the object world, and thereby leaves a gaping wound in our narcissism.

Caveat: the psychoanalytic theory of narcissism

In order for us to proceed with our explanation of what we found in the analysis of Mrs A, we must first describe the basic psychoanalytic theory of narcissism. According to this theory, which was based primarily on the analysis of melancholics and paranoiacs, the prototype for all object relationships is, in earliest infancy, our relationship to our own bodies. The ego is first and foremost a bodily ego, and the first object it discovers in the outside world is its own physical body. Initially this body—which is attached to us wherever we go—is experienced as something alien, a source of peculiar sensations of various types, arising from the superficial and deep sensory receptors (including from passive awareness of movement) and, more importantly, from the major somatic needs, which constantly demand satisfaction and press themselves on our attention in the form of acutely distressing states of colicky, hungry unpleasure.

Freud (1923b) stated that hate is older than love, and our first reaction to this constant source of unpredictable, unwanted stimulation is one of hatred: a wish to be rid of it and to be left in peace—to be allowed to return to the blissful state that existed before the painful caesura of birth. This is something that people who have not studied the psychology of the narcissistic neuroses and psychoses find difficult to accept: the most primitive attitude in all of us towards the external object world—with all its frustrations and privations—is one of *hatred*.

But fortunately there is also another tendency at work in the human mind which is, at bottom, an expression in the subjective world of the indifferent biological processes that gave rise to our existence in the first place. We are referring to the processes of natural selection, and to the sexual and self-preservative drives to which it gave rise. Unless we found a way to adapt to the world and to satisfy our biological needs within it, there is no way that we could have survived as a species. It is from these instinctual sources that the impulse arises in the infantile ego to, as we say, *libidinize* the object world—this source of unpredictable, unwanted stimulation—and to take it into ourselves, to make it a part of our selves. In this way the first love relationship is established—starting with the narcissistic love of our own physical selves, our bodies. But this relationship is from the start (and for obvious reasons) a profoundly ambivalent relationship, for always lurking beneath the surface of our love for the body—and beneath the feeling that it is justly part of our selves, and the belief that it is therefore under our omnipotent control—is the unconscious knowledge that it is really, fundamentally, something *alien*, something *disturbing* our need for tranquillity and *demanding* our attention, something that is, in many respects, far from being under our omnipotent control—and something that really belongs, therefore, or *also* belongs, to the hated *external reality*.

We do not want to go too far into an exegesis of our basic psychoanalytic theory, with which many of the readers of this book will be familiar in any event. We just want to remind the reader of the *ambivalent* nature of our relationship to our own bodies, which forms the prototype of all love relationships. Beyond one's own bodily ego, the next narcissistic object relationship is the relationship with one's mother, which is built up on the model of the relationship to the body. The mother (or other primary care-giver) is another object that is essential to the preservation of life, a source of goodness and relief from unpleasure, and it, too, is therefore libidinized and taken into the beloved self and brought into the sphere of phantasized omnipotent control. But she, too, even more than one's own body, is apt to disabuse that illusion and to injure our narcissistic world-view by revealing herself to be separate and independent and capable of disappearing and of frustrating us and of refusing to do our bidding—in short, of be-traying the fact that she, too, belongs also, after all, to the hated external reality.

Upon the foundations of these early narcissistic cathexes, all our libidinal relations with the outside world of objects are ulti-mately established. These subsequent relationships are progres-sively less egocentric, and during the process of development an important shift occurs in our whole conception of the world, as we reluctantly come to accept that it really is quite separate from us and quite indifferent to our own urgent needs. At this point we move from narcissism to what we call object love. But we will come back to that development in a moment, when we consider the *spatial* disorders of the right-hemisphere syndrome.

We are going into all of this theory in order to remind the reader of what we mean when we say that Mrs A's relationship to the lost body-image that she had introjected was a narcissistic one, and also when we say that this implies that its separate, independ-ent existence had never been fully accepted in the first place, that it had been treated as if it were under her own omnipotent control, that the loss of such an object was intolerable, and that it shattered her infantile sense of omnipotence and forced her to recognize her real dependence on the object world, and thereby left a gaping wound in her narcissism.

What happens when such an object—a narcissistically cath-ected object—is lost, and when it thereby reveals its true colours as a part of the hated external reality, is not only that the loss is denied in the form of an introjection, but also that one's original hatred of that piece of reality is reawakened (or, more correctly, delibidinized). The lost ambivalently loved object is therefore not only set up within one's own self, but also subjected there to all the ruthless, vengeful punishment of the lover scorned. To be more specific, what happens when an ambivalently loved object is lost is that the bound ambivalence unravels, and the object is split in phantasy into absolutely good and absolutely bad parts—that is to say, into absolutely loved and absolutely hated parts—with the result that when it is taken into the self in order to deny the loss of its good qualities, its bad qualities are also, simultaneously, taken into the self. *It is the hatred of this internalized bad aspect of the introjected object that is the source of the violent self-hatred that is so characteristic of melancholia.*

In Mrs A's case, for example, she introjected the perfect image of her own intact body, which she now idealized, in order to preserve it safely inside her. This, as we have explained already, was the emotional basis of her neglect and anosognosia. Yet, simultaneously, she introjected the damaged image of her handicapped body, which had let her down so terribly, and which she hated with the vengeance of a lover scorned. This was the emotional basis of her self-hatred, and therefore of her melancholia. Note that this is not a *normal* reaction to object loss; it is a *pathological* reaction to the loss of a *narcissistically cathected* object. The healthy reaction is the reaction of normal mourning (which was observed in all three *left* perisylvian cases described in chapters five, six, and seven). In normal mourning, one recognizes that the object never was under one's omnipotent control, that even though one needed it so much it was always something separate from the ego, and that it is now gone forever. This recognition triggers the long and painful process of mourning, in which one gradually detaches one's libido from the lost object.

But Mrs A reaction was the pathological one, and this was the cause of her self-directed hatred. When she said consciously that everybody hated her, what she meant unconsciously was that *she* hated *herself*, that she hated the part of herself that she could no longer depend on and that no longer cared for her, the part that was outside the sphere of her omnipotent control, and ultimately, therefore, that she hated reality itself. But the *most* hated aspect of reality, the part of it that she had always depended on so absolutely, and which had now let her down so terribly, was *in reality* inextricable from the very part that was introjected into her own beloved *self*. And *that* is why her self-hatred was such an extremely dangerous situation, liable to end in suicide.

When this interpretation was gradually put to her, Mrs A could see the truth of it, and in so doing she simultaneously admitted—at least momentarily—that she was hemiplegic and hemianopic and so on, and she acknowledged the full implications of her predicament. In this respect, she responded to analytic interpretation in just the same way as Ramachandran's patient had responded to caloric stimulation, and in just the same way as Mrs B and Mr C did fleetingly when their defences broke down spontaneously.

A historical analogy might be drawn here between the effects of caloric stimulation and interpretation, and those of *hypnotic suggestion* and psychoanalytic interpretation. Both techniques bring the repressed to conscious awareness—that is, they *force* the patient to attend to the repressed material—but the analytic technique does so with the conscious cooperation of the patient's ego, and therefore—unlike hypnotic suggestion (or caloric stimulation)—it holds out the promise of a permanent change.

The metapsychology of spatial cognition

So far we have looked analytically at the *emotional* aspects of Mrs A's right-hemisphere syndrome. It was apparent that the neglect arose from the denial of a loss through repression and introjection, that the anosognosia reflected the unconscious belief that the premorbid body-image was still safely preserved inside her, and that the melancholia arose from a narcissistic libidinal disposition towards the lost and introjected object. We have only briefly alluded to the *other* major symptoms that characterize this syndrome— the various disorders of *spatial* behaviour and cognition. Therefore, before we move on to the last two cases, we will briefly make some further remarks on this aspect of the right-hemisphere syndrome. Here, our excursus into the psychoanalytic theory of narcissism will repay us.

We said earlier that all of our libidinal relations with the world of external objects were originally built on the foundations of narcissistic attachments to our bodies and our mothers. This origin provides a clue to some aspects of the disorders of *spatial* cognition that routinely accompany neglect and anosognosia. In short, what happens in these patients—and what we hope we have adequately illustrated with the brief clinical vignettes we have cited—is that their external object cathexes are withdrawn, and their libidinal relations with the outside world regress quite pervasively back to the narcissistic level. In short, *external object cathexes collapse back into the ego*, resulting cognitively in a veritable collapse of external space and, with that, in an abandonment to varying degrees of recognition of the independent existence of external things—of their allocentric, lawful nature. Henceforth, *space is treated narcissistically*, as if it were arranged as the patient *wished* it to be, rather than how it actually *is*. So, if we are not being too laconic, we hope the reader can see how a psychoanalytic approach to this syndrome reveals the underlying unity of the hemineglect, anosognosia, *and* spatial disorders in a way that the conventional cognitive theories do not. These are some of the benefits of exploring the submerged portion of the iceberg in neuropsychological syndromes, and some of the contributions that our "underwater psychology" can make. But we are aware that we are covering a vast amount of theoretical ground in just a few sweeping formulations. It is unfortunate that we cannot here go over all the detailed evidence that we have examined in this regard in our study group in New York (see Kaplan-Solms & Solms, in press).

Preliminary conclusions

Before moving on to the final two cases, let us recap our argument so far. Using the psychoanalytic method of investigation, we have found that, unconsciously, right-hemisphere patients with neglect and anosognosia are far from being unaware of and indifferent to their tragic situations. A small amount of analytic work quickly brings the underlying, profound feelings of depression to the surface. Thus, a patient who appears bland and unconcerned about his or her incapacities one minute will, after a not very deep or elaborate psychoanalytic interpretation, suddenly be fending off floods of tears the next. Observations of this sort, in the first two right-hemisphere cases that we summarized (Mr C and Mrs B), led us to conclude that in these cases their manifest symptoms of anosodiaphoria were in part *defensive*—more specifically, that they were a narcissistic defence against awareness of the loss of a loved object. In the third case, which we have just discussed in some detail (Mrs A), we saw what happens when these defensive manoeuvres fail completely. That patient, who, like the other two, suffered a stroke in the region of the right middle cerebral artery, was overcome by a full-blown clinical depression, the psychoanalysis of which revealed the typical mechanism that Freud first elucidated in his celebrated paper "Mourning and Melancholia" (1917e [1915])—that is, the patient suffered the consequences of a narcissistic introjection of the lost object, which culminated in her intense hatred towards that object being diverted inwards, towards her own beloved self.

These three cases combined lead us to formulate the following hypothesis: behind the cardinal clinical manifestations of the right-hemisphere syndrome there lies *a failure of the process of mourning*. Rather than mourn the loss of their healthy bodies in the normal way (as the *left*-hemisphere patients did: cf. chapters five, six, and seven), *these* patients institute massive defensive measures which are designed to protect them against any awareness of the loss. In short, the cardinal manifestations of the right-hemisphere syndrome are revealed by psychoanalytic research to be, at least in part, *defences against a recognition of loss, and the associated depressive affects*.

The defences in question vary somewhat from case to case, but the underlying common factor is this: *there is a regression in the libidinal cathexis of the lost object from the level of object love to that of narcissism* and, therefore, *a withdrawal of object libido back into the ego*. This necessarily results in what we call a *defusion of the drive cathexis of that object* and therefore in *a splitting of the object into absolutely good and bad parts*, which accounts not only for some of the more bizarre aspects of the emotional symptomatology, but also—in part—for the associated attentional and spatial disorders.

Although this explanation contradicts the simplistic notion that the right hemisphere is specialized for negative affects, we do not think that it altogether contradicts the attention-arousal hypothesis of Heilman (Heilman & van den Abell, 1980) and Mesulam (1981). Nor is it entirely incompatible with the somatic-monitoring hypothesis of Damasio (1994). It merely *adds* something to those hypotheses. In the case of the attention-arousal hypothesis, it points to the fact that *the distribution of attention in the mental apparatus is not an emotionally and motivationally neutral function*. Although it may well be true that attention is not appropriately aroused and distributed in these cases, this is not due simply to damage to a so-called attention-arousal module; rather, it is the result of a defensively motivated *dynamic* process, designed to protect the subject against awareness of an intolerable aspect of reality. Likewise, in the case of the somatic-monitoring hypothesis, we do not think that these patients are emotionally indifferent because they have *lost* bodily awareness; rather, they are indifferent because they are *defending themselves against* their awareness of an intolerable bodily situation.

Whether or not the reader agrees with these more complex psychoanalytic formulations, the essential point remains that the clinical psychoanalytic observations on which they are based—that is to say, the undeniable presence of significant depressive affects in right perisylvian patients, which are usually suppressed, and which are linked directly with perceptions of and ideas about their physical handicaps—strongly suggest that we need to revise (or at the least, to *add* something to) the prevailing cognitive theories of anosognosia, anosodiaphoria, and neglect.

Before we end with a consideration of what new light all of this might cast on the *normal* psychological functions of the right cerebral hemisphere, we would like to report briefly on two further patients with right perisylvian strokes, who presented in the psychoanalytic situation in ways that simply cannot be accounted for by the prevailing cognitive theories but can readily be explained by the alternative, neuro-psychoanalytic theory.

Parenthetically, we must point out that these cases were not especially selected because of the problems they pose for the prevailing neurocognitive theories: rather, they are the only five cases with right perisylvian lesions that have so far been referred to us for psychoanalytic treatment. We turn now to the fourth of these cases.

Case D: paranoia

Mr "D" was an Irishman living, until recently, in London. He was 34 years old at the time that he was referred [to K.K.-S] for psychotherapy. At the age of 32, two-and-a-half years before he was admitted to our rehabilitation unit, he had suffered a sub-arachnoid haemorrhage. Investigations at that time had revealed a posterior communicating artery aneurysm. The bleed was associated with significant spasm in the distribution of the right anterior cerebral and middle cerebral arteries, causing a large, continuous area of infarction in the right frontal, temporal, and parietal lobes (see Fig. 8-5). The aneurysm was clipped by a neurosurgeon attached to our unit.

Considering the extent of his lesion, Mr D was fortunate indeed to have made an excellent physical recovery, and he was able to return to work, albeit at a lower level of employment than before. Whereas he had been working as an estate agent at the time of his stroke, he was now employed as a boiler operator.

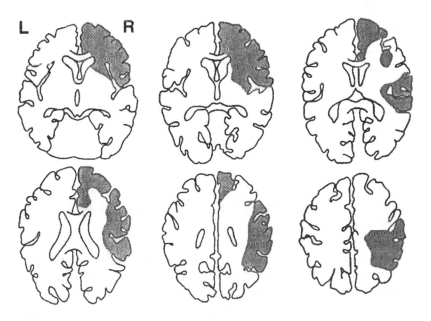

FIGURE 8-5

Although he had initially suffered from the typical neuropsy-chological sequelae of a right-hemisphere stroke—namely, neglect, anosognosia, and spatial disorders—these were recovering, and by the time that he was referred for psychotherapy he was considered to be cognitively nearly normal. His physical deficit, too, was lim-ited to a mild left-sided hemiparesis, which presented essentially as weakness and clumsiness of the left hand. In addition, this hand was subject to paroxysms of clonic twitching.

However, Mr D was absolutely obsessed by this left hand, which he hated passionately and refused to use (even though the neurosurgeon felt that the hand was capable of a good degree of further functional recovery—an opinion with which the physio-therapists concurred). This was, therefore, a case of *misoplegia:* a man with a massive right-hemisphere lesion of the type that fre-quently leads to profound neglect and anosognosia, but who was now presenting clinically with the very *opposite* symptoms—that is, an absolute *obsession* with his left hand and with his physical deficits.

Neuropsychological assessment

On admission to our unit, Mr D underwent a routine neuropsycho-logical assessment. This revealed a mild degree of left hemispatial neglect, which was evident on formal testing, but not in his ordi-nary behaviour. Also, there was considerable left-sided hemiakin-esia—that is, unilateral *motor* neglect. This resulted in a failure to use his hand in situations in which it certainly could have been functionally useful. In addition, this patient reported a total cessa-tion of dreaming, the onset of which he dated to his stroke. Apart from this, and a moderate degree of affective disinhibition, other localizing symptoms and signs could not be demonstrated.

The neuropsychologist noted that Mr D displayed a peculiarly aggressive and negative attitude towards him. In addition, he noted that Mr D seemed hypervigilant and that he was extremely possessive towards his own medical notes. For example, when the neuropsychologist paged through the various scans kept in the envelope at the end of his bed, Mr D leapt up and took them away from him. He would only allow him to look at the images one at a time, and on condition that each scan was returned to the envelope before the next one was looked at. He showed the same suspicious and controlling attitude towards the reading of the written notes in his clinical file. Other staff members reported similar behaviours. They also reported that Mr D was verbally aggressive, towards the staff in particular, and that he tended to pace up and down the corridors of the hospital. He himself described this as "letting off steam", which was an interesting way of putting it, considering the fact that, since his stroke, he was employed as a boiler operator.

Psychoanalytic observations

We want to quote just one clinical vignette from the psychoanalytic treatment of this patient, to illustrate his cardinal emotional symptom—that is, his hatred of his paretic hand: his misoplegia. This is an extract from his seventh session:

> As he sat down in the consulting-room, Mr D told me that he had had a good week-end, and he asked me—in the form of an accusation—why I had not attended the previous ward round. He said that at the ward round the neurosurgeon asked him if he was seeing me—"That's all", he added, "and then he said that my brain scan was fine". Now Mr D exploded with a malignant rage. First he reported, as usual, how disgusting the hospital food was, to the extent that all he had ever enjoyed was his cigarette after each meal. Then he said: "I've spoken to the matron *and* the head sister about it—other patients keep quiet, but I speak my mind." He also informed me that he was discharging himself later that week, no matter what—"they can bring the *whole* British Army to hold me here, but I'm *not* staying. And apart from this place being a *dump*, not *one* bit of improvement have I seen. I'm supposed to get fine movements back in my hand, but look at this; would you think *this* bloody thing is doing anything?—It's useless!" Then, suddenly, Mr D hit his left hand, hard, with his other hand. "I've had *not* more than *one* hour of individual attention since I came here—I could have paid someone myself, to treat me at home. Those OT's—

they're useless—*useless*—I'm going to *smash*—start *smashing* all the furniture in OT up. They don't know what they're doing—they will say I'm improving just to save their own bloody skins." I intervened, and said: "You're not sure whether it is us or your hand you hate. The problem is that your hand is part of yourself, and hating a part of your own self is an impossible situation to be in. For an instant he calmed down, and then he said: "Well, I can see the hospital's predicament, having so many patients ... but my old individual physiotherapist helped me such a lot with my arm and leg ... but I left Belfast before she could work on my hand." After this, he became extremely angry again, and he continued the tirade. "But even when I went for the brain scan the doctor wasn't a medic's backside—he was just a vet ... a *vet*, I'm telling you!" I commented at greater length now, saying much the same thing as before, in different words, and adding that he felt humiliated by all these doctors lording it over him, and he wanted to be treated like a man again, rather than a little boy. While I spoke, Mr D sat still and listened. Then there was a long silence, after which he said: "And I haven't seen the Professor *once*—I saw him in December and he suggested that I come here; and I haven't seen him *once* since then." Suddenly Mr D jumped up and said: "I *can't* live like this. I knew when the surgeon mentioned brain damage, it was the end of my life. I'm lucky I didn't have another bleed, and although this one was very serious, I wish I had! I'm going to commit suicide—that's why I've bought a shotgun!"—and he put his finger in his mouth, then at his temple, and he said, "here ... or here. I would rather be dead—six foot under—I've had a *guts-full!*" While he said this he paced around the room, and I felt that he was trying to stop himself from attacking me, or his hand. (I feared for my safety.) Then he said, "I'll *smash* this hand into a *million* pieces and post the pieces to the surgeon, in envelopes, one by one". Then he mimed the action of smashing it on the radiator. "Like *this*—I would do *this* if you weren't here." I said: "You want to punish him for damaging you, and to damage him back; so you're not sure any more whether your hand is part of him or part of you." Again he calmed down a bit, and he alternated between pacing around and sitting down. "I'm giving my hand six months and if it has not improved, I will come back and ask for an artificial claw". He kept saying "I can't live like this; I'm going to have it amputated." He also seemed to be slipping into a delusional state, and he said: "When I first came into this hospital I *bit* my hand and *spat* the pieces of meat out, because I *can't* stand it!" This certainly never happened in reality. I wanted to reinstate his contact with reality, and started saying "the only way of *knowing* if you would improve was to test things out . . .", but he interrupted me and said; "That's it—bad luck again, it always happens with me! I'd rather know where I stand than go through this." He was extremely angry and distressed, and his larynx was moving rapidly up and down. I said, again, that he needed to take control of the situation; he needed to show he was still in charge.

We hope this is enough to give an adequate impression of this man's emotional state. The clinical picture in his case was dominated by aggressive outbursts, directed towards (1) the hospital staff and everything associated with it, and (2) his own mildly paretic left hand. The psychotherapy sessions usually began with an outpouring of complaints and threats, directed towards either of these objects. Moreover, the two objects of his hostility appeared to be quite interchangeable. That is, emotionally, the hospital and the paretic hand appeared to mean the same thing to Mr D. The left hand was therefore treated *as if it were a part of external reality* rather than a part of his own self. At one point, Mr D actually stated that the hand *felt* as if it did not belong to him. The hand thus represented some part of his own self that he had both *lost* and *disowned*. An analysis of his attitudes in this regard suggested that, in fact, he was trying to turn the *passive* experience of losing it into an *active* experience of disowning it. The painful complex of feelings and ideas associated with the dysfunctional hand involved recognition by the patient of the fact that he was not omnipotent, that he was unable to control reality (even those aspects of reality with which his ego was narcissistically merged, such as his own hand, and the internalized caring mother that it stood for), that he was therefore subject to experiences of loss, including the loss of his adult status, and above all, that he was therefore dependent on others for help in some important aspects of his life. In other words, the fact of the paretic hand represented a *narcissistic injury* that was intolerable to him. This seemed to represent the crux of the psychological symptom complex. At one point in his sessions, Mr D actually recognized consciously his intolerance of these feelings, when he described his situation as "utterly degrading".

Note that Mr D's reaction to this narcissistic injury was to *expel* the hand—and all the bad feelings associated with it—out of the sphere of his beloved omnipotent self and into the hated external reality, to which it now so obviously belonged. There, it was attacked ruthlessly and relentlessly, sometimes by actual physical violence, sometimes in phantasy bordering on delusion (e.g. biting the hand to bits and spitting out the pieces, or chopping it up and posting it to the surgeon). It was noteworthy that these attacks always involved a "disowning" or expulsive aspect.

A *paranoid* constellation is evident in this psychic configuration based on *projection*. In psychoanalysis, we class paranoia together with melancholia as a *narcissistic* neurosis. The world was split rigidly into good and bad, and all the bad was projected outward, including the unwanted parts of his self. Equally, the few "good" objects that Mr D recognized, such as his "unlucky" father, were idealized and blurred with his own self. In the transference, the therapist was sometimes idealized and sometimes denigrated, depending on whether Mr D was able to maintain the phantasy that she was entirely available and understanding. Any indication of her separateness (e.g. when she did not attend the ward-round) precipitated a shift from the one to the other extreme of the split transference.

The obsessive wish to have the hand amputated and replaced by an artificial one or a metal "claw" apparently constituted an attempt by the patient to force external reality to coincide with his internal (omnipotent) phantasy—that is, to have the offending hand *actually* split off from his narcissistically cathected body and replaced by something that was "not me". In this way, too, he could conquer his traumatic loss, by turning passive into active.

The externalization or projection of the hand accounted for its interchangeability with the hospital and everything associated with it. For Mr D, his hand represented something external to himself that was constantly failing him; so he sat, full of hatred, bitterness, and complaints, impatiently waiting for it to be made better. Any recognition of personal involvement in his current imperfect, damaged, and dependent state was intolerable. He did not reflect consciously upon the fact that a sub-arachnoid haemorrhage (caused by a constitutional weakness of his own body) was the source of his illness, nor that improvement in his symptoms would require active cooperation and effort from him personally. Instead, he blamed the surgeon and the rehabilitation staff alternately, either for damaging him or otherwise for failing to make him better.

Rather than recognize that he was, psychologically speaking, a "baby" (patient) heavily dependent on the love and care of a good-enough "mother" (the medical staff) for his survival, Mr D treated the hospital as a neglectful mother, giving him bad ("disgusting") food and useless medications, constantly letting him down in innumerable ways, and never devoting herself properly and exclusively to him. He actively controlled and rejected the mother–hospital, he gave ultimatums and made threats of all types, and eventually he withdrew from her care completely, rather than passively experience the pain of his dependency, imperfection, and loss.

The suicidal aspect of the presentation is also germane. (It was as if Mr D were saying: "If you don't give me the breast exclusively, immediately, and exactly as I want it, then I won't take it at all; I won't take anything in—I will bite, spit, and expel it and smash everything up into bits, including myself, and it will all be your fault, and *that* will teach you a lesson"!) However, the thing that was killed in the suicidal aspect of this phantasy represented something other than his own beloved self; it was a part of his ego which represented sharing, imperfection, loss, and so on, which had been transformed in phantasy into a part of the outside world. This was recognizable in the interchangeability of his threats of suicide, his threats towards his hand, and his threats towards others. In his mind, these were *all* externally directed threats. In other words, *Mr D's worst fear was that the paretic hand, which was perceived as part of the bad, hated external reality, would become permanently attached to him and would thereby contaminate his omnipotent, perfect, and beloved self.* If this narcissistically intolerable situation came about, *his only defence would have been to kill the hand, and the internal object that it represented, and, therefore, to kill himself.*

Thus, in summary, in this case, we see a patient struggling with the fact that a piece of the object world which he had cathected libidinally—namely, his own hand (which was associated unconsciously with his early maternal care)—abandoned him, let him down, started to behave independently, refused to do his bidding, and so on—in short, revealed itself to be not really under his omnipotent control after all.

This narcissistic insult resulted in a regression in the level of the cathexis, from object love to narcissism, with the consequent defusion of the drives, resulting in massive release of destructive impulses and, consequently, a splitting of the object (and therefore the ego) into absolutely "good" and "bad" parts. This created a positively life-threatening situation, similar to what we saw in Mrs A—where an object that the patient regarded with feelings of murderous hate was experienced psychically as being internal to the self. In Mrs A's case this took the form of an *introjection* of the bad lost object, and therefore resulted psychopathologically in a suicidal melancholia, and cognitively in anosognosic neglect of the introjected limb; in Mr D's case, however, there was a further, *projective* aspect to the defensive process, in which he made desperate attempts to *expel* the internal bad object, and therefore the bad part of his split ego, into the hated, indifferent external reality to which it now so obviously belonged. This resulted psychopathologically in an aggressive paranoia, and cognitively in the very opposite of neglect and anosognosia. In this way, Mr D managed to keep melancholia—that is to say, self-directed hatred consequent upon object loss—at bay; instead, he experienced the bad object as coming at him from the *outside* world, in the form of incompetent, neglectful, and disgusting surgeons, hospitals, and mothers, who were constantly trying to imprison him, subjugate him, and force their useless care upon him. In this way, despite the great price that he had to pay in terms of his mental health, Mr D was able to avoid the painful work of normal mourning, which was absolutely intolerable for him.

We hope the reader can see why we feel that this case of right perisylvian damage, like the other three we have discussed thus far, supports our contention that the emotional abnormalities associated with damage to this part of the brain are attributable to *a failure of the process of mourning*. We hope also that the reader can see why we feel that the attention-arousal, somatic-monitoring, and negative-affect hypotheses cannot account for the full range and complexity of right perisylvian clinical presentations as they unfold in the psychoanalytic situation.

We do not see how one can account for a case like that of Mr D in terms of the prevailing hypotheses; he presented in almost every way with the very opposite emotional symptoms to those that these hypotheses would predict. He did not neglect, or fail to attend to his left-hand side: he was positively obsessed by it. Likewise, he did not ignore or fail to notice his hemiparesis: he was unable to get it out of his mind. And he most certainly was not deficient in respect of negative affectivity; he was a seething cauldron of aggression and hatred. We do not see how one can account for a patient who presents in this way within the framework of the prevailing cognitive theories. By contrast, the psychoanalytic theory of defence—the idea that there are positive symptoms that are actively inhibited in the standard form of the right-hemisphere syndrome—is readily able to account for the fact that *the same lesion can produce two diametrically opposite emotional states*.

Case E: alternating paranoia and melancholia

We are mindful of space, so we will just skim over the fifth case, and then move directly to our conclusions regarding the normal psychological functions of the right perisylvian region. This last case in our series, Mr "E", was a 30-year-old man with a right parietal arteriovenous malformation (AVM) draining from the midcerebral artery to the sagittal sinus. The AVM was surgically resected, leaving him with a large avascular area of infarcted brain in the right fronto-parietal region (Fig. 8-6). This left him with a variety of physical handicaps, about which he, like Mr D, felt anything but unconcerned and indifferent.

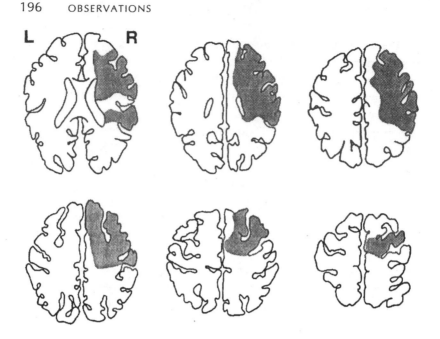

FIGURE 8-6

Psychoanalytic observations

The analytic investigation [by K.K.-S.] revealed that this right perisylvian patient, like all the others we have studied, defended himself against full awareness of his loss by means of a narcissistic organization. He tried to keep depressive affects at bay by identifying himself with the therapeutic staff, rather than with the other patients. He, too, became a provider of help rather than a recipient of it (in phantasy, at least), and in this way he fended off the necessary work of mourning (cf. Mrs B). However, this defence proved highly unsuccessful, and suicidal depressions frequently broke through (cf. Mrs A), which he then secondarily re-defended himself against by means of violent rages against the surgeons, the therapeutic staff, and the hospital, in much the same way as Mr D did. In this way, he—like Mr D—was ultimately able to direct the narcissistic rage outwards, rather than have to kill himself.

The two major ways in which the defences of all five patients broke down, therefore, coincided with two great risks that a regression to narcissism always carries with it. For, according to the psychoanalytic theory of narcissism, the withdrawal of libido from the object world back into the ego is always accompanied by a defusion of the drives—or, to put it in more contemporary terms—by a splitting of the object. The ambivalence that lies buried deeply within all object relationships—that is to say, our mixed feelings towards all love objects, and our recognition that they possess both good and bad attributes—comes apart whenever libidinal object cathexes regress to narcissism. When this happens, the whole object is split into loved and hated parts, which are treated as if they were really separate objects. Herein lies the slippery slope to suicidal melancholia—which arises from the *introjection* of the hated component of the object—and to aggressive paranoia—which arises from a *projection* of it.

Discussion:
the metapsychology of the right cerebral hemisphere

What does all of this tell us about the *deep psychological functions of the right perisylvian convexity*? In a nutshell, what we have seen in all of these cases is a *diminution in whole object relationships* (and therefore in *object love*) and a corresponding *regression to narcissism* (with the *drive defusion* and splitting of the object that that entails, and resultant *primitive defences*). In all of these respects, the right perisylvian cases differed sharply from their left hemispheric counterparts (cf. chapters five, six, and seven), who dealt with loss by means of the process of normal mourning.

On this basis, we would advance the following metapsychological formulation. We think that the right perisylvian convexity is a crucial component of the *neuroanatomical substrate of whole-object representation*, and therefore a *neurophysiological vehicle for whole-object cathexes* and the capacity for mature *object love*. The destruction of the vehicle of whole-object representation, caused by right perisylvian damage, therefore results in a loss of the ability to bind our fundamentally ambivalent attitude towards the real object world, with all its frustrations and privations, and therefore to an inability to relate to objects in a mature and balanced way.

To repeat: we suggest that the right perisylvian convexity is a vehicle for *whole-object cathexes*, that it is a crucial component of the neural substrate for the representation of real external objects *that are felt to be separate from ourselves*. The loss of these concrete things, partly including the representation of one's own body as a thing, which form the foundation of all our love relationships with the real object world, is a severe blow that necessarily results in a regression from object love to narcissism. In other words, right perisylvian damage radically undermines the *means* by which we normally transform infantile narcissistic libido into mature and realistic object love. This is the *specific* factor in the right-hemisphere syndrome which distinguishes it emotionally from the syndromes associated with equivalent lesions in the perisylvian region of the *left* cerebral hemisphere—where objects are represented not concretely but, rather, symbolically, as words rather than things.

The merit of this psychoanalytic account of the normal emotional functions of the right-hemisphere convexity is not only that, unlike the prevailing neuropsychological theories, it is able to accommodate the *full range and complexity* of the emotional presentations of these patients, but also that it is entirely consistent with what we know about the *spatial* functions of the right-hemisphere convexity, which sit uneasily with the existing theories of neglect and anosognosia. We have always known—and today it is beyond dispute—that the right-hemisphere convexity is specialized for the perception and cognition of our relations with concrete external space. What the theory of narcissism provides is a link between these *spatial* aspects and *emotional* aspects of right-hemisphere functioning. *It reminds us that all our relationships with the external object world are, at bottom, driven by our libidinal needs*, which are rooted in our evolutionary biological constitution. The parsimony of our hypothesis in this respect gives us some confidence that we are at least on the right track.

As can be seen, we have not shied away from pushing our formulation to the absolute limits that the clinical evidence will allow, and frankly—in some respects—we have pushed it beyond that. However, as previously stated, at this stage in our attempts to draw a first sketch of how our psychoanalytic model of the mind might be represented in the tissues of the brain, we should not shy away from bold and speculative formulations. We now have a method by means of which we can test these formulations and correct our errors along the way.

CHAPTER NINE

Psychoanalytic observations on four cases of ventromesial frontal damage: "the end of the world"

The beginnings of a general theory

Starting from the principle that object representations (like all memories) are encoded not once but many times over (Freud, 1950a [1887-1902]), we would suggest on the basis of the observations reported in the previous four chapters that objects are represented as a cascade of mnemic traces that stretch from *whole*-object representations (closely tied to concrete perceptual images) encoded at the relatively superficial level of the right perisylvian cortex, through the (symbolic) *word*-presentations that are encoded in the left perisylvian cortex, down to *narcissistic* object representations which we believe (for reasons that will be outlined in this chapter) are structuralized largely on the basis of physiological modifications that occur in the ventromesial frontal region.

This chapter is based on a paper presented by Mark Solms (which summarized earlier clinical presentations by Karen Kaplan-Solms and Mark Solms) at the Neuro-Psychoanalysis Center of the New York Psychoanalytic Institute on 2 October 1997. A version of this chapter appeared, in German, in Solms (1998b).

In other words, when we combine the formulations we outlined in the previous four chapters with the findings from our studies of the ventromesial frontal patients to be described in this chapter, it appears that the ventromesial frontal region is a crucial neuro-anatomical substrate of the more primitive, narcissistic object representations that form the *internal nucleus* of the self-regulatory functions of the ego and superego. These inner representations remained largely intact in the right perisylvian cases just described in chapter eight, but they were almost completely destructuralized in the ventromesial frontal cases that we describe in this chapter.

We only have space to describe these cases very schematically. More detailed clinical reports of these cases can be found in Kaplan-Solms and Solms (in press; process notes based on a series of analytic sessions with the first patient described below were also reported in Kaplan-Solms & Solms, 1996).

Case F: psychosis

The first ventromesial frontal case was that of a beautician, Mrs "F", a 30-year-old dextral South American woman. She was admitted to our hospital through the Accident & Emergency department, in a confused state, following a subarachnoid haemorrhage. An aneurysm of the anterior communicating artery was identified on angiogram, and a CT scan demonstrated—in addition to the bilateral effects of the communicating artery haemorrhage itself—right ventromesial frontal-lobe infarction (in the region of the anterior cerebral artery). The area of bifrontal low density extended posteriorly to include the anterior aspect of the corpus callosum and the basal forebrain nuclei (Fig. 9-1).

In the analytic setting, Mrs F associated freely and naturally—indeed, excessively—in a loose and confused manner. She said more or less whatever came to her mind, and she moved from one topic to the next by means of concrete and tangential associations. Her mind functioned according to principles that were remarkably reminiscent of those that Freud (1915e, p. 186) described as "the special characteristics of the system unconscious". Freud defined

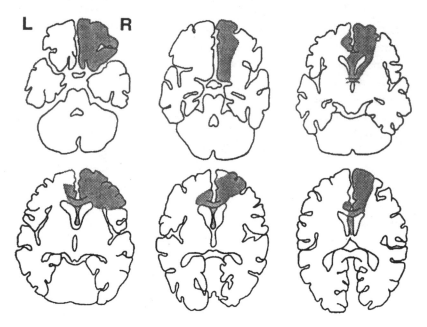

FIGURE 9-1

these characteristics as follows: "[1] exemption from mutual contradiction, [2] primary process (mobility of cathexes), [3] timelessness, and [4] replacement of external by psychical reality."

Contradiction was rife in Mrs F's associations. She seemed to be aware of each idea only as it occurred to her. She moved from one thought to the next without a trace of the former thought remaining behind, and without forming a logical connecting link between them. There appeared to be little or no observing ego. She did not experience doubt. If the currently conscious idea contradicted a previous one entirely (as happened frequently), she seemed to be unaware of this, and therefore she was wholly unperturbed by it.

This way of thinking provided the context for the *timelessness* that she displayed. She was clearly able to remember things, from both the remote and the recent past, but each memory appeared to exist as an island. The memories were not consciously related to one another within a coherent framework. Here, too, an observing ego—that is, a reality-oriented, superordinate reflecting and organizing function—was essentially lacking. Frequently Mrs F was not consciously aware of the fact that she was remembering things, whereas unconsciously traces were being laid down.

She was disorientated in *time*, and her past and present became equivalent for her. She generalized her current problems to her entire life history; conversely, she experienced present events directly according to a model of the past, as if the past were still currently present. Her timelessness also expressed itself in the endless repetitiveness of her associations; she compulsively repeated the same stereotyped communications over and again.

Similar difficulties to those that occurred with regard to time also occurred in other spheres. For example, she conflated her various current ailments, the various hospitals that she had recently attended, the various members of her family, and so on. At times, it appeared almost as if, for this patient, all things were equal.

The isolated and fragmentary thoughts and memories that we have described occurred to Mrs F in the form of concrete, immediate experiences. Perhaps because they were not interrelated and bound by a logico-grammatical or temporal structure, she perceived them passively—as things that occurred spontaneously to her, rather than as information that was at the disposal of a voluntary, directed thought process. It appears that this was far from pleasurable for her. She was no longer able to trust her own mind and body, and to take them for granted, and at times she seemed to fear actual annihilation.

Affects in general were disinhibited, as was, to a certain extent, access to motility. Not only did the disinhibition apply to the intensity of feeling that she was subject to, but also to the freedom with which she expressed and acted upon these feelings. It also applied to the *mobility* or *changeability* of the affective states.

She frequently equated her experiences of mental instability and unreliability with concrete, physical experiences of falling and needing assistance. This type of symbolic equation was a vivid manifestation of *primary-process* thinking. Instead of reflecting on her situation in logical, verbal thoughts, she experienced her mental states concretely, in the form of dream-like visual images; these portrayed her underlying thoughts as concrete, near-hallucinatory experiences, which seemed to depend fundamentally on a process of topographical regression and also to utilize the well-known mechanisms of displacement and condensation (cf. the fifth syndrome, of dream/reality confusion, described in chapter three). Examples of these concrete visual experiences were phantastical images of herself being struck by lightning and walking into invisible glass (which were metaphors for her current predicament) and of her husband being a physical crutch or, literally, a tree (again, a concretized metaphor of the real situation). Here, we recognize the replacement of verbally based thinking by visuospatial forms of thought. The patient herself sometimes complained that she was living as though she were trapped in a dream. Sometimes she was definitely unable to distinguish dreams from reality. In other words, there was a significant weakening of reality-testing.

The concrete visual images that we have just referred to ultimately derived from a single underlying phantasy. This phantasy dominated the patient's experience during the entire period that she was in treatment. An analysis of its various manifestations yielded further evidence of the fourth element in Freud's tetrad of the special characteristics of the unconscious—namely, the *"replacement of external by psychical reality"*.

Description of the dominant transference phantasy

In essence, the phantasy took the following form: "A sick child is being cared for by its mother." In the transference, initially, Mrs F behaved towards her therapist [K.K.-S.] as if she were a sick child and the therapist a caring mother. She communicated to the therapist all that was happening to her, and this was based on the assumption that the therapist was going to help her. The therapist was sympathetic, and Mrs F expressed her anxiety, agitation, and distress openly. A strong feeling of dependency rapidly evolved. She behaved like a sick child pleading for mothering care.

Gradually, however, the quality of the core phantasy of being cared for changed, and she then felt that nothing could be done for her and that the doctors could not help her. The mind and body that had let her down became identified with a mother that did not explain things to her and that did not look after her. She spoke of how terrifying it was to fall when there was no one there to catch

her. These feelings were provoked especially by the breaks between the sessions, which she apparently experienced as complete
abandonments in which she felt that she was being "dropped" by
her therapist, concretely.

She defended herself against the anxieties that were thus generated primarily by means of projection (or, rather, projective identification). Sometimes this took the form of a simple idea: she
wished that she could be with her children, as that made her feel
better. Usually, however, the thought transformed itself into a delusion: it was her *daughter* rather than herself who suffered from
epilepsy, falling, and amnesia; or it was the *therapist* who stayed
in hospital at the end of the session while she went home; or *she*
would not be available when the therapist needed her, rather
than the reverse. Thus, in phantasy, Mrs F was able to become the
caring mother herself, and she obtained a measure of control over
the terrifying separation and annihilation anxieties. Sometimes she
rid herself of her bad feelings in other, similarly concrete ways. In
one session, for example, she projected them in the form of paranoid phantasies of stabbings and betrayals; later in the same session, she apparently evacuated them (in phantasy) through an
actual bowel movement. On other occasions, she employed manic
defences and enacted phantasies of merging with the therapist
(e.g. by sitting in the therapist's chair).

These phenomena were associated with resistances against
talking to her therapist. Mrs F wanted to care for herself, or, alternatively, she wanted to go home and look after her sick children.
She did not want to feel dependent on the therapist's unreliable
presence. Also, when she saw the therapist, it made her think of
things that she did not want to think about; that is, she became
aware of the fact that she felt sick, depressed, and envious. She
experienced her resistance on one occasion in the form of a dream-
like thought, wherein she was being forced by a man to do something that she did not want to.

Whenever she was able to relinquish these defences (usually
towards the middle of a session, when she felt more contained and
"held" by the therapist), she expressed openly and verbally her
despair and anxiety at her lack of improvement. In these moments,
rather than experiencing delusions of being the mother of a sick
child, she admitted instead that it was *she* who wanted to go home

and be cared for by her *own* mother. In one of these lucid moments, in the middle of a session, she stated clearly how she felt:

> "I am *helpless*, and no one knows or understands what things feel like unless they have it themselves. And the doctors are ignorant—they say they don't know what is wrong and they won't tell me—and they can't help me. I'm just sick and no one can help!"

Whenever she felt sufficiently contained to be able to think and express her anxieties in words like this, she was visibly calmer and she felt much better. Interestingly, she simultaneously became far more coherent in her thinking, her memory improved, and she became more orientated in space and time. However, she always lost these gains at the end of each session.

In the final session of her brief treatment, a significant variant of the core phantasy emerged: she told her therapist that her convulsions and delirium had frightened her mother. This was apparently how she understood the therapist's final "abandonment" of her. At the end of the last session, she slipped back into the familiar disorientation and confusion of identity. She confused herself and the therapist (in an introjection of the caring mother), and she confused herself and her daughter (in a projection of the sick child).

Another variation of the core phantasy, which emerged fleetingly throughout the period that she was treated, was one in which the sick child was actively rejected by the mother. The basis for the rejection appeared to be that the child was too messy and was unable to control herself. The activation of this phantasy was usually announced by feelings of shame, for example, at being considered as "crazy" or "clumsy" due to her "forgetting" and "falling" (which were unconsciously equivalent).

The analysis of these phenomena casts further light on the structure of Mrs F's internal world. *It appeared that the loss of an internal reflecting and organizing agency was experienced in phantasy as the loss of a caring and containing mother.* This loss was accompanied by feelings of extreme anxiety.

Whenever she was able to recover this lost agency (i.e. the good object in phantasy) in the concrete form of containment from her therapist as an auxiliary ego and superego, she regained her mental equilibrium to a remarkable degree. However, she was unable to retain these advances. That is, *she was unable to internalize the therapist's containing function*, and she regressed completely in her absence. In the therapist's absence she created a delusional object or object relationship in a desperate attempt to recover her lost contact with a safe and caring mother-figure. In this latter respect, her disorder followed closely the model that was described by Freud in his paper "Neurosis and Psychosis" (1924b), where he wrote: "the delusion is found applied like a patch over the place where originally a rent had appeared in the ego's relation to the external world" (p. 151). The mechanism of psychosis as described by Freud could therefore be recognized in this case in the form of a direct expression of a phantasy of self-cure.

Case H: psychosis

The second case was that of Mr "H", a 65-year-old retired meteorologist. He had a very troubled history, which ultimately culminated in the event that brought him into our neurological rehabilitation unit. Ten days before he was admitted to the unit, he had attempted—in an agitated and apparently intoxicated state—to commit suicide by shooting himself in the right temple. The bullet had entered his skull in the right frontal area, destroying the anterior fossa and enucleating his right eye, crossed over the midline, and remained embedded in the cranium above the left eye, in the region of the left frontal pole. A CT scan of the brain revealed massive haemorrhagic contusion of the ventromesial aspect of the right frontal lobe, which extended across the midline to include the anterior cingulate gyrus and the orbital region of the left frontal lobe (Fig. 9-2). Numerous bone fragments were visualized in this region.

There were striking similarities between Mr H's presentation and that of Mrs F. Once again, the essential features of the case could be defined by the tetrad of functional characteristics that Freud (1915e) attributed to the system *Ucs*. We will quote Freud's summary of these characteristics once again, to remind the reader: "exemption from mutual contradiction, primary process (mobility

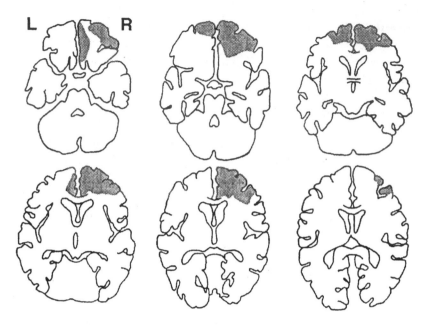

FIGURE 9-2

of cathexes), timelessness, and replacement of external by psychical reality" (p. 186).

We again discuss each of these four elements separately, starting with the *replacement of external reality by psychic reality*. Mr H displayed a pervasive tendency to misperceive external reality on the basis of his internal (and usually wishful) schemata. One instance of this was his delusion that the hospital was a barge or a ferry. This delusion seemed to serve a wishful function, as it always occurred at a point in the session when Mr H became (consciously or preconsciously) aware of his disorientation and amnesia. Anxious (and realistic) questions in this regard were immediately followed and replaced by this delusion. His associations to the delusion that the hospital was a barge suggested that it was based on memories of previous, pleasurable experiences of being in an unfamiliar environment, where he was relieved of the normal routines of working life and where he shared a confined space with strangers (e.g. on a boat-trip in the Caribbean, and on holiday on a barge). Thus, an unpleasant external perception (of being in hospital) was replaced by a pleasurable internal one (of being on holiday). A piece of reality was denied or lost and then replaced by a delusional "patch", in the manner described above by Freud in his (1924b) formulation of the mechanisms of psychosis.

Another example of wishful apperception in this case involved misrecognition of strangers for familiar friends and family members (e.g. he mistook strangers for a deceased friend, and for his wife and for his daughter). Further examples of the projection of internal schemata onto external perceptions occurred in a rabbit's head that he "saw" in his dessert, in a hallucination of a helpful person whom he kept "seeing" in his blind visual field, in a delusion that he left hospital daily by car, and in general denial or unawareness of his own deficits. However, the phantasies that Mr H projected onto reality were not always pleasurable ones. An elaborate phantasy concerning a social worker's control over "comings and goings" at the hospital was an example of an unpleasurable delusion. Unfortunately, the therapist was unable to get to the bottom of that delusion analytically. At times, Mr H seemed to be fleetingly aware of his own inability to distinguish between phantasy and reality. As occurred with Mrs F, he sometimes used his therapist in just this way, as a trusted and reliable auxiliary ego who could test reality for him.

Turning to the second element in Freud's tetrad of the characteristics of the system unconscious, Mr H's *timelessness* seemed to be very closely related to his tendency to replace external reality with internal reality. For Mr H, time was an entirely subjective phenomenon. There were, according to Mr H, various times—the therapist's time, his time, "hospital" time, "municipal" time, "adjusted" time, and so on. His own sense of time always seemed to follow a wishful model—that is, his judgement of time was determined by his wishes, to the near-complete exclusion of external reality. For example, it almost always seemed to be 5:00 p.m. for Mr H (which was his wife's visiting time), or, alternatively, he thought that it was mealtime. The extent to which his desire distorted his external perceptions is perhaps best exemplified by an occasion when he misperceived a "no-smoking" sign as a clockface indicating the time of 5:00 p.m., despite the fact that he had just been told (moments before) that it was not yet 5:00 p.m. On some occasions, he was momentarily aware of the wishful basis of these apperceptions of time and of external reality, and at one point he even described them as wish-fulfilments himself.

An interesting aspect of these phenomena was their comical effect on the therapist. This could be understood—in accordance with Freud's (1905c) theory of humour—as an effect of the unexpected rupture of primary-process mechanisms into secondary-process consciousness. (Mrs F, too, exerted this comical effect on us, despite our full awareness of her equally tragic circumstances.) Another aspect of this comical effect may have been the egocentric quality of Mr H's world, which evoked warm and humorous reactions that were very similar to those that are typically provoked by the innocent vulnerability of a baby and by the playful antics of a young child.

Turning to the third element in Freud's tetrad, the *primary process* quality of much of Mr H's thought and behaviour was very easy to recognize. An interesting aspect of his presentation in this respect was his tendency to speak in vague generalities, abstractions, or allusions, or to think in ways that could be described as ideational circumlocutions. This tendency reflects the "mobility of cathexes" that Freud postulated as the essential basis of primary-process thought—that is, Mr H's thought processes lacked sufficient specificity and thereby lost their normal, bound, logico-grammatical structure and function. A recurring example of this type of thought was Mr H's oblique references to a file at the bottom of his bed, which contained notes about his condition and his clinical progress. This file seemed to represent his own missing memory (and it was therefore a source of security), but it also represented his psychic exposure and lack of privacy (and in this sense it was a source of anxiety and mistrust). Rather than referring to these feelings directly, however, Mr H readily transferred the affective cathexis onto the image of the file. This sort of free displacement of cathexis is normally opposed by the constraints of the secondary process, which, in our view, were largely absent in this case. The recurring nature of the file theme also reflected another aspect of the domination of the primary process in Mr H's case—namely, the stereotypical, repetitive quality of his associations.

Primary-process thinking was also revealed in the occasional occurrence in consciousness of concrete visual images of the sort that were so common in Mrs F. One occurred during the initial

neuropsychological assessment, before the analytic treatment began, when Mr H referred mockingly to a "young puppy" neuropsychologist who was displaying the same "woolly thinking" as
he was supposed to be assessing in the patient. He then said: "Why
doesn't this youngster stop pissing on my leg?" This was a characteristic condensation, of the sort that we are so familiar with from
the psychology of dreams. The condensed, concrete, and visual
quality of this image and the patient's apparent unawareness of the
symbolic meaning of his own communication were typical of the
processes that characterize dreaming thought. Another instance of
such concrete, visual thinking was Mr H's misunderstanding of a
verbal communication, on the basis of an inert visual image in his
mind of aeroplanes in a hangar. A further instance was his repeated reference to crumbling structures in various contexts. This
image—which seemed to carry a variety of meanings simultaneously (once again, by means of condensation)—was apparently
derived from a book that he was reading at the time about the
Great Pyramids at Giza. (The confusion between the various phantasies that this book evoked and his memories and other real
experiences provided numerous examples of the *breakdown in reality-testing* that we discussed above in relation to the first element
in Freud's tetrad.) In fact, the whole "barge" delusion could also be
conceived of as a concrete visual image of this sort, and one sometimes gained the distinct impression in this regard that Mr H was
actually experiencing a dream in his sessions, while completely
awake. (Cf. the fifth syndrome, of dream/reality confusion, in
chapter three.)

The concrete quality of Mr H's thought also deserves attention.
This is perhaps an inevitable consequence of the visual (non-sym-
bolic) nature of unconscious thinking. Despite the fact that Mr H
spoke in a vague and generalized way, which gave the appearance
of abstraction, to a large extent his language actually lost its abstract, logical function. In this respect too, his presentation was
reminiscent of dreaming thought (and of schizophrenia). It seemed
likely that Mr H's relative inability to reflect upon himself might
have arisen directly from a regression to concrete (non-verbal)
thought. The verbal foundations of the superego can also be recognized here. However, he readily made use of his therapist's ego in
this respect: as soon as she made the appropriate connections for

him, he readily accepted them and then momentarily became quite reflective himself. This is a further instance of the destructuralization of the ego and superego that was observed in the case of Mrs F.

Mobility of cathexis could also account for another aspect of this case—that is, Mr H's tendency to accept and to recognize intellectually the accuracy of certain interpretations that were made, without displaying the affect appropriate to such recognition. That is to say, the link between ideas and affects in Mr H's mind was rather weak. For the most part, he was apparently indifferent to his extremely difficult circumstances. It appears that Mr H's affects (sadness and anxiety, for example) were primarily denied, and he become quite irritated when his therapist attributed them to him. However, these attempts were maladaptive and unsuccessful, and his relationship to his affects therefore remained in a constant state of flux.

As for the remaining element in Freud's tetrad, there was abundant evidence in this clinical material of *exemption from mutual contradiction*. For example, Mr H stated that he had an adult son, despite the fact that he recognized simultaneously that the boy had died as a child.

All four of the elements that we have just enumerated are represented in Mr H's frequent use of projective identification. This primitive mechanism (which is more than a defence mechanism) is seen by many analysts as predominant in the system *Ucs*. We would like briefly to draw attention to some of its manifestations in the transference relationship.

Description of the dominant transference phantasy

From the start, Mr H related to his therapist [K.K.-S.] as a helpful figure, who would assist him to re-integrate the bits and pieces of his mind and memory. She was thus apparently equated with the missing part of his own ego—that is, as the containing parental introject who binds together and makes sense of the infant's immediate experiences. This equation was quickly complicated by the superego functions that he then attributed to her, and he therefore began to feel judged, inferior, and exposed. The remnants of his own superego were clearly evident in this latter attitude, but as was the case for Mrs F, they were projectively identified with the therapist and with other members of the hospital staff. In other words, they were not structuralized.

For the most part, however, Mr H did feel contained by his therapist in her role as his auxiliary ego (or his good internal mother). At these times, he conveyed the extent of his disorientation and dependency poignantly. (For example, he said: "It's like being a six-year-old, back at the first day at school—not really knowing or understanding what is going on.") However, although these transitory identifications with her containing function enabled him to experience sadness and anxiety momentarily, they seldom persisted, and his rational insight almost always collapsed at the end of the sessions, just as they had with Mrs F. He then lapsed back into confusion and into spatial and temporal disorientation (i.e. back into primary-process thinking). Sometimes this collapse of his mental integrity manifested in the form of actual (physical) falling, which was especially interesting in view of the fact that Mrs F frequently equated the two phenomena (of mental and physical collapse) in a metaphorical way. (The reader will remember how she constantly complained that she was falling everywhere, although in reality she never actually fell.)

However, the sense of reality that Mr H gained by internalizing his therapist's ego functions during the sessions was frequently too much for him to bear, and his underlying tendency to projectively identify then re-emerged. For example, he disavowed his dawning awareness of his predicament by projecting it into the other patients (the "pathetic cases", as he called them) around him, and he discussed them and their abnormalities in a caring but distant way. One instance of this tendency was his concern about an elderly male patient "with illogical thoughts" whose wife and daughter were "just waiting for him to die". In this way, Mr H successfully protected his consciousness from any sense of his own abnormality and vulnerability.

What preoccupied Mr H most about his fellow patients therefore revealed a great deal about his own internal state. He focused on the dependent isolation of the aphasic patient in the bed next to him, her gross lack of civilized manners, her depression, and the way in which the staff sometimes failed to recognize or accommodate her needs. His emotional attitude towards her was, moreover, decidedly ambivalent: at one moment he displayed great sympathy for her predicament, in the very next he expressed revulsion and disgust. (Here we see another example of Mr H's exemption from mutual contradiction.) Mr H's own (unconscious) ambivalent concern about and enjoyment of his own dependent, incontinent, and troublesome patient-self was evident here. Although it was not possible to uncover the infantile roots of this constellation of thoughts and feelings during the brief period of time in which the therapist saw him, these were clearly related in some way to aspects of urethral erotism and urethral aggression. In this respect, and in his occasional equation of his confused mental state with financial failure, there were echoes of the ideas that so preoccupied the incontinent patient with frontal-lobe disease whom we describe next. As was the case in that patient, Mr H's loss of mental control was accompanied by a physical loss of bladder control (and, to an extent, he seemed to be aware of this regression of his mental functions to a physical level when he himself said one day that "my body controls my mind, not the other way round"). In this respect, the mental "censorship" function seemed to be directly equated with physical urethral control.

However, oral preoccupations were more prevalent than anal or urethral ones in Mr H's case, and in this respect he had more in common with Mrs F than with the next patient we discuss. He enjoyed being indulged like a baby and being relieved of the adult responsibilities that had driven him to attempt suicide, but he simultaneously felt guilty about this regression to dependence and the loss of his adult, masculine status as the breadwinner in his household. This conflict (between a primary dependent impulse and a guilty superego judgement) was also typically dealt with by means of projection (i.e. by means of references to the *other* patients' total passivity, their dependence, their low cultural level, and so on). Similarly, Mr H was sometimes respectful of and at other times derogatory towards the so-called "important work" that was performed by the medical and nursing staff.

An interesting feature of this conflict is that it attested to the persistence of at least some observing-ego, reality-testing, and superego functions. In this respect, Mr H displayed greater mental integrity than did Mrs F. However, as we have already said, these functions were mostly externalized, and they were only con-sciously experienced in the context of his sessions. That is to say, the holding and observing functions that his therapist performed were internalized only for as long as she was concretely present. This was reflected in both the negative and the positive aspects of the transference, wherein the therapist was experienced mostly as a helping, advising, and containing figure, but sometimes as an intrusive, critical, and judging figure. The precarious state of Mr H's ego in this regard was reflected in another aspect of the transference—namely, his ultimate lack of faith in his therapist's competence and ability (and in the ability of the rehabilitation team in general) to test reality accurately on his behalf and to take proper care of him. Similar factors resonated in his occasional, subtle denigration of the therapist by means of his apparent inter-est in and support of rehabilitation and of psychiatry.

Case G: psychosis

The third case we studied was that of Mr "G", a 62-year-old engi-neer. He had spent most of his life in Switzerland but was living and working in London at the time that he was admitted to the neurosurgical unit following a subarachnoid haemorrhage, which resulted in paresis of the left leg and severe mental confusion. An angiogram demonstrated the presence of an aneurysm in the ante-rior communicating artery. It also showed that there was consider-able spasm of the right anterior and middle cerebral arteries. A CT scan (which was taken one month later) showed bilateral, ventro-mesial frontal low density in the anterior cingulate gyrus and basal forebrain, which included a part of the right anterior cerebral ar-tery distribution. This was described as a right mediobasal frontal infarct by the radiologist. The scan also showed areas of infarction in the distribution of the right and left middle cerebral arteries, which resulted in two convexity lesions (Fig. 9-3).

We thought that this patient's presentation in the analytic situ-ation, like that of the previous two patients, was characterized above all by the following two clinical features: first, Mr G dis-played severe mental confusion, the psychological mechanism of

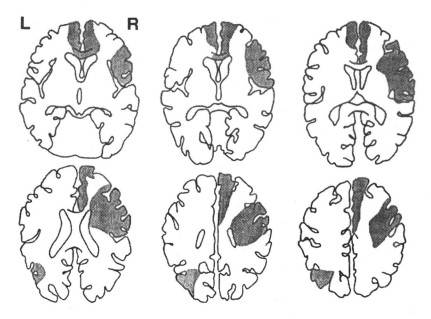

FIGURE 9-3

which we discuss below; second, this confusion was temporarily reversible under favourable conditions.

What was the structure of the mental confusion? It seemed—as was the case in the previous two ventromesial frontal patients—that it displayed all of the fundamental features that Freud (1915e) attributed to the system *Ucs.*

The most striking instance of *exemption from mutual contradiction* was Mr G's belief that he was dead (Cotard's syndrome), a belief from which he could not be dissuaded by factual contradiction or logical argument (cf. chapter six). His belief that he was dead and his daily experience of being alive in hospital existed side by side, despite their mutual incompatibility. Similarly, he believed that his wife was in Switzerland despite the fact that she visited him on the ward every day. However, the loss of a logical faculty was not complete; for example, Mr G demonstrated some awareness of the fact that he might have to give up the idea that he was able to drive, as it gradually dawned on him that this was impossible (under the influence of an identification with the psychotherapist's perspective during a session).

The *primary process* aspect of his presentation was displayed most graphically in his tendency to think in terms of concrete visual images (just as Mrs F had). The essential features of dreaming thought (i.e. condensation, displacement, and visual representation) manifested in these visual images. For example, due to his confusion and loss of memory, he told his therapist [M.S.] that the file containing all his notes had been lost, instead of recognizing his anxiety that he would not be capable of participating in an interview. Similarly, in a moment of resistant chatter during a session, he recognized the situation in the form of a concrete thought—he said, "much of what is on television at the moment is boring". Likewise, at another point, when he seemed to be aware of his inability to find his way around in his thoughts, he referred to the difficulties he was having manoeuvring his wheelchair through the traffic. Also, there were frequent symbolic equations—for example between therapeutic failure, financial failure, and incontinence. These originated in the freedom with which affects attached to one ideational complex were transferred to another. These transfers followed familiar routes of unconscious symbolism (e.g. faeces equals money), and verbal links were used concretely (e.g. a financial deal has "fallen through" equals incontinence; or "I have made a mess" of the financial deal equals "I have made a mess" in my pants). The same phenomena (of displacement and condensation) could be described as a difficulty in keeping separate groups of ideas apart. These tendencies were expressed in his habit of speaking (and actually thinking) in a tangential way. Other aspects of primary-process thinking were evident; first, many of his delusions were plainly wishful (e.g. he believed that he could drive, that he was going home, and that he was an important committee-member). Second, theoretical possibilities became concrete facts (e.g. his fear that his wife might have an affair with the therapist became the "fact" that his wife was having an affair with him).

The problem of *timelessness* served to illustrate further the difficulty that Mr G had in keeping his thoughts and memories separate from one another. The majority of his temporal confusions can be explained in this way. For example, he reacted to a setback in his rehabilitation as if it were a financial setback that had occurred (in reality) eight months previously. Also, he mistook his analytic sessions for a course that he had attended at his company's expense some years before, and he confused his current illness with the Second World War. In other respects, his timelessness appeared to be a direct result of his memory loss. For example, when his therapist asked him how old he was, he replied, "Twenty-five, or perhaps thirty. I don't know exactly because I was dreadfully ill for a period, and that part seems to be missing" (he was actually 62). Another factor, which we have mentioned already, emerged in his representation of theoretical possibilities (which were usually hypothetical possibilities) as if they were actual occurrences in the present.

The *replacement of external by psychic reality* was, to a certain extent, implicit in all the features of his presentation which have been discussed so far. Phantasies were often treated as if they were reality. Numerous examples included the following: he believed that he was dead, that his wife was in Switzerland, that his dreams were actual occurrences, that he could drive, that he was attending a course rather than undergoing rehabilitation, that he had been dropped from a football team when he was moved from his ward, that a ward-sister and his therapist were people he knew from Switzerland, that the therapist was having an affair with his wife, and so on. However, the breakdown of reality-testing was incomplete. For example, he said of his inability to distinguish dreams from reality, "how can you tell?"; he would also often defer to his therapist's judgement, saying that he was "on the other side of the fence"; and he frequently suggested that it would be a good idea to obtain an independent opinion on the real state of affairs from a trusted third person. Accordingly, this patient's use of projection was less frequent and impenetrable than Mrs F's.

A further feature of Mr G's presentation was his disinhibition. This, too, was a partial tendency only, which was exemplified in frequent arguments with the nursing and therapeutic staff, and in angry outbursts at his wife, occasional tearfulness, and rapid shifts of mood.

These features made it possible to obtain an unusually vivid impression of some of the dominant phantasies in this patient's subjective mental life. His major preoccupation and primary response to his illness seemed to be the loss of his status as a potent adult male. He experienced this loss as a deep humiliation. The humiliation was strongly associated with a concomitant loss of bowel control.

Brief sample of the analytic process

We briefly summarize in this section the analytic process across the first few sessions to illustrate how he presented clinically.

His relationship to his therapist was, for the most part, strongly positive. From the first session, he immediately responded to him as someone with whom he could discuss his troubles frankly. His first concern was his loss: he told the therapist, with some distress, that the file containing his notes had been lost. Interpretation of the immediate anxiety led to a distinct improvement in his mental state, and he told the therapist in a surprisingly coherent way about his loss of status, his shattered self-image, and the importance of recovery to him. However the confusion returned whenever the therapist withdrew ego support during the session, and when he left at the end.

In the following session, his internal sense of humiliation was externalized in relation to the therapeutic staff, who, he said, had been rude to him because he had wandered into the wrong ward. At this point, his mental state (in this instance, in relation to his spatial disorientation) was linked for the first time, through association, with a loss of bowel and bladder control. The therapist was identified as a benign superego figure; he resolved to speak honestly with him about his humiliating experiences "even if it's embarrassing". Nevertheless, the humiliation proved to be too much for him, and he slipped into a wishful delusion.

In the third session, the possibility of being moved to another ward led to a regression into confusion, with strong references to topographical questions. Once again, interpretation of the underlying anxiety had significant (albeit transient) effects: Mr G spoke coherently about his fear that he was being dropped from the rehabilitation programme because he was too burdensome for the staff. His lucidity was sustained by ongoing interpretation. Withdrawal of ego support led to gradual loss of coherence. A comment that was perceived as patronizing led to an outburst—he was tired of being pushed around. His strong sensitivity to his loss of status had been provoked. The opportunity to speak his mind, however, led to gradual improvement, and the therapist was perceived again as a benign superego figure until the end of the session, when confusion returned.

In the fourth session, Mr G described how upset he was at being excluded from a game on the ward on the grounds that he had made a fool of himself (i.e. from his point of view). Further associations led to a painful awareness of his loss of independence—with special reference to financial independence—and he eventually burst into tears. His humiliation was yet again too much for him, and he regressed to a more concrete mode of thought. Psychological pain (caused by demanding therapists) was equated with physical pain, and a possible unconscious phantasy of being bullied to perform on the toilet soon dominated his associations (which were now interspersed with defiant expressions of self-assertion). At the end of the session, he regressed completely and had an argument with his wife, which was clearly motivated by the same defiance that he had expressed in the session.

The following session was also dominated by the theme of exclusion or demotion from the adult world. This manifested in the form of delusions that expressed, firstly, his wish to be treated as an adult, and, secondly, his fear of being displaced by someone who was more potent than himself. Interpretation of the underlying anxiety again led to a marked shift in his mental state and the emergence of a therapeutic alliance. Withdrawal of ego support at the end of the session once again led to a regression to confusion.

A setback in the ward—which was perceived by the patient as an exclusion or demotion due to narcissistic inadequacy—led to a sudden shift in the transference. The therapist became a deceitful, unreliable superego figure. A traumatic, passive experience of rejection was reversed, and he actively rejected the therapist, as well as the entire rehabilitation programme. Despite vigorous interpretation, the confusion persisted. Mr G expressed the need for a different ego-support figure; he needed to consult a third person in order to judge reality, as his therapist was no longer fully trustworthy. Simultaneously, the perceived failure on the ward was then confused with financial failure, and it was for reasons of financial advice that he needed ego support. Mr G's loss of confidence in his therapist's ability to help him to control his thoughts was experienced by him as an inability to control his bowel. This gave an indication of the therapist's previous role in the transference. He had unconsciously used his therapist as an internalized figure who helped him to control his sphincter. At this point, it was evident that his masculine potency was equated directly with the firmness of his stools (on the model of "stool equals penis").

These themes persisted in the following session. His internal chaos and sense of failure continued to be experienced physically in the form of actual diarrhoea, and in phantasy as a financial disaster about which he felt guilty (or ashamed). His projected superego figures were people who believed that he owed them money, or that he had let them down financially, and he had to "face the music." The feeling of total loss of internal control and superego support was momentarily perceived as actual death.

The confusion also persisted into the final session in this sequence. He reported a dream (which he had initially mistaken for reality) in which he was informed by a superego figure—immediately after his stroke—that he had died. This dream was connected with thoughts about religious truth and his sense of reality; however, due to the depth of his confusion during this session, it remained essentially obscure.

In summary, the stroke and its sequelae were apparently perceived by this patient as a humiliating loss of sphincter control, which was equated with loss of adult status and loss of masculine potency. We think that it is not too wild a speculation to suggest that, at least in part, he perceived the rehabilitation programme (including his analytic sessions) as repetitions of a toilet-training situation. The staff (and psychotherapist) were perceived as superego figures who either (a) helped him to gain control over his sphincter (i.e. who provided ego support) or (b) rejected him due to his inability to regulate his bowel movements in an appropriate way. In the former, benign situation, the patient was able temporarily to internalize ego support and thereby to achieve considerable control over his thoughts, which resulted in a wide range of ego and superego capacities. However, these capacities were lost immediately, as soon as external support was withdrawn or perceived as withdrawn. He then experienced the (re-externalized) superego as rejecting and excluding, and, in humiliating mental pain—caused by the loss of his narcissistic ideal through physical incontinence—he regressed to a state of psychotic confusion.

The mechanism underlying the psychotic symptoms in this case can, once again, be understood according to Freud's (1911c [1910], 1924b) formulation. A loss of contact with reality ("the end of the world") is followed by "an attempt at recovery, a process of reconstruction", either in the form of a delusional phantasy that carries with it all the hallmarks of primary-process thinking, or, alternatively, by a concrete internalization in the analytic situation of the mental structure that was lost (which was represented in phantasy by an observing, regulating, and inhibiting figure).

Case I: encapsulated psychosis

The final case, Miss "I", was quite different from our other three patients with ventromesial frontal lesions. Nevertheless, there were some important similarities. In fact, we thought that she presented with many of the same symptoms as the other three patients, but that she differed from them in that these symptoms appeared in a highly circumscribed—one could say, encapsulated—form only.

Miss I was a 32-year-old dextral secretary. She was Canadian but had been living in Britain for a few years, together with her Scottish fiancée, in Edinburgh. It was her misfortune to be visiting London during the racial riots that occurred there some years ago. Miss I and her fiancée were driving through London and unwittingly went into the area where the rioting was at its worst. They were attacked by a violent mob. A brick was thrown at their car, which smashed through the passenger side of the windscreen and struck Miss I on the right forehead. She sustained a large, open skull fracture, with depression of the right frontal bone and destruction of her zygomatic complex. She suffered a brief loss of consciousness but awoke rapidly, and she was talking when she was admitted to hospital. She was also responsive to verbal commands.

After a sequestrectomy was performed, an MRI scan revealed an extensive medial frontal-lobe lesion. The area of low density extended posteriorly to include the anterior aspect of both cingulate gyri, but it was more extensive on the right. Unlike the other three frontal-lobe cases that we discussed above, this lesion spared the ventral frontal region. That is, it was a relatively dorsal lesion (Fig. 9-4), in comparison to the previous three cases, which has important implications. In addition, air was present in the anterior horns of both lateral ventricles. After Miss I's surgery, she was confused for two days. She recovered rapidly from this confused state but not completely, as will be seen in a moment.

The overriding feature of her presentation in the analytic situation was the presence of encapsulated psychotic symptomatology. This took the form of an isolated breakdown of reality-testing, primarily in relation to paranoid phantasies, in the context of essential preservation of the observing ego and other superego functions.

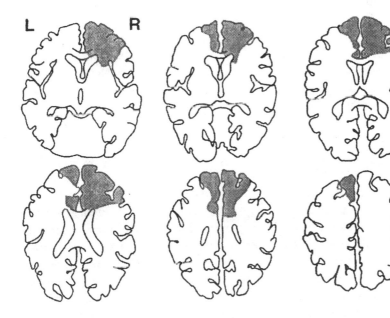

FIGURE 9-4

During her psychotherapeutic sessions, Miss I recalled two traumatic childhood memories, which were clearly associated with her current trauma and appeared to throw the structure of her mind into some relief. The first of these memories involved an early hospitalization for acute gastroenteritis. This event seemed to match her current experience of sudden and traumatic impingement upon her tranquil and safe worlds of suburban Vancouver and Edinburgh. The memory was brought to mind through discussion of her current sense of invasion. It was not possible to ascertain what Miss I's unconscious phantasy had been in relation to her symptoms at that time, nor to illuminate the enormous disruption of her safe routines and of the sense of control over her bodily boundaries, which the experience must have represented. However, she reacted to her current experience of the intrusiveness of both the hospital staff and the medical procedures by refusing to use the bedpan, until she was forced to do so by means of the administration of laxatives. This reaction also seemed, to a certain extent, to represent a premorbid character defence (i.e. anal retentiveness, affective isolation, obsessional control, etc.).

The real experience of acute diarrhoea in infancy could have provided a prototype for her current conviction that phantasies sometimes do become realities. That is, the infantile experience may have provided a prototype for the current breakdown in her reality-testing. This childhood memory also seemed to be closely connected in Miss I's mind to her fear that she had been abandoned by her family, and it was recapitulated, in the nascent transference, in her difficulty in ending sessions. (She said about her early hospitalization, "whenever they left, I cried and cried".) In essence, the infantile experience apparently revealed an aspect of Miss I's current unconscious phantasy: she felt (or feared) that she had lost control over her mind and mental boundaries according to an unconscious model of having lost control over her bowel and bodily boundaries. Her phantasies "poured out" like diarrhoea (and, as was the case with the other patients we have just considered, her disinhibited thoughts were, in fact, equated by her with diarrhoea). Miss I's sense of shame at her incontinent phantasies also suggested an anal component (at the same time as it illustrated the relative integrity of her observing superego). Her loss of self-esteem, too, was evidently connected with this unconscious phantasy (i.e. the unconscious phantasy of loss of the good internal faeces, and of loss of pride in her ability to control her sphincter). Premorbidly, Miss I took great pride in her good intelligence, her good memory, and her highly developed ability to control her feelings. The unconscious equation between her mind and her bowel was again conspicuous.

The second traumatic memory that she associated with her current situation dated back to puberty. She remembered a scene in which her mother had lost her sanity and had attempted to commit suicide: Miss I had walked into the bathroom and found her father on the floor, on top of her mother, while he was trying to prevent her from killing herself. On the basis of this prototype (and the unconscious phantasies associated with it), Miss I apparently experienced her own, current traumatic experience as a violent sexual assault. Here, too, the notion that phantasies sometimes do become realities was prominent. Her mother seemed to have suffered from excessive sexual jealousy, but, ironically, her father really did have an affair and this had led to her mother's psychotic depression. This memory had links with two important aspects of Miss I's current mental state—firstly, her fears and phantasies of aggressive sexual penetration, and, secondly, her ambivalent identification with her mother.

We discuss the fears and phantasies of aggressive sexual penetration first. This constellation of feelings and ideas (i.e. violent rape phantasies) formed the essential core of Miss I's encapsulated psychotic symptomatology. The child-like fears of vampires, bad things, people outside breaking into her home while she slept, and of snakes in or under her bed revealed the breakdown of reality-testing most clearly. These fears were linked with her complaints about the penetrative intrusiveness of the medical staff and medical procedures. This link was apparent from the outset, when she said: "I am sick of people poking around. I never want another injection or anything else again." She went on to describe how she currently felt very frightened of being attacked, especially at night. These fears took the form of a fear of vampires in particular and related in part to her feeling of invasion by the medical procedures. She once thought she heard a bat outside, but she often found that she heard noises and discovered that there were none. As regards the vampires, she slept with garlic under her pillow or on her neck—she had even brought a clove to the hospital, but had not used it.

Brief sample of the analytic process

Aspects of the sexual phantasy underlying these feelings and behaviours emerged gradually during a series of sessions that we now briefly summarize. In the first session, Miss I contrasted London's harsh, penetrating, and intrusive qualities with the homely, quiet tranquillity of Edinburgh and Vancouver. (Here, she appeared to be evaluating her therapist [K.K.-S.] in this regard, in order to decide which category she belonged to.) She then described the bitter hatred that she felt towards her attackers. In this same session, she described the frightening (bathroom) scene involving her parents. In the next session, she described how she had resisted attempts by the emergency medical staff to undress her, immediately after the accident. This was her first reference to the theme that we mentioned above—namely, the idea that "phantasies can become realities". In the third session, she described her current aversion to sexual intercourse and linked this explicitly with her wish not to be penetrated, and to her sexual jealousy (these conscious anxieties were apparently foreign to her premorbidly). The underlying sexual phantasy was thus revealed for the first time—as was her identification with her mother (which we will discuss in a moment). In this session, she also described how her privacy and her bodily space were constantly being invaded by the hospital staff, and she described her characteristic (i.e. anal) way of protecting herself (by means of her refusal to use the bedpan). She complained a great deal about all the brutal medical procedures that she had been subjected to, and described the wounds, bruises, and scars that these had left her with, in some detail. The original assault and these hospital "assaults" were closely linked in her mind. The underlying sexual phantasy was vividly revealed in her description of the catheter that the (male) doctor had painfully and repeatedly inserted into her, and which was too large for her small blood vessels. In this same session, the patient herself linked her loss of libido (i.e. her loss of interest in sexual intercourse) to her fear of being invaded. In the following session, she described the episode of infantile gastroenteritis (in response to a comment by her therapist about her sense of being invaded). She then described her phobic anxieties about snakes, which were clearly and directly linked to her fears of phallic penetration. For example, in the dream material that she reported, the unconscious equation—snake equals penis—was barely disguised (the snakes crawled up her vagina). In the final session in this sequence, she reported her dislike of lying on her back, as it made her feel "vulnerable" (once again, the sexual allusion was evident).

In short, Miss I experienced her traumatic assault according to an unconscious model of a violent rape; this phantasy then persisted in the post-traumatic period and coloured her experience of the hospital environment. Moreover, on the basis of a preconscious suspicion that phantasies sometimes do become realities (which was reinforced by her mother's experience, as well as by her own infantile gastroenteritis) this traumatic sexual phantasy periodically overwhelmed her reality-testing. Miss I reacted to this psychic situation in some near-psychotic ways (e.g. she painted crosses on her forehead and hid cloves of garlic under the pillow), but she also responded in more subtle ways (e.g. she lost sexual drive and interest in her appearance). Her disinclination to make herself attractive (and her paranoid fears that people were staring at her) seemed to have had another childhood referent—namely, her aversion to being the centre of attention at school. This, too, seems to have had an unconscious sexual meaning (namely, fear of her own sexual attractiveness or exhibitionism). Miss I's manner of defending herself against these runaway forces were reinforced by her memory of the earlier, infantile trauma. (In short, her attempts at re-instituting reality-testing at the mental level equalled a closing of her vagina and a refusal to allow entry of the penis at the genital level; these in turn were equivalents of the shutting of her sphincter and the maintenance of the inside–outside bodily boundary, at the anal level). As was the case for Mrs F, Mr G, and Mr H— the other three cases with ventromesial frontal lesions—the easy regression from symbolic thinking to concrete bodily action was readily evident.

We would now like to discuss the other theme that was linked with Miss I's memory of the traumatic bathroom scene—namely, her ambivalent identification with her mother. In her first analytic session, Miss I reported anxiously that her mother had suffered a mental breakdown. She feared that her own current symptoms meant that she, too, was having a mental breakdown—in other words, that she would lose touch with reality completely, and that she would become dependent on hospitals and drugs. She reacted to this increased identification in two ways: first, she attempted to deny or minimize the extent of her mother's pathology; second, she attempted to distance herself from her mother and from madness in general. For example, when Miss I described the bathroom scene mentioned above (i.e. her mother's suicide attempt), she disassociated herself from her own shock and horror by displacing these feelings onto her father. (She reacted to her current trauma in exactly the same way.) Also, despite all the evidence to the contrary, which she herself recounted, she insisted that her mother was not mentally ill—and that she was "very strong" and "remarkably strong". (She described her own premorbid control over her emotions and her eating in similar terms.) In one session, she described her boyfriend's (and her father's) aggressive outrage in response to her own assault, while she herself, on the other hand, remained remarkably calm and affectively bland. This reflected her anal character defence, and her tendency to develop phobias and paranoid ideas (i.e. her isolation of affect and her projection of aggression). In the same session, she also described her loss of interest in her appearance, which may well have repeated her mother's behaviour during her own (i.e. her mother's) depression—although such a memory was not explicitly reported. She also displayed some interest in her therapist's private and professional life, and she seemed to be using her as an auxiliary reality-testing figure, specifically with regard to the implied question, "Am I mad?" (This reminded us, though in a more subtle form, of the wholesale internalization of the therapist's ego functions which Mrs F, Mr G, and Mr H exhibited.) Miss I had difficulty separating from her therapist at the end of the session. However, she also seemed to be assessing her, in order to determine whether she was good or bad. In one session, she described her own sexual jealousy, and how unrealistic (or "crazy") it was. This linked her material directly to her mother's pathology, and it revealed a strong unconscious identification with her. However, Miss I did not recognize this link consciously. In another session, she described her infantile gastroenteritis—which was the result of something bad that she had eaten. She reported that since then, she had always been very careful about what she ate. She also described (with visible alarm) the frightening mental hospital that was situated near her childhood home, with its aggressive and masturbating patients. This description carried the strongest affect that she had expressed, throughout her brief period of treatment. In the final session, she expressed enormous relief that she was leaving the hospital, with its "penetrating" intrusiveness and its "bad smells".

Description of the dominant transference phantasy

All of this material illuminated Miss I's analytic relationship to her therapist. At an (unconscious) oral level, she seemed to be assessing the therapist in the following way: "Is this person something good and safe to eat, or is she something bad and toxic that will make me lose control over my bowels (and my thoughts)?" This, in turn, clarified the nature of her relationship to her internalized mother. She seemed to experience the effect of her traumatic assault as an identification with her mad mother (and with all the attendant dangers of unrestrained sexuality), and she also experienced it as an introjection of her bad mother, which was associated with the risk of food that invaded her and overwhelmed her bodily boundaries. Her reaction conveyed a concerted attempt to dis-identify with the mad mother and to project this unreliable and poisonous bad mother outwards. The latter was apparently the source of her paranoia and of her unstable reality-testing. Miss I no longer trusted her internal mother—with whom she felt more identified than ever before. When she was a child, she used to go to her mother's bed for comfort, but at the time that the therapist saw her she was alone with her fears, and quite overcome by them. There was no longer a truly safe place.

We have thus far described the state of her mind in terms of the subjective, unconscious phantasies involved. From an objective, metapsychological viewpoint, we could describe the same process as a destructuralization of the maternal aspects of her superego—

that is, as a *re-externalization of her primary maternal introjects*. In this respect, the essential mechanism is similar to that which we observed in other cases with ventromesial frontal disease, although it occurred in a far more circumscribed manner and to a much more limited extent.

From a psychological viewpoint, the encapsulated nature of her symptomatology can be understood in terms of her continued reliance upon the perceived strength and protectiveness of her father (and of her boyfriend, and of her therapist in the paternal transference). From the anatomical viewpoint, this might correlate with the relative preservation of the ventral frontal cortex in this case, and most of the left frontal lobe.

It is perhaps important to note in this regard that in contrast to Mrs F, Mr G, and Mr H, the fluctuations in Miss I's reality-testing and her mental control did not depend solely on her therapist's concrete, real proximity as an ego support figure. She retained a far greater degree of superego structuralization, and, accordingly, fluctuations in her mental state were regulated by internal factors to a much greater extent.

Discussion:
the metapsychology of the ventromesial frontal region

On the basis of these four cases, we wish to advance the following hypothesis regarding the functional contribution that this brain region makes to the metapsychological organization of the human mental apparatus as a whole. We try to formulate our hypothesis as precisely as possible, but readers should not be disappointed by the relatively general terms we have to use during this preliminary stage in our work. Our hypothesis is this: *the ventromesial frontal cortex performs the fundamental economic transformation that inhibits the primary process of the mind*. The economic transformation that we are referring to is the process that Freud described as *"binding"*. In other words, this part of the brain is the anatomical locus—or at least a crucial component of the anatomical network—subserving the physiological realization of the secondary process as a whole.

Few depth psychological functions could be more important than this one. Numerous implications flow from this hypothesis, and it is easy to see how they relate to the clinical material that we summarized above. For example, *a disturbance of this economic function will inevitably disturb the whole medium of the influence of reality upon the mind,* and therefore the essential basis of the *reality principle,* and of *ego structuralization* and *superego inhibition* in general, together with a wide range of more specific mental operations and processes, variously described under the headings of *censorship, repression, reality-testing, judgement,* and the like. That is how we understand the breakdown of all these processes in the clinical material presented in this chapter. Above all, that is how we conceptualize the destructuralization of their narcissistic introjects ("the end of the world"), and consequent regression to psychosis.

In the general theoretical model that we present in the final chapter of this book, we suggest that the cerebral cortex as a whole should be conceived of as being composed of a cascade of mechanisms derived from the perceptual systems, which select out specific features of the external and internal environments during an ongoing process of association. These selective processes, once they have been established, act as a series of "stimulus barriers", which protect the mental apparatus from excessive arousal in response to familiar stimuli. These barriers are the mnemic systems, which form the very fabric of the ego. We suggest that although these systems are initially formed under the influence of external reality, they gradually become internalized in an overlearned form that neuropsychologists describe under the headings of semantic memory, procedural learning, and the like. Once they have been internalized, these filters—which form of a set of implicit, unconscious expectations—exert a controlling influence over all subsequent perceptual and motor experiences.

We have equated this whole internalizing and organizing process with what in psychoanalysis is described as the *structuralization of the ego.* Against this background, we suggest that the prefrontal region (which receives its input from both the internally and the externally directed perceptual systems, and which represents the deepest stratum of mnemic analysis and the basis of motor action), once it has been structuralized in this way, exerts a controlling influence over all the more superficial systems of the cortex. Most neuropsychologists agree that this anatomical region forms a reflexive "superstructure" over all other brain structures.

An essential point is this: what is structuralized in the prefrontal region is a highly abstract set of connections of a particular type. These connections are fundamentally *sequential* in nature (as opposed to the simultaneous patterns of connectivity that predominate in the posterior cerebral cortices). The structure of these sequential connections was originally formed under the direct influence of the verbalizations of those adults who mediate the world to the young child. *The child uses this internalized set of connections to gradually differentiate, organize, and gain control over its thinking and actions.* Following a critical period in the development of prefrontal tissue, which occurs around the fifth year of life, these abstract, sequential codes—which psychologists describe as "inner speech"—become firmly structuralized, and the child thereby achieves a very secure form of mental control over its own thinking and behaviour. Once this has happened, the whole of the child's mental life is fundamentally reorganized, according to an abstract set of connections that are—amongst other things—uniquely suited to reflexive functioning. The child simultaneously shifts from a fundamentally atemporal ("timeless"), visuospatial mode of thinking to a fundamentally verbal and sequential (or propositional) mode.

In our general theoretical formulation (chapter ten), we link some of these unique properties of internal speech to some of the special attributes of the spoken word, and we argue that the internalization and structuralization of the parental voice enables the child to stand apart from its own subjective processes, and, using the categorical, nominal, and certain other properties of language, to evaluate its own thoughts and behaviour in an abstract way. The propositional qualities of language also enable the child to plan a sequence of activities in relation to a differentiated internal scheme, the goal of which need not be concretely present. This enables the child to subordinate its thought and behaviour to an abstract, goal-directed programme.

At the physiological level, this ability is expressed in the manner in which the prefrontal region—via its rich interconnections with core-brain structures—influences the rate, sequence, and pattern of neuronal firing throughout the cerebral cortex. This is described as the voluntary and selective arousal function of the prefrontal region, and of the ventromesial region in particular. A breakdown of this function is expressed physiologically in a condition that Luria (1980) described as "equalization of excitability of traces". In this condition, the highly differentiated, selective arousal function of the prefrontal region—which is performed directly with the aid of internal speech—breaks down. In the clinical material summarized above, we saw this phenomenon clearly, and the material illustrated why we have linked this selective arousal function of the frontal region with the group of psychological functions that we include under headings such as "reality-testing" and "censorship". Breakdowns of these functions are, we have contended, manifestations in the psychological sphere of a breakdown of the selective arousal function of the prefrontal region in the physiological sphere. This is the essential consequence of the meta-psychological process of "binding".

A bridge to the basic neurosciences

Before outlining our general theoretical conclusions in the final chapter of this book, we would like tangentially to link the conclusions we have reached in the present chapter with some formulations outlined in an interesting book by Allan Schore (1994), *Affect Regulation and the Origin of the Self: The Neurobiology of Emotional Development*.

Schore's central thesis is that "the early social environment, mediated by the primary caregiver, directly influences the evolution of structures in the brain responsible for the future socioemotional development of the child" (p. 62). In successive chapters, his book surveys the different literature presenting levels of evidence relevant to this thesis, in an impressive sweep that incorporates data drawn from such disparate fields as mother–infant observation and molecular biology. The resultant model is one that explicates in exemplary detail the precise mechanisms by means of which the infant brain might internalize and structuralize the affect-regulating functions of the mother, in circumscribed neural tissues, at specifiable points in its epigenetic history.

Schore's model focuses primarily on the ventromesial frontal cortex, which he conceptualizes as the inhibitory component of a motivational system that originates in subcortical limbic and brainstem structures, the physical maturation of which he demonstrates is significantly guided by certain aspects of early mother–infant interaction. *The ventromesial frontal cortex is thereby shown to almost literally embody an internalized, containing mother.*

In the first part of his book, Schore presents evidence to support the proposal that the maturation of the ventromesial frontal cortex

> begins in a specific critical period which commences at the end of the first year of human infancy. It is hypothesized that maternal regulated high intensity socioaffective stimulation provided in the ontogenetic niche, specifically occurring in dyadic psychobiologically attuned, arousal amplifying, face to face reciprocal gaze transactions, generates and sustains positive affect in the dyad. These transactions induce particular neuroendocrine changes which facilitate the expansive innervation of deep sites in orbitofrontal areas, especially in the early maturing visuospatial right hemisphere, of ascending subcortical axons of a neurochemical circuit of the limbic system—the sympathetic ventral tegmental limbic circuit. This imprinting experience initiates the maturation of a frontolimbic excitatory system that is responsible for the ontogenetic adaptations in the inceptive phase of [Mahler's] practicing critical period—behavioral hyperactivity, high levels of positive affect and play behavior, and subsequently the establishment of the capacity to form an interactive representational model that underlies an early functional system of affect regulation. [p. 65]

In the second part of his book, evidence is presented to support the hypothesis that the following significant development occurs with the onset of socialization procedures:

> The 14- to 16-month-old infant's psychobiological response to stressful socializing transactions is frequently a state of hypoarousal. These stage-typical stress states, accompanied by a different pattern of psychoneuroendocrine alterations, serve

as an optimal socioaffective stimulus for the expansion of the other limbic circuit, the parasympathetic lateral limbic circuit. The experience-dependent wiring of this circuit into the orbito-frontal cortex allows for the emergence of an efficient and adaptive inhibitory system. A competition between the [earlier] sympathetic and the parasympathetic limbic circuits underlies a parcellation process that produces a mature differentiated orbitofrontal system at about 18 months, the end of the critical period. This reorganization is responsible for a loss of the earlier ontogenetic adaptations, and the emergence of more complex representational and more efficient affect regulatory functions. [p. 66]

We hope readers can see why we are drawing this book to their attention. It is not only because Schore's experimentally based con-clusions are so compatible with our own clinical findings. We have said before that the method we are recommending is not the final step in our quest to correlate psychoanalysis with neuroscience; it is only the very first step. We have also said that once we have established gross correlations of the type that this method facili-tates, we will have obtained a theoretical foothold on the neuro-scientific literature which becomes the gateway for establishing far more elaborate bridges between psychoanalysis and basic neuro-scientific research. Schore's book reviews precisely that portion of the basic science literature that is most relevant to the part of the brain that our clinico-anatomical research has made accessible to psychoanalytic study. The strength of Schore's book lies in its com-prehensive, up-to-date review of the relevant literature, and in its successful synthesis of the disparate data. Sadly, its weakness lies in precisely the area that concerns us most: its relatively simplistic approach to psychoanalytic theory.

For example, the modulatory (so-called tension-discharging) principles outlined in Freudian affect theory are said by Schore to have been replaced in contemporary psychoanalysis by the notion that "the infant's behavior is primarily object seeking from the start" (p. 24). This assertion ignores the fact that what the "object-seeking" infant is seeking is *pleasure* (or relief from unpleasure), and that the attraction to the object only arises because the object is capable of meeting the infant's needs (i.e. ultimately, of reducing drive tension). This is the essence of Freudian affect theory: by a process of natural selection, pleasurable sensations gradually become attached to those objects and activities that are most likely to satisfy the libidinal drives (and thereby, ultimately, preserve the species; Solms & Nersessian, 1999a).

However, according to Schore:

> [Freud's] views are not supported by recent neurochemical research which indicates that activation and not deactivation of a specific reward circuit, the ventral tegmental dopaminergic system, mediates elation. In contrast to Freud's assertion that pleasure is maintained only in a quiescent state, infant elation is known to be associated with heightened activation of the excitatory, energy-mobilizing sympathetic component of the autonomic nervous system. . . . These findings do, however, confirm the developmental conceptualizations offered by [modern object relations theory and attachment theory] . . . Stern (1990) suggests that pleasure is associated with moderate stimulation (excitation) not at a falling or zero excitation, where Freud [1920g] had placed it. [pp. 84–85]

These remarks are based on a prevalent misunderstanding of Freudian affect theory—a theory that revolves centrally around the vicissitudes of *unbound* excitation, not the gross level of excitation in the system. In fact, Freud's conception of the relation between emotional feeling states and underlying modifications in quantities of excitation culminated in a viewpoint that is not at all contradicted by recent findings:

> We . . . relate pleasure and unpleasure to the quantity of excitation that is present in the mind but is not in any way "bound"; and we relate them in such a manner that unpleasure corresponds to an increase in the quantity of [unbound] excitation and pleasure to a diminution. *What we are implying by this is not a simple relation between the strength of the feelings of pleasure and unpleasure and the corresponding modifications in the quantity of excitation*; least of all—in view of all we have been taught by psychophysiology—are we suggesting any directly proportional ratio: the factor that determines the feeling is probably the amount of increase or diminution in a given period of time. Experiment might possibly play a part here, but it is not advis-

able for us analysts to go into the problem further so long as our way is not pointed by definite observations. [Freud, 1920g, p. 8][1]

We would be interested to know what Schore makes of this (more complex and accurate) formulation of Freudian affect theory, in the light of contemporary knowledge of ventromesial frontal neurodynamics. A possible starting point for his analysis might have been his contrast between the energy-expending and energy-conserving properties of the ventral (dopaminergic) and lateral (noradrenergic) tegmental-limbic circuits, respectively. To us, evidence for the view that the dopaminergic circuit is associated with libidinal drive discharge (and the anticipation of such discharge) is so strong as to almost dissuade analysis (see Solms, 1997a, in press [a]). There is similarly compelling evidence to suggest that the noradrenergic circuit is, at least in part, associated with the binding of libidinal energies (inhibition of drive discharge).[2] If this correlation is upheld, it would provide us with a very significant foothold on which some metapsychological processes might become accessible to basic neurobiological description.

We hope readers can see what conceptual vistas this sort of thinking opens up for us. We have discussed Schore's book in order to illustrate this point: once we have established on clinico-anatomical grounds that the ventromesial frontal region appears to perform the fundamental economic transformation that inhibits the primary process of the mind, then we have a viable conceptual bridge to basic neuroscientific research which can further enlighten us as to the neurochemical correlates and the physiological mechanism of this binding, right down to the molecular level. The research that Schore reviews suggests that this transformation might involve the inhibition of dopaminergic mesial cortical and limbic

---

[1] Further complications in the relation between feelings of pleasure and unpleasure and the corresponding modifications in quantities of excitation were introduced with Freud's consideration of the capacity of the ego to *anticipate* such quantitative modifications on the basis of qualitative events (cf. Freud, 1926d [1925]; Solms & Nersessian, 1999a).

[2] When seeking the physical correlates of metapsychological concepts, it is important to remember that Freud's conception of mind–body relations was that of dual-aspect monism, not simple isomorphism (see Solms, 1997b).

circuits (which appear to subserve primary instinctual purposes) by competing noradrenergic mediobasal frontal circuits that are formed directly under the influence of early object relationships.

We know that these are speculative remarks, but we hope that we have made the point that clinico-anatomical correlation will soon make it possible for us to pursue metapsychological lines of research at the basic neuroscience level.

Concluding remarks

We may now begin to draw back, in order to survey our findings as a whole. We have reported psychoanalytic observations on three groups of patients with damage to different anatomical areas. The patients in the first group (left perisylvian convexity: chapters five, six, and seven) presented with disparate cognitive deficits, revealing a series of interconnected metapsychological mechanisms that we attributed to different anatomical regions within the left perisylvian convexity. All of these mechanisms were linked with the metapsychological functions of *words* (both as a means of communication and as a tool for cognitive operations). The patients in the second group (right perisylvian convexity: chapter eight) presented with disorders of *object* representation. Specifically, in these cases the capacity to represent objects *realistically* was lost, and the patients fell back upon narcissistic modes of representing and relating to objects. The mechanism of these disorders was essentially akin to that of the narcissistic neuroses (e.g. melancholia, paranoia). Finally, in the third group of patients (ventromesial frontal region: this chapter), even the *narcissistic* (inner) objects were destructuralized, as the very fabric of the ego and superego unravelled, due to a failure of the most basic inhibitory mechanisms of the mind. The mechanism of these disorders was therefore akin to that of the psychoses.

In part III, we place these three anatomical regions into a broader context and attempt to formulate a general theory of how the mental apparatus might be represented in the tissues of the human brain *as a whole*. In doing so, we are relying partly on analytic observations of the kind that we have reported in part II, not only in the 12 cases described but also in 23 additional cases (not reported here) with damage in other parts of the brain. Nevertheless, many gaps in our analytic observational data remain. We have attempted to fill these gaps—as an interim measure—with reasonable inferences drawn from existing neuropsychological and psychoanalytic knowledge.

It goes without saying that all of these inferences must be treated as highly tentative. A heuristic general theory is nevertheless useful at this point, even if it serves only as a springboard for conceptualizing the contradictory empirical material that will almost certainly arise from a more systematic application of the method described in this book. We hope that our readers—and fellow investigators—will treat the formulations presented in part III in this spirit.

INTEGRATION

CHAPTER TEN

Towards a neuroanatomy of the mental apparatus

In this chapter, we propose a general model of how the human mental apparatus—as we conceive of it in psychoanalysis—might be represented in the tissues of the brain. Since this is a first approach at something unknown, it goes without saying that our proposals are subject to substantial revision. The hypotheses that we present are based on a small amount of empirical data, derived from psychoanalytic investigations of 35 patients with localized cerebral lesions, 12 of whom we described in part II. In all likelihood, our perspective on these problems will alter radically as we continue to test our hypotheses against clinical reality. However, excessive caution should not prevent from us pausing at this point to gain a first, schematic perspective on what our efforts have yielded thus far. The aim of a preliminary overview of this sort is for us to take our bearings for the research that still needs

This chapter is based on a lecture presented to the Neuro-Psychoanalysis Center of the New York Psychoanalytic Institute on 4 June 1994. Versions of this chapter were published in Solms (1996b) and, in German, in Solms (1998c).

to be done if we are properly to rejoin psychoanalysis with the neurosciences.

The first problem that we face when we attempt to integrate psychoanalytic observations with neuroscientific knowledge is that of having to decide which conceptual frames of reference to use. For reasons that we outlined in part I, we have chosen to be guided on the one hand by the classical metapsychological concepts of Sigmund Freud, and on the other hand by the dynamic neuro-psychological model of Aleksandr Romanovich Luria. We chose these relatively conservative models for the following two reasons: first, in our view, they still represent the most comprehensive models that we have of the two domains we are attempting to correlate, and, second, these two approaches to the human mind are conceptually and methodologically compatible with one another.

We will not repeat the arguments we have presented already in support of these conclusions. Instead, we think it useful to preface our conclusions by re-orienting ourselves to the broader problem that we are grappling with—that is, the problem of the relationship between the brain and the mind. We shall follow the general framework that Freud developed in this regard. His approach was quite unique—and it opened up conceptual vistas that have seldom been intellectually appreciated, let alone scientifically explored (see Solms, 1997b). We therefore preface this chapter by quoting some long extracts from Freud's *Outline of Psycho-Analysis* (1940a [1938]). This monograph outlined his final reflections on this important problem. In the opening pages, Freud wrote the following lines:

> Psycho-analysis makes a basic assumption, the discussion of which is reserved to philosophical thought but the justification for which lies in results. We know two kinds of things about what we call our psyche (or mental life): firstly, its bodily organ and scene of action, the brain (or nervous system) and, on the other hand, our acts of consciousness, which are immediate data and cannot be further explained by any sort of description. Everything that lies between is unknown to us, and the data do not include any direct relation between these two terminal points of our knowledge. If it existed, it would at the most afford an exact localization of the processes of consciousness and would give us no further help towards understanding them.

Our two hypotheses start out from these ends or beginnings of our knowledge. The first is concerned with localization. We assume that mental life is the function of an apparatus to which we ascribe the characteristics of being extended in space and of being made up of several portions—which we imagine, that is, as something resembling a telescope or microscope or something of the kind. Notwithstanding some earlier attempts in the same direction, the consistent working-out of a conception such as this is a scientific novelty. [pp. 144–145]

Freud then went on to describe the basic arrangement of this spatial apparatus—which he divided topographically into id, ego, superego—before he described the biological processes that drive it. (We will return to these subjects shortly.) Freud then proceeded to state his second fundamental hypothesis:

I have described the structure of the psychical apparatus and the energies and forces which are active in it, and I have traced in a prominent example the way in which those energies (in the main, the libido) organize themselves into a physiological function which serves the purpose of the preservation of the species. There was nothing in all this to demonstrate the quite peculiar quality of what is psychical, apart, of course, from the empirical fact that this apparatus and these energies are the basis of the functions which we describe as our mental life. I will now turn to something which is uniquely characteristic of what is psychical, and which, indeed, according to a very widely held opinion, coincides with it to the exclusion of all else.

The starting-point for this investigation is provided by a fact without parallel, which defies all explanation and description—the fact of consciousness. . . . If anyone speaks of consciousness we know immediately and from our most personal experience what is meant by it. Many people, both inside and outside science, are satisfied with the assumption that consciousness alone is psychical; in that case nothing remains for psychology but to discriminate among psychical phenomena between perceptions, feelings, thought-processes and volitions. It is generally agreed, however, that these conscious processes do not form unbroken sequences which are complete in themselves; there would thus be no alternative left to assuming that there are physical and somatic processes which are concomitant with the psychical ones and which we should necessarily have to recognize as more complete than the psychical sequences, since some of them would have conscious processes parallel to them but others would not. If so, it would of course become plausible to lay the stress in psychology on these somatic processes, to see in *them* the true essence of what is psychical and to look for some other assessment of the conscious processes. The majority of philosophers, however, as well as many other people, dispute this and declare that the idea of something psychical being unconscious is self-contradictory.

But that is precisely what psycho-analysis is obliged to assert, and this is its second fundamental hypothesis. It explains the supposedly somatic concomitant phenomena as being what is truly psychical, and thus in the first instance it disregards the quality of consciousness . . .

Now it would look as if this dispute between psychoanalysis and philosophy is concerned only with a trifling matter of definition—the question of whether the name "psychical" should be applied to one or another sequence of phenomena. In fact, however, this step has become of the highest significance. Whereas the psychology of consciousness never went beyond the broken sequences which were obviously dependent upon something else, the other view, which held that the psychical is unconscious in itself, enabled psychology to take its place as a natural science like any other. The processes with which it is concerned are in themselves just as unknowable as those dealt with by other sciences, by chemistry and physics for example; but it is possible to establish the laws which they obey and to follow the mutual relations and interdependences unbroken over long stretches—in short, to arrive at what is described as an "understanding" of the field of natural phenomena in question. This cannot be effected without framing fresh hypotheses and creating fresh concepts; but these are not to be despised as evidence of embarrassment on our part but deserve on the contrary to be appreciated as an enrichment of science. They can lay claim to the same value as approximations that belong to the corresponding intellectual scaffolding found in other natural sciences, and we look forward to their being modified, correlated and more precisely determined as further experience is accumulated and sifted. So too it will be entirely in accordance with our expectations if the basic concepts and principles of the new science (instinct, nervous energy, etc.) remain for a considerable time no less indeterminate than those of the older sciences (force, mass, attraction, etc.).

Every science is based on observations and experiences arrived at through the medium of our psychical apparatus. But since our science has as its subject that apparatus itself, the analogy ends here. We make our observations through the medium of the same perceptual apparatus, precisely with the help of the breaks in the sequence of "psychical" [conscious] events: we fill in what is omitted by making plausible inferences and translating it into conscious material. In this way we construct, as it were, a sequence of conscious events complementary to the unconscious psychical processes. The relative certainty of our psychical science is based upon the binding force of these inferences. Anyone who enters deeply into our work will find that our technique holds its ground against any criticism. [pp. 157–159]

Freud then goes on to draw a distinction between the different classes of psychical quality—conscious, preconscious, and unconscious—and to describe the psychological laws that define their modes of functioning. Then, after providing a number of detailed examples of this way of thinking about the mind, he concludes with the following words:

The hypothesis we have adopted of a psychical apparatus extended in space, expediently put together, developed by the exigencies of life, which gives rise to the phenomena of consciousness only at one particular point and under certain conditions—this hypothesis has put us in a position to establish psychology on foundations similar to those of any other science, such, for instance, as physics. In our science as in others the problem is the same: behind the attributes (qualities) of the object under examination which are presented directly to our perception, we have to discover something else which is more independent of the particular receptive capacity of our sense organs and which approximates more closely to what may be supposed to be the real state of affairs. We have no hope of being able to reach the latter itself, since it is evident that everything new that we have inferred must nevertheless be translated back into the language of our perceptions, from which it is simply impossible to free ourselves. But herein lies the very nature and limitation of our science. It is as though we were to say in physics: "If we could see clearly enough we should find that what appears to be a solid body is made up of particles of such and such shape and size occupying such and such relative positions." In the meantime we try to increase the efficiency of our sense organs to the furthest possible extent by artificial aids; but it may be expected that all such efforts will fail to affect the ultimate outcome. Reality in itself will always remain "unknowable". [p. 196]

We hope that the reader will agree that it was well worth while to remind ourselves of these remarks of Freud's. We believe that they clarify beautifully the essential nature of the task we are engaged in, and the place it occupies in relation to the scientific goals of psychoanalysis as a whole.[1] What classical behavioural neurology attempted to do was to explain the broken sequences of consciousness in terms of an underlying sequence of *physical* events. According to Freud's conceptualization, this approach had two shortcomings. Although it held out the promise of an exact localization of the processes of consciousness, it gave us no help towards understanding them. This was because it sought to explain conscious events by reference to non-mental events. It therefore looked to another science for the true essence of what was psychical. This effectively removed consciousness from the domain of natural science. Freud's alternative approach was to treat the non-conscious events causing our acts of consciousness as if they, too, were conscious mental events—that is, he decided to translate them, as it were, into the language of conscious perception. This conceptual leap generated an independent causal domain of (conscious and unconscious) mental events, and it thereby enabled psychoanalysis to take its place as a natural science like any other. With this step, the mental unconscious—the unknowable thing that underlies our acts of consciousness—became the true object of study of scientific depth psychology.

From the point of view of modern neuroscience, however, this approach has significant shortcomings too. By ignoring the neuro-

---

[1] Cf. Freud's remark to Groddeck (letter dated 5 June 1917): "the unconscious is the proper mediator between the somatic and the mental, perhaps the long-sought 'missing link'" (Groddeck, 1977, p. 38)

logical manifestation of the mental apparatus—that is, by ignoring the second "terminal point of our knowledge" of the mind—Freud removed his conception of the unconscious from the field of physical science. This insulated psychoanalysis from all of the methodological and practical advantages that attach to physical science. It thereafter became impossible for psychoanalysts to take advantage of physical technologies that—to paraphrase Freud—have increased the efficiency of our sense organs to the furthest possible extent by artificial aids. The development of physical aids of this sort has led to an explosion of neuroscientific knowledge in recent years, which has increased one-hundred-fold our understanding of the system that Freud described as the "bodily organ or scene of action" of our mental life. However, because psychoanalysis has constructed its picture of the unconscious solely from data and inferences derived from subjective consciousness, we cannot link up our psychological model of the mind with the enormous advances that have occurred in our understanding of its objective realization—that is, "the brain (or nervous system)". Although it is true, as Freud said, that it is simply impossible for us to free ourselves from the limits of conscious perception, and we must therefore accept that the unconscious in itself will always remain "unknowable", it is also true that psychoanalysis has effectively ignored a great portion of the data that may be derived from our externally oriented perceptions. By limiting itself in this way to only half the available data, psychoanalysis has not only restricted the possibilities for gaining pure knowledge of the mental apparatus, it has renounced our capacity to apply this knowledge to influence the mental apparatus through physical means.[2] This insulation of psychoanalysis from advances in physical science has had inevitable consequences for its standing in the public sphere. We cannot deny these facts, even if we may legitimately console ourselves with the knowledge that our relative ignorance and impotence in relation to psychic reality is a direct consequence of the manner in which the mental apparatus is constructed.

---

[2] Cf. Freud (1940a [1938]): "The future may teach us to exercise a direct influence, by means of particular chemical substances, on the amounts of energy and their distribution in the mental apparatus. It may be that there are still undreamt-of possibilities of therapy" (p. 182).

We might well ask ourselves—as an aside—why it should be that the psyche, or mental life, is presented to us in two different forms, once as a bodily organ and again as our acts of consciousness. Of course, we cannot answer this question unequivocally; it is one of the great mysteries of life. However, we may suspect that the dual aspect of the psyche is a necessary outcome of the fact that we are consciously aware both of ourselves and of our external context at one and the same time, and a sharp distinction between these two things has obvious survival value in view of the biological facts that Freud subsumed under the concept of "specific action" (Freud, 1950 [1895]).

When Freud pioneered his new branch of science, in which the mind-as-part-of-reality was studied systematically for the first time, there were of course good reasons for keeping it separate from developments in the established neurological sciences. We have discussed these reasons in the opening chapter of this book. However, as we saw in chapters two and four, the situation has now changed in a number of important respects. First, due to the efforts of the pioneers of psychoanalysis during the first century of its existence, we now have a solid foothold on the psychological nature of the events that are interpolated between our acts of consciousness. We do not doubt that the future will bring innumerable further advances in our knowledge, but the basic structure and fundamental working principles of these unconscious mental events are now known to us. To use the terminology that Freud employed in the passages we quoted a few moments ago, we now have a psychological "understanding" of the unconscious. Second, due primarily to the astonishing advances that have occurred in the field of scientific technology, we now have a far better grasp of the basic structure and working principles of the brain than we had one hundred—or even fifty—years ago. We have, in short, a solid neurological "understanding" of the organ of the mind—or, to use Freud's terminology again, of its "bodily scene of action". Third, and most importantly from our point of view, due to an important methodological advance associated with the name of Luria we now have a viable means of correlating these two "terminal points of our knowledge". This new method—the method of "dynamic localization"—was generated by Luria's (1973) reconceptualization of the classical theories of function and localization, as we have discussed before. There is nothing to stop us from using this method to study the psychological functions that constitute the human mental apparatus as we conceive of it in psychoanalysis and, thereby, from dynamically localizing the major constituents of Freud's psychological model in the anatomical structures of the brain.

Combining these three advances, therefore, we are now in a position to plot the relationship between two unbroken sequences of natural events: the psychic sequence of conscious and unconscious mental events on the one hand, and the material sequence of physical brain events on the other. We can therefore correlate what we have been able to discover in psychoanalysis from the viewpoint of psychic reality with what we have been able to discover in neuroscience from the viewpoint of material reality. We are, in short, in a position to correlate what we know about the mental apparatus from both of the two terminal points in our knowledge of it.

We are now going to summarize what we know in this regard, on the basis of the limited amount of work that we have done over the past few years, using the method of dynamic localization. Before we do so, however, we would like to point out that the neurological model of the mental apparatus that we are going to describe is not in any respect "more real" than our more familiar psychological model of it. We are simply describing the same thing from a different point of view—that is, *we are simply describing the mental apparatus as it is presented to us as a piece of material reality.* In doing so, we are trying to *correlate* our two perspectives on the unconscious "thing in itself", we are not aiming to *reduce* the psychic perspective to the physical one, any more than a competent translator aims to reduce one language to another. If anything, it makes more sense to attempt to reduce the body to the mind— since we cannot know the body independently of its realization in the perceptual systems of the mind (see Solms, 1997b). The aim of a depth neuropsychology is not to replace our psychic model of the mind with a physical one. Rather, our aim is to supplement the traditional viewpoints of metapsychology with a new, *"physical" point of view.* The aim is to gain an additional perspective on something that can never be known directly. If one thinks of the blind men and the elephant, it will be appreciated what an advantage this can be. It is our sincere belief that the brain, like our acts of consciousness, provides us with a second "beacon-light in the darkness of depth psychology" (Freud, 1923b, p. 18).

So let us see, then, what sort of picture emerges if we attempt to describe the human mental apparatus from a physical point of view. We will try and keep our presentation as simple as possible, so that the overall pattern of relations can be clearly seen. Naturally, this means that we are not going to be able to go into detail.

The reception, analysis, and storage of information

It seems appropriate to start from the few observations that Freud himself made with regard to the localization of his topographical systems. Freud always localized the system *Pcpt.-Cs.* within the cerebral cortex (see, for example, Freud, 1920g, p. 24). In Freud's 1896 revision of his "Project" model of the mind (1950 [1895]), he equated these cortical zones with the "ω" system of neurones (letter to Fliess dated 1 January 1896). Earlier, in his (1891b) monograph on aphasia, he identified the unimodal sensory cortices that subserve the four main modalities of human consciousness— namely, vision, hearing, kinaesthesis, and tactile sensation—as the "cornerstones" of this perceptual system. During Freud's lifetime, the cerebral representation of the senses of smell and taste and the subcomponents of "general sensation" were not yet accurately determined. However, in line with the basic principle that the primary sensory modalities may be localized within relatively circumscribed regions of the cortex, it seems reasonable for us to include these more obscure sensory modalities within the general schema of the "system *Pcpt.*".

All of this places the system *Pcpt.* within the posterior cortex of the brain, which Luria (1973) described as a functional unit devoted to the reception, analysis, and storage of information (Fig. 10-1). On the basis of modern neuroscientific knowledge, it is possible to specify with some precision the exact physiological characteristics of these unimodal cortical regions (for a comprehensive review of these intricate facts, see Creuzfeldt, 1995).

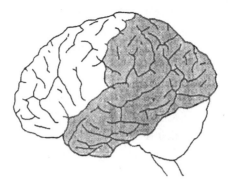

FIGURE 10-1

However, we would like to remind the reader that although Freud felt that it was justifiable to localize the elementary modalities of perceptual consciousness within the unimodal sensory zones of the cortex, he always emphasized two important qualifications in respect of this narrow localization. The first qualification was that by the time a stimulus from the periphery reaches the cortex, it has already undergone a number of significant transformations at the subcortical level (see Freud 1990/1888, 1891b, 1893-94). These subcortical transformations represent the contribution of the "ψ" system of neurones (in Freud's 1895 "Project" model). We may equate this system with the sensory receptors themselves, together with all the ganglia and nuclei with which they are connected during their passage along the spinal cord and cranial nerves, through the modality-specific nuclei of the brainstem and thalamus, towards the cortex. Due to the influence of this intermediate subcortical system, Freud asserted that the outside world is not "projected" onto our consciousness in any direct fashion; rather, it is "represented" there, in accordance with various functional criteria that are integral to the anatomical structures and physiological properties of the peripheral sensory apparatus. Thus, even at the level of external perception, our so-called "immediate acts of consciousness" have a long and complicated history. On the basis of this qualification, we think that it is reasonable for us to include the peripheral and subcortical modality-specific sensory systems within our anatomical picture of the system *Pcpt.-Cs.*

The second point that Freud emphasized, as early as 1891, was that the unimodal cortical zones represent ideal points in an anatomical network that, in reality, continues in an uninterrupted fashion. We localize these zones because their anatomical boundaries correspond relatively directly with the basic psychological categories that constitute conscious perception. However, in reality, perceptual consciousness always and only arises within an ongoing process of association, especially with respect to "downstream" executive and attentional systems (see below).

What we are leaving out of account in this picture of the system *Pcpt.-Cs.* is the important complication that Freud added when he later asserted that consciousness had, as it were, *two perceptual surfaces*. So far we have only considered the first of these surfaces, which is directed outward, towards the external world. The second perceptual surface of consciousness is directed inward, and it registers the quantitative processes in the interior of the mental apparatus within a range of affective qualities. For reasons discussed elsewhere (Solms, 1996), we have proposed that the limbic lobe of Broca can be conceived of as the "unimodal" cortical zone for this modality of perceptual consciousness (Fig. 10-2). According to that formulation, the subcortical and corticoid nuclei and tracts that constitute the limbic system proper, together with their deeper connections in the interior of the brainstem and spinal cord, and ultimately with the internal organs of the body, are analogous to the externally directed sensorimotor apparatus that links the

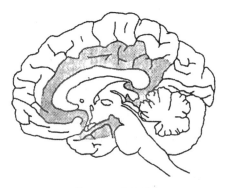

FIGURE 10-2

cortical convexity with the peripheral organs of the body (cf. Damasio, 1999). The limbic cortex is thus the central termination of a complex, internally directed sensorimotor apparatus.

(In saying this, we are trying to be as plain as possible and are using the most concrete means of expression. We hope that readers will not think we are being too obscure, therefore, if we remind them that we can only know these things *indirectly*, as they are represented to us in consciousness, at the two terminal points of our knowledge. This means that the object representations that we know as the physical organs of the body—and that includes the nervous system—are just one of the two fundamental ways in which we represent an unknowable reality; these representations of material reality are no more real in themselves than the subjective phantasies that we uncover in psychoanalysis, concerning the psychic reality of an internal world [see Solms, 1995b, 1997b]. But as we say, we are trying to be as plain as possible.)

It is perhaps questionable whether we are justified in including the subcortical components of this so-called internal sensory apparatus within the system *Pcpt.-Cs.*, because—as will be seen later—they obey fundamentally different laws to the anatomical systems subserving external perception. Luria also did not include them within the perceptual unit of his (1973) theoretical model. Instead, he included them within the unit for regulating cortical tone and waking, which we discuss later.

Before we can get to these deeper levels of the brain, however, we have to pass through an intermediate system of neurones, which separates the externally directed component of perceptual consciousness from the interior of the apparatus. In the "Project" model (1950 [1895]), this intermediate system was the "ψ" system of neurones—or, more specifically, to begin with, the pallium component of the ψ system. In the modified model that Freud later sketched in Chapter 7 of the *Interpretation of Dreams* (1900a), these psychic systems were depicted as a series of mnemic transcriptions, which stretched from the perceptual periphery down to the system *Ucs.* itself. In these mnemic systems, perceptual experiences are registered repeatedly in a number of different transcriptions, according to various functional criteria. In his later, "structural" model of the mind (1923b), Freud included these systems within the functional domain of the ego.

We must therefore now turn our attention to the ego. The ego is a highly complex and differentiated apparatus, which Freud studied from a great many viewpoints in different periods of his scientific development. We have space to consider only a few of them here. According to the structural model, the ego corresponds to that portion of the id that has been modified during ontogenesis by the influence of external reality. For this reason, Freud argued, the system *Pcpt.-Cs.* (which abuts directly on external reality) forms the nucleus of the ego. We can therefore once again take our anatomical bearings in the metapsychological writings of Freud. He wrote in *The Ego and the Id* (1923b) that

> the ego is first and foremost a bodily ego; it is not merely a surface entity, but is itself the projection of a surface. If we wish to find an anatomical analogy for it we can best identify it with the "cortical homunculus" of the anatomists, which stands on its head in the cortex, sticks up its heels, faces backwards and, as we know, has its speech-area on the left-hand side. [p. 26]

To this passage Freud added the following explanatory footnote:

> I.e., the ego is ultimately derived from bodily sensations, chiefly from those springing from the surface of the body. It may thus be regarded as a mental projection of the surface of the body, besides, as we have seen, representing the superficies of the mental apparatus. [p. 26, n. 1]

On the basis of this passage, and our own observations, we may conclude from the *physical* point of view that the unimodal cortical zones form the nucleus of the ego. But the ego's nucleus is not the ego itself. It is the topographical and genetic origin of the ego. In order to understand something about the anatomical and physiological representation of the ego itself (and especially of its structural, dynamic, and economic functions), we need to consider the brain structures that, as it were, "grow out of" the unimodal cortical zones.

These structures are—in Luria's (1973) and Mesulam's (1985, 1998) models of the brain—the heteromodal cortical zones on the posterior surfaces of the hemispheres. These zones make up the remainder of the unit for the reception, analysis, and storage of information, and they connect the various unimodal cortical analysers with one another. We said earlier that Freud described these regions of the mental apparatus as a series of mnemic transcriptions, which register and re-register perceptions in accordance with a sequence of functional criteria. Freud was not sure what these criteria were—but he guessed that the first one probably represented simultaneous relationships between perceptual events, whereas a later one might represent the sequential relations between them.

How are we to represent these systems from the *physical* point of view? In fact, this aspect of neuroscience has been very thoroughly explored. The basic facts are the following. During the first months and years of life the cortical regions that lie between the unimodal cortical "projection" zones gradually evolve. This evolution expresses the development of a highly complicated matrix of cortical and thalamic connections. These connections select out certain features of the flood of information arising from the sensory modalities, and they combine these features into complex synthetic patterns. The details of these processes can be studied in any modern textbook of perceptual anatomy and physiology (e.g. Creuzfeldt, 1995; Mesulam, 1998). Once again, we are only mentioning some general principles that are of interest to us.

The first principle that we would like to emphasize is that these synthetic functions, which may legitimately be conceived of as the very building blocks of our knowledge of the world, are by no means predetermined. Although there are certainly strong species-specific patterns of connectivity, the connections themselves develop epigenetically under the direct influence of early perceptual experience. Once these connections have been established, they form a gradual morphological transition from primary to secondary and tertiary cortex. All of this is done in accordance with the needs of the organism, which are conveyed via a second system of connections, which we discuss a little later. All of these connections together constitute the physical expression of the function of memory. The connections are expressed at the cellular level in a number of different ways, depending on the stage in the maturational process of the brain at which they are encoded, on the anatomical level at which they occur, and on the degree of permanence of the morphological changes that they represent. As we have said, some of the connections appear to be genetically pre-wired, which implies that they are almost impossible to shift. Other connections occur during critical maturational periods of neuronal migration and synaptic selection. The patterning of these connections is initially very sensitive to internal and external events (they are "activity-dependent"), but thereafter the connections become relatively permanent. Yet other, more short-term connections occur at the level of synaptic permeability. Across this morphological transition, the connections that encode relatively permanent, long-term, and remote memories gradually fine away into the connections that encode transient, short-term memories and certain forms of attention (cf. the concepts of habituation and sensitization). Those readers who are interested in how these complex processes are mediated at the basic cellular level may profitably consult two accessible papers by Eric Kandel (1979, 1983). These papers describe some of the physiological mechanisms that we now believe underlie the process that Freud described as "facilitation" in his 1895 "Project".

We hope we are not giving too static an account of these systems. Not only are we dealing with a set of anatomical connections that change to varying degrees throughout the life of the individual, but we are also dealing with a set of physiological connections that are constantly shifting, from moment to moment, in relation to an evanescent matrix of interrelated variables, some of which have nothing to do with what we call "memory". We mention some of these variables later, when we discuss the arousal systems and the executive systems of the brain. These latter variables play an extremely significant part in determining the direction taken by these processes. They also determine when and whether consciousness will be attached to a particular part of the process ("working memory").

However, the point we are wanting to make now is that within the posterior cortical regions themselves, on the basis of physiological and lesion studies, we have been able to identify the basic functional features that are encoded at certain points in this ongoing process of association. We know, for example, on the basis of various converging lines of evidence, that the process that we describe psychologically as "whole-object representation" occurs at a relatively deep level of analysis, associated with the contribution of the heteromodal cortical zones of the right cerebral hemisphere

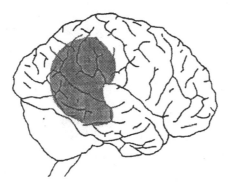

FIGURE 10-3

(Fig. 10-3), which is where concrete information derived from all the major external sensory analysers converges. (In the heteromodal zones there is a high degree of lateral differentiation between the hemispheres.)

During early stages of development, the morphological arrangement and physiological functions of the heteromodal cortex are hierarchically dependent on the unimodal cortex (and ultimately on the peripheral receptors), which, in Freud's terminology, formed the nucleus of the ego. However, according to Luria (1973), once certain critical periods have passed, the direction of the hierarchy reverses itself. This is very important. Previously conscious sensorimotor acts that have become automatized and internalized at deeper levels of analysis, and the associative connections between them ultimately encoded within the heteromodal cortical zones (see chapter seven, pp. 144–147), gradually come to structure the activities of the unimodal sensory analysers. Thus, for example, heteromodal "whole-object" representations come to dominate the fragmentary perceptual operations that are performed at the unimodal cortical level. To put it differently, after certain critical periods, we no longer deliberately analyse each perceptual scene into of a variety of significant features, and then deliberately integrate them in semantic "directories" (Mesulam, 1998). Instead, we project our *expectations* onto the perceptual scene, in the form of complex associative representations, and we only adjust these projections if our expectations are not met. This is an important part of the psychological mechanism that Freud described as "wishful mnemic cathexes", which in turn is closely associated with the concept of "identity of perception". These processes are central to the clinical phenomenon of "transference". We will shortly say something about the dynamic and economic mechanisms that regulate wishful cathexes of the perceptual system.

The developmental process that we have just described, whereby certain habitual perceptual associations are internalized and automatized in heteromodal cortico-thalamic "directories" (Mesulam, 1998), corresponds to an important part of what in psychoanalysis is described as the "structuralization of the ego". This is how perceptual experience transforms a portion of undifferentiated id into the associative mnemic structure of the ego. We will return to this subject again later.

First, we would like to remind the reader—in line with the general framework we have adopted—that it would be a serious mistake to conclude from what we have said (despite the way we are saying it) that the subjective mental contents that we experience as memories or phantasies actually *reside* in these structuralized neuronal connections. And it would be no less a mistake to conclude that the conscious perceptual experiences that we described earlier can actually be *found* in the unimodal cortical zones. One will never find a thought inside a piece of tissue. What we are attempting to do is to map the *lawful relationship* that exists between the two terminal points in our knowledge. This lawful relationship is expressed in the form of dynamic localizations. The fact that such laws exist suggests that these are two perspectives on a unitary underlying process. But the two types of knowledge they generate are still two different things, and the underlying process can still not be seen directly (Solms, 1997b). This should be kept in mind as we proceed, because it applies to every dynamic localization that we describe in this chapter. When we say that a particular mental function can be reduced analytically to a number of component parts that correlate with the activities of an equal number of anatomical regions, we have described a lawful relation between two different causal domains. We think that this might best be thought of as something like a *translation*.

We would now like to follow up a hint offered by Henry Edelheit (1969). According to him, the process of consciously analysing the perceptual world into biologically significant components, and then gradually internalizing those components so that they come to represent permanent memories which translate into perceptual expectations, corresponds to the establishment of the psychological structures known as "stimulus barriers".[3] Stimulus barriers form the very fabric of the ego. They make it possible for the organism to protect itself—by recognizing and selecting certain regular perceptual patterns—against the overwhelming flood of information that constantly arises from the world. Without this selective process, the organism would be in an almost constant state of excited arousal.[4] We cannot discuss the reasons for this until we have considered the connections between the perceptual-mnestic systems and the deeper systems that regulate arousal. However, it is important to emphasize immediately that, although the stimulus barriers face outward as it were, the arousal comes from within.

We said earlier that the two cerebral hemispheres encode perceptual memories according to different criteria, or, to put it another way, that the two posterior convexities represent different ego structures. In the *right* cerebral hemisphere, on the basis of perceptions derived initially from the bodily ego, an internalized representation of the spatial relationships in the external object world is gradually established in the mind. We said earlier that these relationships are encoded as whole objects at the hetero-modal cortical level. We have described in chapter eight how these internalized representations of the external world collapse following damage to this part of the brain—how the patient regresses from whole- to part-object relationships and from object-love to narcissism, at the same time as his or her cognitive representations of external space collapse into the ego. However, something quite different happens following lesions to the heteromodal zones of

---

[3] We are here generalizing and elaborating an observation that Edelheit made with specific reference to *phoneme* discrimination (cf. Edelheit, 1969, p. 386).

[4] We use the anthropomorphic phrase "the organism protects itself" rather than something like "salient information is selected for further processing" for the reason that, from the subjective viewpoint, an excited state of arousal in which the organism is forced to respond equally to all stimuli necessarily produces ego fragmentation or annihilation. The "I" is overwhelmed by a multitude of "its".

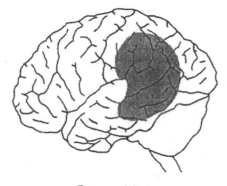

FIGURE 10-4

the *left* posterior convexity (Fig. 10-4). This links up with Freud's (1923b) remark to the effect that the bodily ego wears its "cap of hearing" on the left-hand side only.

The essential point here is that whereas the external world is (very loosely speaking) represented as a series of *things* in the posterior zones of the right cerebral hemisphere, it is re-represented by a series of *words* in the corresponding zones of the left hemisphere. This is ultimately due to the fact that in the left-hemisphere mnemic systems, reality is represented primarily in terms of its audioverbal rather than visuospatial qualities (see chapters five, six, and seven). In the first instance, audioverbal qualities, too, are "things". However, because the audioverbal connections are later organized into a closed lexical system, which is in turn organized by a set of logico-grammatical rules, they re-transcribe the open-ended connections of the object presentations in a manner that may legitimately be described as symbolic (cf. Creuzfeldt, 1995). This feature of speech bestows special economic and dynamic advantages upon it, with the result that our most efficient mnestic and cognitive processes are always verbally mediated. Not all of these economic and dynamic properties of speech can be linked with the functions of the *posterior* cortical zones, however, as we shall see shortly.

Moreover, the mnemic systems of the ego do not analyse perceptual information arising from the outside world alone. A considerable portion of their activity is taken up with internally generated processes that are stimulated from endogenous sources of activation. These internally generated activities of the mnemic systems correspond in large measure to the function that we call "thinking". As will be seen later, the most essential components of this process are regulated by mechanisms that are situated *outside* the posterior cortico-thalamic region; however, it is in the posterior cortico-thalamic region that they are brought into *associative contact* with the unimodal perceptual systems that mediate *conscious qualities*. The left-hemisphere posterior cortical zones make an essential contribution here (cf. chapter six). Thus, words—being originally derived from perceptions—render the thought processes occurring in the depths of the ego *conscious*.

Words also render thought processes more efficient and reliable; for, once thinking is attached to speech, it is structured by a fixed set of logico-grammatical rules. Freud discussed these relationships in detail in Part 3 of his "Project" (1950 [1895]), where he described normal psychic processes (cf. our chapter seven). As he showed there, speech also makes it possible for us to communicate our internal thought processes in a way that can be understood by the other minds around us. We discussed this aspect of the function of speech in chapter five. We will say something more about this function shortly.

However, first we would like to remind readers that—according to Freud—all of this does not mean that *thing*-presentations are incapable of becoming conscious, or that we are incapable of thinking in visual or spatial consciousness; it only means that the visuospatial type of internally generated cognition is less efficient than the audioverbal type. This view was confirmed by our analysis of the right-hemisphere syndrome (chapter eight), which—contrary to the expectations of some psychoanalytic authors—revealed that these cortical zones subserve *ego* functions (or perceptual–mnestic functions) rather than *id* functions (or the functions of the system *Ucs.*). Here we should also remind readers of the role that the internally directed surface of perceptual consciousness plays in this regard. It attaches subjective *value* to mental states, and on this basis it plays an essential role in many perceptual–mnestic processes (see below).

Due to the exceptional position of the auditory sphere in human mental life, the distinction between audioverbal and visuospatial perception has still other important consequences (see

Isakower, 1939). The exceptional position of hearing is primarily due to the fact that the audioverbal modality is more closely bound up with self-consciousness than is the visuospatial modality, which is more closely bound up with object-consciousness.

According to Freud's analysis of the aphasias (to which Edelheit, 1969, drew particular attention), the origin of this distinction lies in the fact that one constantly hears one's own vocalizations. For this reason, during the process of language development, speech is perfected through the auditory modality by critically listening to oneself and modifying one's own vocalizations until they match the vocalizations of one's parents. In this respect, one treats an aspect of one's own self as though it were an external object. This applies far less to one's visual image of oneself, and less still to the tactile, somatosensory, and other forms of sensation. The internalization of this attribute of speech makes it uniquely suitable for the purposes of self-reflective thought.

In order to trace these themes further, it is necessary for us to shift from the posterior cortical surfaces—that is, from the unit for the reception, analysis, and storage of information—to the anterior cortical structures, which constitute a functional unit for the programming, regulating, and verifying activity. Before we do that, however, we must first say something about the *arousal* systems of the brain, which we have mentioned more than once already.

Modulating cortical tone and waking

The arousal systems are responsible for what Mesulam (1985) has described as the "state-dependent" functions of the brain, which he contrasted with the "channel-dependent" functions of the perceptual–mnestic systems. Although we now have at our disposal detailed knowledge regarding the functional organization of this part of the brain, we will only mention some general principles of interest here.

We said earlier that the limbic lobe, which we described as the "unimodal" cortical zone for internal perception, formed the upper end of this primitive functional unit. The basic role of this unit is the modulation of cortical tone and waking. Its core component is

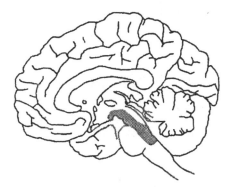

FIGURE 10-5

traditionally described as the "ascending activating system", which includes the parabrachial nuclei, periaqueductal grey, reticular formation, raphe nuclei, locus coeruleus, and ventral tegmental area (Fig. 10-5). This unit also includes the limbic system proper. Unlike neurones in the perceptual–mnestic ("channel-dependent") systems of the brain, the neurones of this unit do not respond only (or primarily) to discrete, modality-specific stimuli. They are rich in receptors that respond to gradual and relatively non-specific changes in the *state* of the organism, some of which are communicated by peptides and hormones in addition to the classical neurotransmitters (see Damasio, 1999; Panksepp, 1998, 1999). These anatomical and physiological properties bestow unique functional attributes upon this deep region of the brain. Principal among these is the fact that its neurones modulate the state of activity of the *externally* directed neurones by increasing or decreasing their discharge rates and thresholds. This affects the *level* (as opposed to the contents)[5] of consciousness and thereby alters parameters such as arousal, vigilance, and attention. In saying this, one can immediately see what an important role this region of the brain must play in the psychological functions we have discussed already.

---

[5] The distinction between the level and contents of consciousness corresponds in part to the distinction that Freud drew between "ideational traces" and "quotas of affect" (see Solms, 1996a; Solms & Nersessian, 1999a, 1999b).

The major sources of stimulation that influence these core systems are the following. First, there are the intrinsic cycles of the hypothalamus and related nuclei. These cycles mediate various innate biological rhythms, which (due to their circularity) may justifiably be described as "timeless". The 90-minute cycle that underlies the phenomenon of REM sleep—and its diurnal equivalent—is one example of this sort. These cycles can be influenced chemically. This introduces the second source of endogenous arousal, which is the chemical processes of the body—that is, metabolic and humoral processes. These processes fluctuate in a less predictable fashion. This second source of arousal is closely linked with a set of inborn behavioural automatisms, such as masticatory, copulatory, stalking, and other stereotyped behaviours, which are encoded in the form of "instincts" (see Panksepp, 1998, 1999). Instinctual behaviours can be triggered by the chemical state of the organism, but also by a different source of arousal. This is the origin of their unpredictability. This other (third) source is the outside world. Here we have the physiological basis for attention, which Freud discussed at length in his early metapsychological writings. Attention has tonic and phasic components. Tonic arousal of the perceptual systems underlies the "evenly suspended" form of attention that determines our background level of interest. This form of cathexis seems to be an important component of the mechanism that directs consciousness from internal sources. Attention of this form enables the organism to recognize certain patterns of external stimulation when they are represented by the posterior perceptual-mnemic systems. These patterns are associated with previous "experiences of satisfaction" and with potentially noxious experiences (see LeDoux, 1996). These perceptions provoke phasic arousal reactions. The "basic emotions" are prototypical examples of this kind of arousal. As can be seen, the degree of phasic attention that a perception warrants is essentially determined by the previous *experiences* of the organism. In other words, this form of attention is closely connected witn *memory*. However, the templates upon which these experience-dependent codes are traced are largely innate (see Panksepp, 1999; Solms & Nersessian, 1999a). Naturally, the internal state of the organism—as conveyed by its metabolic and humoral state—constantly affects these processes (Damasio, 1999).

Memory is invoked by the external absence of an object of internal need. This state of frustration is the prototypical situation whereby consciousness is attached to a need. In this way, the various sources of arousal combine with one another. All of these involuntary processes are also affected by a fourth (voluntary) source of arousal, which we describe in the next section.

In view of what we have said, it will come as no surprise to learn that we view the cortical arousal processes, which have their epicentre in the ascending activating system, as the physiological correlates of those mental processes that in psychoanalysis are conceptualized with the postulate of "psychical energy". The ascending activating system may therefore be loosely described—to use Freud's figurative terminology—as the great "reservoir of libido". It is probably no accident that most psychopharmacological agents act directly upon the single neurotransmitters sourced in nuclei of this system.

We would like to draw attention in this regard to two specific aspects of arousal-system functioning. First, although core-brain activation may be stimulated into action from a variety of sources, including the outside world, the activation process *itself* is always an endogenous one. Whatever the original source of activation may have been, the level of cortical tone is ultimately mediated by these core systems of the brain. Here we have a possible neurophysiological correlate of a fundamental metapsychological principle— namely, the principle that endogenous psychic energy is the single driving force of the mental apparatus. Second, although there are specific, epigenetically determined links between certain sources of and certain responses to arousal, the relatively diffuse organization of the "state-dependent" systems of the brain makes it possible for one source of activation to coalesce with another, and for one form of arousal to become confused with another. (A striking example of this is provided by the "seeking" system discussed briefly in chapter three; see Panksepp, 1998, for details). Here we have possible neurophysiological correlates of the fundamental metapsychological principles that state that "quotas of affect" are only loosely tied to ideas, and that the source of an instinct is only loosely tied to its object. These correlates provide the foundations for a physiological understanding of displacement and condensation and other forms of "substitute formation." (However, this refers only to the economic aspect of these mechanisms.) These facts also provide us with a physiological foothold on the principle of "specific action": an endogenous source of arousal may have non-specific effects, but only a specific action will remove the metabolic or other need that stimulated the process in the first place. Successful actions provide "experiences of satisfaction", which establish connections between specific sources of arousal on the one hand and specific perceptual–mnestic configurations on the other.

We have described elsewhere (Solms, 1994) how the activatory and mnemic connections between deep brain systems and the cortex, which we have just been discussing, provide the anatomical and physiological basis for the whole mode of psychic functioning that Freud designated as "primary process". We described this process as a non-adaptive mechanism by which a state of arousal, activated by a pressing need—which has been registered (by limbic structures) as a state of unpleasure—is temporarily reduced by an uninhibited cathexis of the structuralized (neocortical) introjects we have mentioned. This results in an immediate process of discharge along the mnemic paths laid down by previous experiences of satisfaction. This unmediated process of cortical activation produces (in its most direct form) a hallucination or a stereotypical motor discharge. Some interesting parallels seem to exist between this primitive mode of functioning and the pathological mechanism of epilepsy (see Solms, 1994). This has implications for a physiological understanding of Freud's dual-instinct theory, which is another subject we return to later.

We hope that it is clear from what has been said so far that we are proposing that this functional unit of the brain should be conceived of as being the physical realization of the "instinctual" pole of the mind. To put it differently: we are suggesting that the ascending activating system, together with its limbic connections— that is, the whole region that Luria (1973) defined as the unit for modulating cortical tone and waking—is the anatomical and physiological correlate of the mental agency that in psychoanalysis is described as the "id". However, we also hope that it is clear from what we have said that—from both the anatomical and physiological points of view—these structures are inseparable from those of the posterior cortical convexity and the internal milieu of the body. This applies all the more so to the immature organism.

Programming, regulating, and verifying activity

The third functional unit in Luria's (1973) scheme is the unit for programming, regulating, and verifying activity. By shifting our attention from core brain structures to this unit, we are shifting our attention from the instinctual to the executive pole of the mind.

In Freud's first topographical model—as he depicted it in Chapter 7 of *The Interpretation of Dreams* (1900a)—this takes us to the "motor" end of the apparatus. This is the topographical locus of the system *Pcs.* and, behind that, of the "censorship". The executive pole of the mind is therefore also its *inhibitory* pole. In terms of Freud's structural model of the mental apparatus, this is the locus of the ego in its dynamic manifestation. It is, therefore, once again, surprisingly easy for us to find our anatomical bearings in Freud's metapsychological writings.[6]

---

[6] This is primarily due to the fact that Freud's topographical models of the mind involved a description of mental life as if it were "the function of an apparatus to which we ascribe the characteristic of being extended in space and of being made up of several portions" (1940a [1938], p. 145). As Freud himself implicitly stated, this hypothesis started from an anatomical model (cf. his comment, cited above at the beginning of the chapter, to the effect that "Our two hypotheses start from [both of] these ends or beginnings of our knowledge. The *first* is concerned with localization ..."). The anatomical model referred to was explicitly developed in Freud's (1891b) monograph on aphasia. Freud's *second* fundamental hypothesis started from "the fact of consciousness" (1940a [1938], p. 158). It is certainly more difficult to find one's anatomical bearings in models derived from the hypothesis of psychic quality than models of psychic locality.

We would like to take this opportunity to suggest that some of the controversies currently surrounding Freudian metapsychology could be resolved if we pursued this line of thinking further and added a "subjective" point of view to our classical metapsychology. A "subjective" viewpoint—which has the significant clinical advantage of approximating closely to the patient's own experience—generates models of unconscious phantasy in which unconscious events are described as if they were acts of consciousness (see Solms, in press [c]).

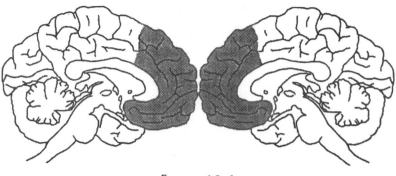

FIGURE 10-6

The anatomical structures that regulate the executive and inhibitory functions of the mind are the frontal lobes of the brain, and the prefrontal divisions in particular (Fig. 10-6). In one respect, the prefrontal region could be described—with some justification—as just a further system of mnemic transcriptions of the perceptual information derived from the outside world. Accordingly, Mesulam (1985) describes the dorsolateral frontal lobes, like the posterior lobes, as "channel-dependent". In this respect, it could be said that the prefrontal region represents the deepest layer of structuralization of perceptual information. For this is precisely what it is. The perceptual–mnestic processes encoded in the posterior cortical regions are associated via well-defined cortico-cortical and thalamo-cortical tracts with the anterior divisions of the brain, where they are re-coded, according to different functional criteria, into programmes of goal-directed activity. These programmes form the basis for a further sequence of transcriptions which terminate in motor discharge. Furthermore, if we take account of the reversal of the information-processing hierarchy which occurs when the prefrontal region is fully structuralized, then we can understand why it is that the deepest mnemic systems eventually come to exert executive control not only over the motor system, but also over the posterior (perceptual) systems, which—as it were—taught them everything they know.

This hierarchical reversal also enables us to understand how the system Pcs. gains access to perceptual consciousness. In this way, it not only attaches conscious qualities to its own internal processes, it also controls the distribution of cathexes that govern perceptual consciousness. This casts light on the vexed question of the "direction of flow" of cortical perceptual processes (cf. Brown, 1988).

On the basis of clinical studies, we can specify the functional principle by which the frontal cortico-thalamic region structures its cognitive activities. Whereas the posterior systems operate in parallel and synthesize information into *simultaneous* (spatial and quasi-spatial) patterns, the anterior systems operate in series and re-transcribe these patterns into *sequential* (attentional and executive) programmes (Luria, 1966). If one recalls the hierarchical capability of the prefrontal region to organize the activities of the other cortical systems, one can see how these two cortical functional units together generate the two great classes of abstraction that structure our entire conception of the world. These two classes of abstraction are *space* and *time*—or, rather, as Freud wrote in an unpublished draft manuscript discovered by Ilse Grubrich-Simitis (1993), *matter* and time. In that draft, Freud described these two categories of abstraction as the ego's "shield[s] against stimuli". This tallies well with the general model of the cortex that we are trying to develop here. Following *lesions* to the cerebral cortex, we see in the aphasias, apraxias, and agnosias these great abstractions disintegrate and dissolve. Then we are reminded again, with an understandable sense of shock, just how subjective and ephemeral is our construction of the world (cf. Solms, 1997b).

But, by putting it this way, we are leaving out of account at least half of our picture of the mind. The prefrontal region is not only interpolated between the perceptual–mnestic and the motor systems of the brain, it also interposes itself between motor discharge and the instinctual pole of the mind. By reminding ourselves of this fact (i.e. that the prefrontal lobes are interpolated between the motor systems and both of the two major sources of mental stimulation—the external and the internal worlds), we recognize the full dependent relations of the structural ego, in its primary role as mediator between the various forces in the mind (Freud, 1923b). We are reminded also of Luria's (1973) comment to the effect that the prefrontal lobes form a "superstructure" over all other parts of the brain. We have already said quite a bit about the interactive relationship between the prefrontal region and the perceptual system; we would now like to turn our attention to its interrelationships with the instinctual forces in the mind.

We should first point out, in line with what we know already about the nature of psychic energy, that the process of motor discharge, which we described earlier as the termination of a process of association that begins at the perceptual periphery, does not receive its driving force from the external world. Motor processes, no less than sensory ones, are energized from endogenous sources. But here we must not forget that the frontal region does not only control motor discharge itself; it also mediates all the complex executive processes that precede (and in many respects prevent) motor release.

The prefrontal region structures these processes by—to paraphrase Freud—"interpolating the activity of *thought* between the demand made by an instinct and the action that satisfies it". It does this by inhibiting the stereotypical primary process that is mediated by the limbic/posterior-cortical axis and by *binding* the psychic energy that would otherwise proceed freely to motor discharge. Here, incidentally, we have the fourth (voluntary) source of arousal acting upon the activating system that we mentioned in the previous section. The prefrontal lobes marshal the energy resources of the core brain systems for the purposes of voluntary, goal-directed activities. This *bound* energy provides the essential basis for all of the ego's dynamic functions (see chapter nine).

The binding of psychic energy is made possible—according to Freud's "Project" model—by maintaining a constant state of cathexis of what he described as the "nuclear" zones of the ψ system of neurones. On the basis of clinical data (chapter nine), we have concluded that the ventromesial frontal region is a central anatomical locus of this critical economic function. The importance of this region for all of the ego's functions is demonstrated by the adynamic and confabulatory states that arise from deep frontal lesions, resulting in pathological states of generalized inertia and in a general breakdown of the selective basis for goal-directed activity, which expresses itself in its most severe form as a dreamlike state of consciousness. This economic transformation underlies central aspects of the function of "reality-testing" as well as the function of "censorship". (Luria has argued, incidentally, in an unpublished letter to Jason Brown, that the physiological mechanism of all focal disturbances of higher cortical functions in man might ultimately be reduced to disruptions of the sequencing and selection of local patterns of neuronal firing—that is, to local disturbances of plasticity and selectivity of cortical discharge, which are expressed as pathologically inert or equalized traces and as pathologically unstable or inhibited traces of a particular zone.) Here we recognize the regulatory influence of the prefrontal region over all posterior cortical functions. On this view, all the aphasias, apraxias, and ag-nosias may be interpreted as *localized regressions from secondary to primary process*.

Freud always said that our understanding of the mind would be advanced immeasurably if we could understand the physical basis of the economic transformation of freely mobile energy into bound psychic energy. He was surely right. Incidentally, the ego's ultimate hierarchical dependence on the id is laid bare by the helplessness of the ego in the states of hypoarousal that are caused by deep brainstem lesions. In these cases, there is, as it were, no energy to bind. Before we leave this subject, we would like to remind readers of the central role that *language* plays in the transformation of freely mobile energy into bound energy.

We have said that the prefrontal region is, in one respect, just a further mnemic system, which encodes the information arising from the sensorimotor periphery at a topographically deeper and genetically more mature level of analysis. In accordance with what we have said already about the topographical and genetic sequence of events in the posterior cortical region, it comes as no surprise to learn that what is structuralized in the prefrontal region is neither a unimodal aspect of perceptual reality nor a concrete "thing-presentation", but, rather, a purely symbolic "word-presentation"; that is to say, what is re-transcribed at the prefrontal level is something derived from the highest level of abstraction of which posterior cortex is capable. In this we pick up once more the threads of our earlier comments about the special role of speech in the dynamic functions of the ego.

The essential basis for the transformation that this form of verbal representation involves seems to be the sequential nature of frontal syntheses. This enables prefrontal cortex to inhibit stereo-typical behaviours with the aid of the predicative and proposi-tional structure of language. It enables the mental apparatus to organize its activities in terms of "first this and then that" pro-grammes, and to inhibit discharge in terms of "if this, then that" structures. The profound effects that this tool has upon the activa-tory process is revealed by what happens to the form and structure of our thoughts in dreams, where it is no longer available to us. Freud subsumed these negative characteristics of dreaming under the general heading of "considerations of visual representability". These characteristics, incidentally, together with those of conden-sation and displacement, reveal the anatomical structure of the regressive process that underlies dreaming, as we have demon-strated elsewhere (Solms, 1997a) and summarized in chapter three. What characterizes the neuropsychology of dreaming is, above all else, the absence of any contribution from the prefrontal convexity (cf. Braun et al., 1997). This results in an almost total dependence of dreams on spatial and quasi-spatial—that is, *simultaneous*—forms of synthesis.

We have already mentioned the fact that the verbal codes that come to be represented by the prefrontal cortex in the form of "internal speech" originally derive from the perceptual cortex and therefore ultimately from the outside world. We have also discussed how the mnemic traces derived from these reality per-ceptions gradually structuralize a portion of the id into the psychic organization known as the ego. On this basis, the prefrontal lobes—which represent (from the physical point of view) the deep-est and last layers of ego structuralization—come to be organized as a set of internal propositions, which were originally modelled on the concrete utterances of the parents. We have also described how, following a certain critical maturational period, the dependent re-lations between inside and outside reverse themselves, and the prefrontal lobes come to control the highest executive functions of the mind. On this basis, we would now like to suggest that the physical maturation of the prefrontal region coincides with the great wave of repression that marks the onset of the latency period. The consequent reorganization of mnemic contents and processes in terms of the propositional structure of inner speech therefore represents the neuropsychological foundation of the phenomenon of infantile amnesia. As is well known, these events—which define a critical moment in mental development—have numerous other fundamental ramifications, all of which, in our view, can be related in detail to these simple neuropsychological formulations.

Before we can end our overview of the putative neurological organization of the mental apparatus, we must make some brief remarks about the relationship of these processes to the structuralization of the superego. We mentioned earlier the important role that auditory self-reflection and critical comparisons between one's own speech and the speech of one's parents plays during the process of language development. This feature of speech—which enables the child to look critically upon itself as if it were an external object—lays the structural bedrock for the superego. This is because the child not only attempts to mould its speech to match the form of the verbal utterances of its parents, but also strives to modify its behaviour to conform with the content of those utterances. As this deeply encoded aspect of the sensorimotor world is structuralized, along with all of its associative connections in the pleasure–unpleasure series, the child gradually develops the capacity to critically observe its own behaviour on the basis of a running internal commentary. This makes it possible for the child to inhibit its behavioural impulses on the basis of its own ideals and standards. For, as Freud wrote in *The Ego and the Id* (1923b), the internal voice of the superego does not only say "you *ought to be* like this", it also says "you *may not be* like this" (p. 34). We have seen in clinical studies (chapter nine) what happens when the regions of the brain that mediate these functions are damaged, with the result that the parental voice is destructuralized.[7]

The functions of the superego are especially closely bound up with the ventromesial regions of the prefrontal lobe, which is the point at which the prefrontal lobe merges into the limbic system

---

[7] The primitive mechanism of "projective identification" also arises from a destructualization of the ego. In projective identification, the very fabric of the ego is (re)externalized. This process is vividly illustrated in the cases reported in chapter nine.

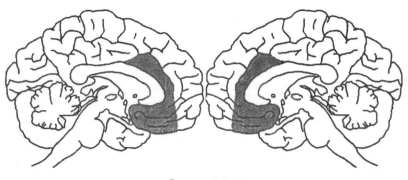

FIGURE 10-7

(Fig. 10-7). This intermediate zone probably represents the ultimate—or at least the deepest—stimulus barrier that the ego has at
its disposal. On this basis, the superego forms a barrier that protects the ego from the incessant demands of instinctual life. This
makes sense of Freud's statements to the effect that "whereas the
ego is essentially the representative of the external world, of reality, the super-ego stands in contrast to it as the representative of
the internal world, of the id" (1923b, p. 36) and that "the ego forms
its super-ego out of the id" (p. 38). The double origin of the superego, which is derived from audioverbal perception on the one
hand and a structuralization of the demands of the internal drives
on the other, makes it difficult to "localize" in any conventional
sense (cf. Freud, 1923b, p. 36). However, if we take account of
Freud's comments to the effect that the superego, with perceptual
consciousness, forms a second "nucleus" of the ego (Freud, 1927d,
p. 164), then we arrive at the following general picture. The ego
and superego may be described as a set of mnemic systems—that
is to say, as a set of structuralized internalizations—that function
as a series of stimulus barriers, occupying the region between the
perceptual systems at the one end and the instinctual drives at the
other. It is at the instinctual end that these barriers merge with the
superego. This means that the deepest level in the hierarchy of the
ego's perceptually derived systems is also a second nucleus. The
superego is thus both the most abstract and the most primitive
part of the ego.

Summary

We are now at last in a position to draw *a schematic picture of the mental apparatus as a whole,* from the viewpoint of its physical realization. As we describe this picture, we will try to indicate its essential relations with other metapsychological points of view.

The ego begins, genetically and topographically, but not structurally and economically, at the periphery of the body, with the sensory end-organs that convey coded information derived from the outside world to the cortex. However, this information is not projected directly onto the cortex; it is analysed and synthesized, in accordance with myriad functional criteria, within the grey matter of the spinal cord, the cranial nerve nuclei in the brainstem, and modality-specific parts of the thalamus, on its way to the unimodal cortical zones (Fig. 10-8). This anatomical apparatus corresponds roughly to the system *Pcpt.* of the mental apparatus, from which, as we have said, the ego is originally derived. The peripheral perceptual apparatus provides the ego with its first protective barriers against stimuli. These barriers are probably genetically predetermined and therefore incapable of memory (cf. the ψ system in Freud's "Project"). The unimodal cortical zones (the ω system of the "Project") are ideal anatomical points, which, from the physiological point of view, merge directly into the heteromodal cortical zones, which we conceive of as being the beginning of the mnemic systems of the ego (the φ systems). The unimodal cortex registers

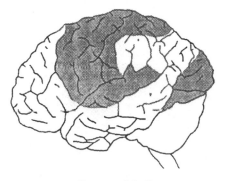

FIGURE 10-8

the various qualities of perceptual consciousness. The mnemic systems that occupy the posterior cortico-thalamic convexity re-register and re-transcribe external perceptual information in "directories", in accordance with a very wide variety of functional criteria (Mesulam, 1998). Many of these criteria can be specified on the basis of modern neuropsychological and physiological studies. The global principle involves associative linking of selected features of the incoming information into simultaneous (spatial and quasi-spatial) patterns. Certain significant patterns are encoded at progressively deeper levels. We describe this process metapsychologically as the structuralization of the ego. Once an associative pattern has been structuralized, it acts as a stimulus barrier. The perceptual systems provide the ego with stimulus barriers too, but those barriers are largely pre-wired and therefore reflect phylogenetic selections (made according to the laws of natural selection). The stimulus barriers in the interior of the ego (although they are constrained by phylogenetic templates) are also structuralized in accordance with ontogenetic experience. These structuralizations occur predominantly in heteromodal cortico-thalamic zones (Fig. 10-9). In the right hemisphere (at this level), they correspond roughly to "whole-object" representations. These representations provide an important stimulus barrier. They organize the sea of modality-specific sensory events into a relatively stable set of meaningful and recognizable "things". Once these introjections have been structuralized, they exert a projective influence over peripheral perceptual events. All of this is achieved in accordance

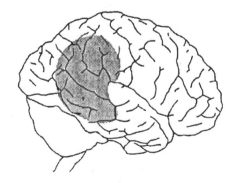

FIGURE 10-9

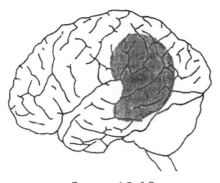

FIGURE 10-10

with the needs of the organism, which are conveyed via a second system of connections, which we will mention in a moment.

The next level of posterior mnemic transcription occurs in the heteromodal cortical zones of the left cerebral hemisphere (Fig. 10-10). Here, concrete whole-object presentations of a primarily visuospatial type are associated with abstract quasi-spatial presentations of an audioverbal type. This level of transcription (which establishes the connections between "things" and "words") is described—by both Freud and Luria—as a process of symbolization. The symbolic transcriptions provide an especially powerful shield against stimuli, because they organize the infinite diversity of real external things into a fixed lexicon of categories. Thus, every possible experience of a particular type is reduced to a single word. In a very concrete sense, it can therefore be said that words protect us against things.

At this point, we must shift our attention to the motor end of the apparatus. This is the dynamic and economic epicentre of the ego. The deepest layers of this part of the ego are realized in the prefrontal cortical region (Fig. 10-11). The transition from posterior to anterior tertiary zones associates the lexical system of word-presentations with a system of logico-grammatical rules. The simultaneous patterns of information are now transcribed into successive, sequential programmes. These programmes provide the structure for propositional speech. The tertiary frontal cortex also integrates this verbally encoded perceptual information with powerful stimuli arising from the interior of the apparatus. In this way, the logico-grammatical and propositional codes, which are

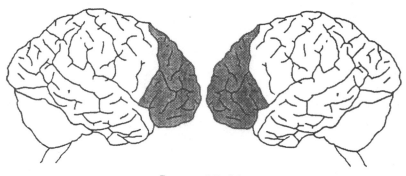

FIGURE 10-11

structured as successive syntheses, are used at the deepest levels of the ego to bind and organize the internally generated drives. The mediobasal prefrontal zone, which blends into the limbic system, is the anatomical locus of this fundamental economic transformation. At this point, the ego blurs with the superego, which forms the ego's deepest stimulus barrier and performs numerous important self-regulatory functions. The bound energy that is generated by this transformation provides the essential foundation for all of the ego's executive functions.

The cortical expanse that occupies the region between this inhibitory nucleus of the ego and its primary motor cortex is the last to mature in development. It codes the deep propositional sequences, through a series of re-transcriptions, into actual patterns of motor activity (see Passingham, 1993). Thus, from the premotor and motor cortex (Fig. 10-12), the ego exerts its controlling

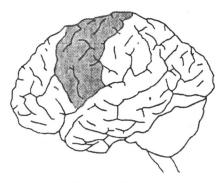

FIGURE 10-12

influence over the musculoskeletal system. Throughout, however, there are abundant interconnections with various subcortical structures. There are manifold reciprocal interconnections with the posterior cortical regions, basal ganglia, thalamus, and cerebellum. Once the prefrontal region has been structuralized (which occurs largely around the fifth or sixth year of life, but continues until late adolescence), it exerts a powerful regulatory effect over all cerebral activities. For example, it not only exerts a controlling and binding influence over motor discharge, it also regulates perceptual discharge and thereby binds projection (which prevents hallucination). This global effect of prefrontal structuralization is described as the "secondary process".

To sum up: the ego as a whole coincides anatomically with the entire cortico-thalamic expanse that separates the external and internal worlds. The ego begins in the unimodal perceptual and motor zones on the outer surface of the cortex and terminates in the ring of the limbic cortex which surrounds the brain's interior. Its basic function is to *mediate* between the internal and external worlds, a function that it performs by establishing a series of "barriers" between its two sensorimotor surfaces. These barriers are formed in the process of development, on the basis of mnemic registrations of connections between internal and external perceptions. They interpose memory between impulse and action, and they subserve attention, judgement, and thinking. However, the anatomical boundaries of the ego should not be confused with its functional sphere of influence (just as, in classical metapsychology, topography should not be confused with dynamics). The control that the prefrontal region exerts over the core activating structures is an excellent example of this distinction. Moreover, we should also not forget that the ego is both master and servant of the forces that it regulates.

The id, for its part, has its epicentre in the vital grey structures that surround the fourth ventricle (Fig. 10-13). From there, it extends its influence rostrally, via the ascending activating system. This system is regulated, in accordance with automatic rules, by the vital grey structures just mentioned and by the hypothalamus in particular (Fig. 10-14). The hypothalamus, in turn, reacts to the vital needs of the body, via the autonomic and endocrine systems. It also has its own intrinsic cycles. The ascending activating system

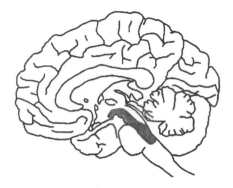

FIGURE 10-13

is influenced indirectly, first, by information arising from the posterior cortical regions, the value of which is mediated by biological desires and dangers, and, second, by the goal-directed programmes that are formulated with the aid of language in anterior cortical regions. Thus, the id influences and is influenced by reality indirectly, through the mediation of its ego, which it developed with experience from its outer cortical layers. Throughout development, the id seems to retain relatively free access to the posterior cortical layers (see chapter three). This may be because the posterior cortex apparently directs its inhibitory activities towards *external* sources of danger. However, the cathectic process in the posterior cortex is closely monitored and controlled from the anterior cortical regions.

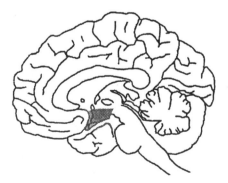

FIGURE 10-14

If we extend our "physical point of view" of the mental apparatus to its logical extreme, we would have to say that whereas the sensory and motor organs at the periphery of the body are under the purview of the ego, the vital organs in the interior of the body fall within the domain of the id. Under that heading, we would include the internal and reproductive organs. In fact—on biological grounds—we might say that the reproductive system forms the nucleus of the id. This simplified classification would also have to find a way to account for the many functional relations that certainly exist between the viscera and the periphery. However, this line of thinking takes us outside the field of neuroscience and into the realm of psychosomatic medicine, which is beyond the limits of our competence. Nevertheless, before leaving the subject, we would like to point out that the id, although it seems to reside in the deepest recesses of both the mind and the body, is in direct contact with the outside world in three important places. The viscera emerge from under the skin in the mucous orifices of the mouth, the anus, and the genitals. We recognize these orifices—which we might hesitantly describe as the "sensorimotor" organs of the id—as the familiar erogenous zones of our classical libido theory.

We end with one or two words about the drives. The libido, and especially its narrowly sexual components, is accessible (in principle) to chemical means of analysis. It is firmly rooted in the physical processes of certain tissues of the body. The self-preservative component of Eros is more difficult to concretize, but might well be connected in some intimate way with the various "basic emotion command systems" described by Panksepp (1998), perhaps together with the binding activities that we have attributed to the ventromesial frontal region, among other things. These complex physiological arrangements (which can only occur in highly differentiated organisms) are certainly fundamental to the adaptive trends of the ego. This makes it possible for us to link the destructive drive, in turn, with a more primitive physiological tendency of nervous tissue. This tendency expresses itself in the pathological states of equalization and inertia that Luria detected at the heart of every neuropsychological symptom. Perhaps this primitive tendency finds its most direct expression in the stereotypical phenomena of epilepsy.

Closing remarks

With this very schematic summary, we conclude our provisional overview of what we currently know about the physical realization of the mental apparatus, as we conceive of it in psychoanalysis. Our summary of the neuropsychological organization of dreaming (chapter three) illustrates the way in which particular mental functions are performed by means of concerted patterns of interaction between the basic functional units—or mental agencies—that we have discussed in this chapter. The principles that we applied to dreaming in this respect apply to all complex mental functions. In this way, it is possible to piece together a reasonably comprehensive picture of the neurological organization of many other mental functions that interest us in psychoanalysis, such as "repression" and "attention" and "reality-testing". However, we are very much aware of the gaps and inconsistencies that still exist in the model we have described. Some of these deficiencies could have been rectified had we had more space to consider *all* of the findings accumulated in the clinical studies that we have conducted over the past 14 years. In this book, it has been our intention to provide only an *introductory* overview based on a selection from these findings. We very much hope that the interested reader will consult our detailed reports of these studies (Kaplan-Solms & Solms, in press). However, we freely admit that most of the shortcomings of our presentation are due to a simple lack of knowledge.

Above all, we hope that some readers will be motivated by what we have written in this book to apply the method of dynamic localization themselves, and thereby to contribute to the enormous scientific task that lies before our discipline. (A new journal, entitled *Neuro-Psychoanalysis*, dedicated to this task has recently been established.) At the very least, we hope that we have been able to convince our readers of the principle that this method provides psychoanalysis with an empirical gateway to the basic neurosciences. We truly believe that this is the way forward for those of us in psychoanalysis who would like to add a physical point of view to the profound instrument that Freud devised for investigating the "unknowable" reality inside us.

NOTES ON NEUROSCIENTIFIC TERMINOLOGY

Oliver Turnbull, Ph.D.
University of Wales, Bangor

The terminology used in neuroscience in general, and neuropsychology in particular, can often be complex and confusing. Below is a
glossary of the neuroscientific terms used in this text. It is not intended
as a *comprehensive* glossary of such terminology, given that there are
many issues of neuroscientific interest not covered in the present
volume. For more information, see the general neuropsychology and
neuroanatomy texts referred to at the end of this section.

A few general principles:

(i) The prefix **"a-"** refers to "loss of". Thus, agraphia means loss
of writing ability.

(ii) The prefix **"dys-"** is used in two ways. It may refer to a "partial loss of", such that a mild agraphia might be described as a dysgraphia. Alternatively, the "dys-" prefix refers to a developmental
(congenital) disorder, as in the case of developmental dyslexia.

(iii) Other commonly used prefixes are:

"hemi-" (half)
"quad-" (quarter)
"para-" (next to, or similar to)
"pre-" (in front of)
"sub-" (under)

(iv) Other commonly used anatomical terms are:

"anterior" (in front of)
"contralateral" (on the opposite side to)
"dorsal" (upper)
"inferior" (below)

"lateral" (to the side of)

"medial" or "mesial" (towards the middle of)

"posterior" (behind)

"superior" (above)

"ventral" (lower)

(v) When two terms are linked together by a hyphen, the initial term takes on the "-o" suffix. Thus, a lesion involving the frontal and parietal lobes is a "fronto-parietal" lesion; a disorder of visual and spatial ability is a "visuo-spatial" disorder.

(vi) A **symptom** is something which a patient complains of (a sore throat). A **sign** is something which an examiner tests for (blood pressure). A **syndrome** is a constellation of signs and symptoms which have the power to predict the site of a lesion, or the cause of a pathology.

(vii) Neuropsychological (and neurological) disorders are typically defined by exclusion. Thus, a patient has a "deficit" of a function if he or she cannot do x, where this deficit cannot be accounted for in terms of impairment of y and z. This type of argument often makes definitions seem cumbersome. However, it is necessary because any given psychological ability (e.g. reading, skilled movement) requires the contribution of multiple processes, including some processes that may not be psychological at all (the visual ability of the eye, in the case of reading; the motor ability of the body, in the case of skilled movement).

Glossary of Terms Used in This Book

acalculia: a disorder of mathematical ability, which may be a primary impairment of arithmetical operations ("is 6>4"?; "is 3+2=5"?), or a secondary consequence of a different neuropsychological deficit (cf. spatial acalculia).

acalculia, spatial: a disorder of mathematical ability, which is typically secondary to a more general deficit of visuo-spatial ability after posterior (parietal) cerebral lesions. Here elementary arithmetical operations are intact, but the patient fails to align numbers in the correct column, or "carry" numbers correctly.

acoustico-mnestic aphasia: see aphasia, acoustico-mnestic.

adynamia: a poverty of spontaneous and voluntary action, in which patients are relatively inactive, and remain passive unless roused. They can act when instructed with specific commands, but easily sink back to listlessness when left to their own devices. The disorder extends to the domain of language, where conversation is limited to single utterances, or repetition of the examiner's question (echolalia). Severe cases present as an akinetic mutism (i.e. motionless silence).

agnosia, finger: definition varies greatly in the literature, but most commonly a difficulty in identifying the relative position of the fingers ("what finger is between the ring and index finger"), which may be part of a general deficit of spatial ability. A core feature of the Gerstmann syndrome.

agnosia, object: a disorder of the ability to recognize objects, in the presence of normal "elementary" sensory abilities. It is most commonly described in the visual domain, in which case patients cannot recognize visual objects (e.g. a dog), though they would be able to recognize the sound of a bark, and could recognize the animal through touch. The lesion site typically involves posterior cortical areas.

agraphia: a disorder of the ability to write that is not due to paralysis or muscular weakness. It may be a primary impairment of the ability to recall/reproduce individual letters, or a secondary consequence of a related neuropsychological deficit (e.g. aphasia).

agraphia, aphasic: an acquired disorder of writing, secondary to a primary disorder of language (i.e. aphasia).

agraphia, apraxic: a disorder of writing, where the primary deficit is an inability to construct the shape of individual letters.

alexia: a disorder of the ability to read. It may be an impairment of the ability to recognize individual letters (cf. literal alexia), or it may involve an ability to read letters but an inability to rapidly recognize letter-strings (letter-by-letter reading).

alexia, literal: an inability to read by virtue of an impairment of the ability to recognize individual letters.

amnesia: a disorder of memory. Typically, the term is used to describe a well-known pattern of impairment known as the "general amnesic syndrome". This involves a loss of recent memory ability (memory for the last few minutes, days, weeks, and months), in the presence of normal working memory (memory for events of the last few seconds or tens of seconds).

amnesia, confabulatory: a disorder of memory (amnesia) which is embedded in a state in which the patient holds false beliefs about the world, and therefore produces false memories instead of no memories (e.g. that the examiner and the patient were at school together, when this is obviously untrue)..

amygdala: a small brain structure (almond-shaped, hence the name) lying embedded in the anterior temporal lobe. It is known to be important in the perception and expression of the emotions of anger and fear.

anosodiaphoria: an indifference, or lack of concern, about illness. It is commonly found in patients recovering from anosognosia.

anosognosia: in the general sense, a denial of illness, found most commonly in acute neurological disease. The classical form of the disorder is one of denial of hemiplegia (commonly of left hemiplegia after a right hemisphere lesion). Denial also occurs in other neuropsychological disorders (e.g. cortical blindness, Wernicke's aphasia). In more chronic cases it often recovers to a milder condition: anosodiaphoria.

aphasia: a disorder of language following from brain damage or disease. The lesion site almost invariably involves the convexity of the left hemisphere in patients with conventional cerebral dominance. It is a disorder of the abstract mechanisms of language, and not merely of spoken speech (the most common means of producing language). Thus, it also affects other language output systems, especially writing (see aphasic agraphia).

aphasia, Broca's: a disorder of language, primarily affecting language production, and typically classified as a "non-fluent" aphasia. Patients have difficulty producing fluent speech, more easily producing nouns than verbs than function words. Thus the sentence "The dog is running" will be produced as "dog . . . running", or in more severe cases merely "dog". It typically occurs after left hemisphere inferior frontal lesions, especially involving Broca's area.

aphasia, acoustico-mnestic: a disorder of language, primarily affecting short-term audio-verbal memory. Language comprehension is far better than that of a Wernicke's aphasic, and language production has none of the loss of function words seen in Broca's aphasia. However, patients have difficulty holding the content of the last few phrases "in mind" in order to examine them at leisure. This classification is that of A.R. Luria, and in many respects his acoustico-mnestic aphasia resembles the traditional aphasiological category of "conduction" aphasia.

aphasia, global: a disorder of language affecting both production and comprehension. It can loosely be regarded as a combination of both Wernicke's and Broca's aphasia. The lesion site is typically large, involving much of the left hemispheric convexity.

aphasia, Wernicke's: a disorder of language, affecting primarily language comprehension. Patients cannot distinguish between similar speech sounds ("b" vs. "d"), and hence cannot understand language, especially in the demanding situation of everyday connected speech. Language production is affected, but the halting nonfluency of Broca's aphasia is absent, so that the disorder is typically classified as a "fluent" aphasia. The patient's productions are often non-sensical, consisting of a "word-salad" of commonplace phrases, which are individually intelligible, but incomprehensible in context. Thus: "Earlier I went to see the man, and sat on the fence and she took lots of dogs to the clouds in the kennels where they...". Many such patients also seem unaware of their language disorder (cf. anosognosia). It typically occurs after left hemisphere superior temporal lobe lesions, especially involving Wernicke's area.

aphasia, transcortical: a disorder of language with relative preservation of repetition. The term "transcortical" is based on a classical (and probably incorrect) account of the cause of the disorder. There are two clear types. In transcortical sensory aphasia, patients cannot comprehend language, but can repeat. This typically occurs after posterior left hemisphere lesions. In transcortical motor aphasia, patients cannot produce language spontaneously, but can repeat (cf. adynamia). This typically occurs after left hemisphere (and bilateral) frontal lesions.

aphasic agraphia: see agraphia, aphasic.

apraxia: a disorder of skilled voluntary movement that is not due to paralysis or muscular weakness. It can occur in a number of domains (constructional, dressing, ideomotor, limb-kinetic, oral).

apraxia, constructional: a disorder of skilled voluntary movement, affecting the ability to construct objects in either two dimensions (e.g. drawing) or three dimensions (e.g. block construction). It is commonly associated with other visuo-spatial disorders, and usually follows from lesions to the posterior convexity (especially on the right).

apraxia, dressing: a disorder of skilled voluntary movement, affecting the ability to dress—for example by orienting clothes incorrectly, placing the incorrect limb in a sleeve or trouser leg, or failing entirely to dress part of the body. It is commonly associated with other visuo-spatial disorders, with failure to dress half of the body being a common accompaniment of hemi-spatial neglect.

apraxia, ideomotor: a disorder of skilled voluntary movement, affecting the ability to produce spatially-appropriate movements in relation to the use of objects (or parts of the body). It is typically much worse for pantomime or imitation than for real object use. In relation to objects, it can be seen in actions such as stirring a tea cup, sawing, and sewing. In relation to the body, it can be seen in actions such as saluting, waving goodbye and shaking hands. It is typically found after lesions to the left posterior convexity.

apraxia, limb-kinetic: a disorder of skilled voluntary movement, affecting fine-motor skills (e.g. picking a coin up from a table). It remains a controversial diagnosis because of uncertainty as to whether the disorder may be due to mild paralysis or muscular weakness (see apraxia).

apraxia, oral: an acquired disorder of skilled voluntary movement, affecting the oral musculature. Patients are unable to place their articulatory organs into the appropriate position, or to change the position of the articulators rapidly. The disorder reflects disruption at the level of movement, and there are no selective effects on various parts of language (nouns, verbs, etc.) so that the disorder is not regarded as an aphasia.

apraxic agraphia: see agraphia, apraxic.

aprosodia: a disorder of the non-linguistic features of speech production (the "music" of speech), such as intonation, rhythm, inflection, timbre, and melody. It typically follows from lesions to the convexity of the right hemisphere.

brainstem: the most ancient part of the brain, whose lower part is continuous with the spinal cord (cf. forebrain). It is composed of three main parts (mid-brain, pons, and medulla). It contains (a) fibre pathways travelling to and from the spinal cord and cerebellum, (b) nuclei which control a range of visceral functions, such as heart-rate and respiration, and (c) nuclei which modulate the general level of activation of the cerebral cortex.

Broca's aphasia: see aphasia, Broca's.

Broca's area: the region in the inferior and posterior frontal lobe of the left hemisphere that is assumed to be involved in cases of Broca's aphasia.

clinico-anatomical correlation: a method of investigation, with its origins in internal medicine, which seeks to link the signs and symptoms exhibited by a patient with the parts of the body that are diseased. Thus, a patient complains of acute pain in the right lower abdomen (the clinical finding), and in surgery the appendix is found to be inflamed (the anatomical finding). The reliability of relationships of this type have made this a central approach in clinical medicine.

confabulatory amnesia: see amnesia, confabulatory.

constructional apraxia: see apraxia, constructional.

cortical tone: the extent to which the cerebral cortex is activated by subcortical structures, especially the reticular formation of the upper brain stem. Disorders of cortical tone lead to under-aroused and drowsy states.

convexity: refers to the lateral surface of the cerebral hemispheres, which have the curved shape of a convex organ. This anatomical term distinguishes the outer surfaces of the cerebral hemispheres from the medial surfaces and from subcortical structures.

deep dyslexia: see dyslexia, deep.

disinhibition: a disorder of the control of behaviour and affect. Such patients act impulsively, fail to maintain sustained attention, and are socially inappropriate. The disorder is typically associated with (bilateral) lesions of the inferior or ventral surfaces of the frontal lobes.

disorientation: a disturbance of the ability to know ones "position" in the world. Most commonly it is used to mean a disturbance of knowledge of location (disorientation for place) in patients who do not know where they are, or have difficulty navigating in their environment (see "visuo-spatial"). It may also apply to a loss of knowledge of the year, month, day, or time (disorientation for time), and in extreme cases for patients who do not know who they are (disorientation for person).

dressing apraxia: see apraxia, dressing.

dysexecutive disorders: result from a disturbance of executive function, i.e. the regulation, management, and supervision of more elementary cognitive abilities. Such disorders are typically (though not invariably) seen after lesions to the frontal lobes, especially when the lesion is bilateral.

dyslexia: a disorder of reading. Typically regarded as either a mild form of alexia or a developmental (congenital) form of reading disorder.

dyslexia, surface: a disorder of reading (see alexia) in which the patient uses letter-to-sound (grapheme to phoneme) rules. Thus, the patient can read regular words ("camel"), and non-words ("pood"). However, they cannot read irregular words ("yacht").

dyslexia, deep: a disorder of reading (see alexia) in which the patient reads through a "whole word" route. Thus, the patient can read regular words ("camel"), and irregular words ("yacht"). However, they cannot read non-words ("pood"). Such patients also produce semantic substitutions (see paraphasia) such as reading "chair" for "table".

equipotentiality: the classical argument that all parts of the brain have an equal role to play in a given psychological function. It carries the implication that the extent of psychological deficit after brain injury is proportional to the size of the lesion, rather than its location. It is often regarded as a position opposite that of localizationism, and in its extreme form has been more or less discredited by modern neuropsychology.

executive function: it is assumed that humans share a core set of elementary cognitive abilities (for arithmetic, object recognition, visual attention, etc.). These are (broadly speaking) subserved by the posterior cerebral hemispheres and a range of subcortical structures. The executive system is designed to "control" these elementary systems, i.e. to regulate, manage, and supervise them. Executive functions seem to be (at least largely) subserved by the frontal lobes, especially by the most anterior (pre-frontal) regions (see dysexecutive disorders).

finger agnosia: see agnosia, finger.

forebrain: the higher brain, excluding the brain stem and cerebellum. It consists of two cerebral hemispheres, and contains a number of large nuclei, such as the caudate, putamen, globus pallidus, hippocampus, and amygdala.

Gerstmann syndrome: a set of four neuropsychological deficits: finger agnosia, acalculia, left-right disorientation, and dysgraphia. Over the years there has been controversy about the merits of regarding the set of signs as a true syndrome. The full set of deficits is regarded as indicating a lesion to the left inferior parietal lobe.

global aphasia: see aphasia, global.

hemiakinesia: a disorder of the spontaneous and voluntary use of one half of the body. The patient must be able to move the limb, and yet generally fails to move it, to meet the diagnostic criterion. The disorder most commonly involves the left side, after a right-sided lesion, and is typically part of the more general neglect syndrome.

hemianopia: blindness of one half of the visual field. The disorder involves the same region of the visual field in both eyes, either left or right.

hemi-neglect: see "neglect".

hemiparesis: muscular weakness affecting one side of the body, typically on the side opposite (contralateral) to the lesion.

hemiplegia: muscular paralysis affecting one side of the body, typically on the side opposite (contralateral) to the lesion.

hemi-spatial neglect: see "neglect".

hippocampus: a structure that lies in the ventro-medial part of the temporal lobe, known to be vital in the formation of episodic (conscious and personal) memories. The anatomical structure of the hippocampus resembles a sea horse in cross section, hence its name.

ideomotor apraxia: see apraxia, ideomotor.

jargonaphasia: a disorder of language in which production consists of a large proportion of nonwords ("darple", "sidot") that bear no clear relationship to the target words. It is commonly associated with a language comprehension deficit and may recover into a Wernicke's aphasia.

literal alexia: see alexia, literal.

limbic system: a set of highly interconnected subcortical structures, which many neuroscientists feel are linked together in a functionally significant way. Neuroscientists differ over the precise list, and some feel it is a meaningless term. The following structures occur in most definitions: hypothalamus (especially the mamillary body), thalamus (especially the anterior and dorso-medial nuclei), amygdala, hippocampus, fornix, anterior cingulate gyrus, and the basal forebrain nuclei.

limb-kinetic apraxia: see apraxia, limb-kinetic.

localization: the argument that particular psychological functions are subserved by specific parts of the brain. This may be a single brain region, or more likely an interconnected system. There is indisputable evidence for the localization of certain elementary neurological functions (e.g. early vision and motor action), but greater disagreement about the extent to which higher psychological functions are localized. The localizationist position is often contrasted with that of equipotentialism.

misoplegia: hatred of the hemiparetic limb. Sometimes found in patients with right posterior lesions, they show an active dislike of the affected side. Patients often do not regard the limb as part of themselves, and may personify it with a name ("the stump"). They sometimes attempt to damage it.

neglect: also known as hemi-spatial neglect, or unilateral neglect, a lateralised disorder of attention in which the patient fails to attend to one side of space. It is typically the left side of space that is "neglected" (in patients with right-sided lesions).

nervous system: the arrangement of neurons and support cells that receives information from various regions of the body, integrates it with information from the outside world, and controls the process of action. The entire nervous system consists of the brain and spinal cord (the central nervous system) and the enormous number of nerves running to and from the periphery (the peripheral nervous system), including the special senses (vision, smell, etc.).

neuroanatomy: the study of the structure of the nervous system, including the location of various anatomical regions of interest, the extent of their interconnection, and the range of their variability in the normal population.

neurology: a clinical discipline that investigates the ways in which the nervous system becomes damaged or diseased, the symptoms and signs this produces, and possible treatments for these conditions. The discipline is primarily interested in disorders of the nervous system, rather than in the way that it works in healthy individuals (though, of course, one must know about the latter in order to understand the former). The discipline is interested in the entire nervous system, only a part of which is concerned with psychological processes.

neurophysiology: the study of the physical functioning of the nervous system—at the molecular and cellular (and even the systems) level.

Physiological functions need have no direct relevance to psychological issues, though clearly there are many instances in which findings in neurophysiology have psychological implications.

neuropsychology: the study of the neurological basis of psychological life. It involves the clinical and research investigation of humans with brain pathology, and the investigation of neurologically normal individuals using special technologies. Neuropsychology also embraces the experimental study of brain/behaviour relationships in lower animals.

oral apraxia: see apraxia, oral.

paramnesia: a disorder of memory in which the patient produces memories or beliefs about people and places that are demonstrably false, or even impossible. It is typically associated with an unawareness of deficit on the part of the patient (cf. anosognosia). The patient often defends the false memory or belief in the face of further questioning, or even objective evidence.

paraphasia: a language production error which is similar in some way to the intended production. It may involve an error at the level of the phoneme ("hobspital" instead of "hospital") or at the semantic level ("knife" instead of "fork").

praxis: skilled movement. A disturbance of this function is described as apraxia, or dyspraxia.

quadrantanopia: blindness of one quarter of the visual field. The disorder involves the same region of the visual field in both eyes, and can involve either the left or right upper, or left or right lower, visual fields.

surface dyslexia: see dyslexia, surface.

topographical agnosia: a disorder of navigation and orientation due to a failure to recognize or use the landmarks that become visible as one traverses a route.

topographical amnesia: a disorder of navigation and orientation due to a failure in monitoring and updating one's position relative to a starting point. It is often part of a more general visuo-spatial deficit. In spite of use of the term "amnesia", the term would not be used to describe the failure in route learning found in a patient with amnesia.

transcortical aphasia: see aphasia, transcortical.

ventro-mesial frontal lobe: the region in the lower (i.e. ventral) and medial (or mesial) regions of the frontal lobes.

visuo-spatial abilities: in general terms, the ability to know (and recall) the location, the inter-relation, of objects in the world. Disorders of various aspects of this complex psychological function include difficulty copying drawings, locating objects to act upon them, and navigating in the environment.

Wernicke's aphasia: see aphasia, Wernicke's.

Wernicke's area: the region in the superior and posterior temporal lobe of the left hemisphere that is assumed to be disrupted in cases of Wernicke's aphasia.

Further Reading

Neuropsychology:

Banich, M. T. (1997). *Neuropsychology: The Neural Basis of Mental Functioning*. Boston: Houghton Mifflin.

Bradshaw, J. L. & Mattingley, J. B. (1995). *Clinical Neuropsychology: Behavioural and Brain Science*. San Diego, CA: Academic Press.

Feinberg, T. E. & Farah, M. J. (1997). *Behavioral Neurology and Neuropsychology*. New York: McGraw Hill.

Heilman, K. M. & Valenstein, E. (1985). *Clinical Neuropsychology*. Oxford: Oxford University Press.

Kolb, B. & Wishaw, I. P. (1990). *Fundamentals of Human Neuropsychology*. New York: Freeman.

Luria, A. R. (1973). *The Working Brain*. New York: Basic Books.

McCarthy, R. A. & Warrington, E. K. (1990). *Cognitive Neuropsychology: A Clinical Introduction*. San Diego, CA: Academic Press.

Martin, G. N. (1998). *Human Neuropsychology*. London: Prentice Hall.

Solms, M. & Turnbull, O. (in press). *The Brain and the Inner World: An Introduction to the Neuroscience of Subjective Experience*. New York: Other Press.

Walsh, K. W. (1985). *Neuropsychology: A Clinical Approach*. New York: Churchill Livingstone.

Neuroanatomy:

Pinel, J. P. J. & Edwards, M. (1998). *A Colorful Introduction to the Anatomy of the Human Brain*. Boston: Allyn & Bacon. [A gentle introduction for beginners]

Afifi, A. K. & Bergman, R. A. (1998). *Functional Neuroanatomy*. New York: McGraw Hill.

REFERENCES

Accardo, P. (1982). Freud on diplegia: commentary and translation. *Am. J. Dis. Child.*, *136*: 452.

Amacher, P. (1954). Freud's neurological education and its influence on psychoanalytic theory. *Psychological Issues*, 4 (Monograph 16).

Angelini, A. (1988). *La psicoanalisi in Russia: Dai precursori agli anni Trenta*. Rome: Liguori Editore.

Anton, G. (1899). Über die Selbstwahrnehmung der Herderkrankungen des Gehirns durch den Kranken bein Rindenblindheit und Rindentaubheit. *Archiv für Psychiatrie*, *32*: 86–127.

Babinski, J. (1914). Contribution à l'étude des troubles mantaux dans l'hemiplégie organique cérébrale (anosognosie). *Revue Neurologique*, *27*: 845–848.

Bernfeld, S. (1951). Sigmund Freud, MD. 1882–1885. *International Journal of Psycho-Analysis*, *32*: 204.

Bisiach, E., Rusconi, M., & Vallar, G. (1991). Remission of somatoparaphrenic delusion through vestibular stimulation. *Neuropsychologia*, *29*: 1029–1031.

Braun, A., et al. (1997). Regional cerebral blood flow throughout the sleep–wake cycle. *Brain*, *120*: 1173–1197.

Brown, J. W. (1988). *The Life of the Mind*. Mahwah, NJ: Lawrence Erlbaum Associates.

Charcot, J.-M. (1889). *Lectures on the Diseases of the Nervous System, Vol. 1*. London: New Sydenham Society.

Cole, M. (1979). "Introduction: The Historical Context" and "Epilogue: A Portrait of Luria". In: A. R. Luria, *The Making of Mind: A Personal Account of Soviet Psychology*. Cambridge, MA: Harvard University Press.

Creuzfeldt, O. (1995). *Cortex Cerebri: Performance, Structural and Functional Organization of the Cortex*. New York & Oxford: Oxford University Press.

Damasio, A. (1994). *Descartes' Error: Emotion, Reason, and the Human Brain*. New York: Grosset/Putnam.

Damasio, A. (1999). *The Feeling of What Happens*. New York: Harcourt Brace.

Du Bois-Reymond, E. (1842). *Zwei grosse Naturforscher des 19. Jahrhunderts: Ein Briefwechsel zwischen Emil Du Bois-Reymond und Karl Ludwig*. Leipzig: J. A. Barth, 1927.

Edelheit, H. (1969). Speech and psychic structure: the vocal-auditory organization of the ego. *Journal of the American Psychoanalytic Association, 17*: 381–412.

Fechner, G. (1860). *Elemente der Psychophysik*. Leipzig: J. A. Barth.

Freud, S. (1887a). Review of Averbeck's "Die akute Neurasthenie". *S.E., 1*: 35.

Freud, S. (1888–89). Preface to the translation of Bernheim's *Suggestion*. *S.E., 1*: 73.

Freud, S. (1888b). Hysteria. *S.E., 1*: 41.

Freud, S. (1891b). *On Aphasia: A Critical Study*, trans. E. Stengel. London: Imago, 1953.

Freud, S. (1892–94). Preface and footnotes to the translation of Charcot's *Tuesday Lectures*. *S.E., 1*: 133.

Freud, S. (1893c). Some points for a comparative study of organic and hysterical motor paralyses. *S.E., 1*: 157.

Freud, S. (1893f). Charcot. *S.E., 3*: 9.

Freud, S. (1893–94). Aphasie. In: A. Bum & M. Schnirer (Eds.), *Diagnostisches Lexikon für praktische Ärzte*. Vienna.

Freud, S. (1895b). On the grounds for detaching a particular syndrome from neurasthenia under the the description "anxiety neurosis". *S.E., 3*: 87.

Freud, S. (1900a). *The Interpretation of Dreams. S.E., 4 & 5.*

Freud, S. (1904a). Freud's psycho-analytic procedure. *S.E., 7:* 249.

Freud, S. (1905c). *Jokes and Their Relation to the Unconscious. S.E., 8.*

Freud, S. (1905e). Fragment of an analysis of a case of hysteria. *S.E., 7:* 3.

Freud, S. (1910a). Five lectures on psycho-analysis. *S.E., 11:* 3.

Freud, S. (1911c [1910]). Psycho-analytic notes on an autobiographical account of a case of paranoia (Dementia paranoides). *S.E., 12:* 3.

Freud, S. (1912e). Recommendations to physicians practising psycho-analysis. *S.E., 12:* 111.

Freud, S. (1913m). On psycho-analysis. *S.E., 12:* 207.

Freud, S. (1914c). On narcissism: an introduction. *S.E., 14:* 69.

Freud, S. (1914d). On the history of the psycho-analytic movement. *S.E., 14:* 3.

Freud, S. (1915e). The unconscious. *S.E., 14:* 161.

Freud, S. (1916–17). *Introductory Lectures on Psycho-Analyis. S.E., 15 & 16.*

Freud, S. (1917e [1915]). Mourning and melancholia. *S.E., 14:* 243.

Freud, S. (1920g). *Beyond the Pleasure Principle. S.E., 18:* 7.

Freud, S. (1923a). Two encyclopaedia articles. *S.E., 18:* 235.

Freud, S. (1923b). *The Ego and the Id. S.E., 19:* 3.

Freud, S. (1924b). Neurosis and psychosis. *S.E., 19:* 149.

Freud, S. (1924f). A short account of psycho-analysis. *S.E., 19:* 191.

Freud, S. (1925d). *An Autobiographical Study. S.E., 20:* 3.

Freud, S. (1926d [1925]). *Inhibitions, Symptoms and Anxiety. S.E., 20:* 87.

Freud, S. (1926e). *The Question of Lay Analysis. S.E., 20:* 179.

Freud, S. (1927d). Humour. *S.E., 21:* 161.

Freud, S. (1937d). Constructions in analysis. *S.E., 23:* 257.

Freud, S. (1939a [1937–39]). *Moses and Monotheism. S.E., 23:* 3.

Freud, S. (1940a [1938]). *An Outline of Psycho-Analysis. S.E., 23:* 141.

Freud, S. (1950 [1895]). A project for a scientific psychology. *S.E., 1:* 281.

Freud, S. (1950a [1887–1902]). *The Origins of Psycho-Analysis.* New York: Basic Books.

Freud, S. (1956a [1886]). Report on my studies in Paris and Berlin. *S.E., 1:* 3.

Freud, S. (1990/1888). Aphasia. In: M. Solms & M. Saling (Eds.), *A Moment of Transition: Two Neuroscientific Articles by Sigmund Freud.* London: Karnac Books.

Goetz, C., Bonduelle, M., & Gelfand, T. (1995). *Charcot: Constructing Neurology*. New York & Oxford: Oxford University Press.

Grinstein, A. (1956–1975). *Index of Psychoanalytic Writings*. New York: International Universities Press.

Groddeck, G. (1977). *The Meaning of Illness*. London: Hogarth Press.

Grubrich-Simitis, I. (1993). *Zurück zu Freuds Texten: Stumme Dokumente sprechen machen*. Frankfurt: Fischer Verlag.

Harlow, J. (1868). Recovery from passage of an iron bar through the head. *Massachusetts Medical Society Publ.*, 2: 327–347.

Heilman, K., & van den Abell, T. (1980). Right hemisphere dominance for attention: the mechanisms underlying hemispheric asymmetries of attention (neglect). *Neurology*, 30: 327–330.

Heilman, K., & Satz, P. (1983). *Neuropsychology of Human Emotion*. New York: Guilford Press.

Isakower, O. (1939). On the exceptional position of the auditory sphere. *International Journal of Psycho-Analysis*, 20: 340–348.

Jaroshevsky, M. (1989). *Lev Vygotsky*. Moscow: Progress Publishers.

Jelliffe, S. E. (1937). Sigmund Freud as a neurologist: some notes on his earlier neurobiological and clinical studies. *Journal of Nervous and Mental Disease*, 85: 696.

Jones, E. (1916). The theory of symbolism. In: *Papers on Psycho-Analysis*. London Ballière, Tindall & Cox.

Joravsky, D. (1974). A great Soviet psychologist. *New York Revierw of Books* (16 May), 21: 22–25.

Kandel, E. (1979). Psychotherapy and the single synapse. *New England Journal of Medicine*, 301: 1028–1037.

Kandel, E. (1983). From metapsychology to molecular biology: explorations into the nature of anxiety. *American Journal of Psychiatry*, 140: 1277–1293.

Kaplan-Solms, K., & Solms, M. (1996). Psychoanalytic observations on a case of frontal-limbic disease. *Journal of Clinical Psychoanalysis*, 5: 405–438.

Kaplan-Solms, K., & Solms, M. (in press). Proceedings of the Neuro-Psychoanalysis Center of the New York Psychoanalytic Institute. *Neuro-Psychoanalytic Dialogues*, 2.

Kosslyn, S. (1994). *Image and Brain*. Cambridge, MA: MIT.

Kozulin, A. (1984). *Psychology in Utopia: Toward a Social History of Soviet Psychology*. Cambridge, MA: MIT.

LeDoux, J. (1996). *The Emotional Brain*. London: Weidenfeld & Nicolson.

Leon, R. (1982). Luria y el psicoanalisis en Rusia. *Rev. de Psic. Gral. y Apl.*, *37*: 105–128.

Levin, K. (1978). *Freud's Early Psychology of the Neuroses: A Historical Perspective*. Pittsburgh, PA: University of Pittsburgh Press.

Lobner, H., & Levitin, V. (1978). A short account of Freudism: notes on the history of psychoanalysis in the USSR. *Sigmund Freud Haus Bulletin*, *2*:5–30.

Luria, A. R. (1922a). Kasan. *Internationale Zeitschrift für Psychoanalyse*, *8*: 390.

Luria, A. R. (1922b). Kasaner psychoananlytische Vereinigung (Sitzungsbericht). *Internationale Zeitschrift für Psychoanalyse*, *8*: 523–525.

Luria, A. R. (1923a). Review of K. Sotonin, *Die Temperamente*. *Internationale Zeitschrift für Psychoanalyse*, *9*: 102–103.

Luria, A. R. (1923b). Review of K. Sotonin, *Die Idee der philosophischen Klinik*. *Internationale Zeitschrift für Psychoanalyse*, *9*: 103–105.

Luria, A. R. (1923c). Kasaner psychoanalytischer Vereinigung (Sitzungsbericht). *Internationale Zeitschrift für Psychoanalyse*, *9*: 114–117.

Luria, A. R. (1923d). Kasaner psychoanalytischer Vereinigung (Sitzungsbericht). *Internationale Zeitschrift für Psychoanalyse*, *9*: 238–239.

Luria, A. R. (1923e). *Psikhoanaliz v svete osnovnykh tendencij sovremennoj psikhologii*. Kazan.

Luria, A. R. (1923f). Russland. *Internationale Zeitschrift für Psychoanalyse*, *9*: 113–114.

Luria, A. R. (1924a). Russische psychoanalytischer Gesellschaft (Sitzungsbericht). *Internationale Zeitschrift für Psychoanalyse*, *10*: 113–115.

Luria, A. R. (1924b). Russische psychoanalytischer Gesellschaft (Mitgliedverzeichnis). *Internationale Zeitschrift für Psychoanalyse*, *10*: 243.

Luria, A. R. (1925a). Psikhoanaliz, kak sistema monistischeskoj psikhologii. In: K. N. Kornilov (Ed.), *Psykhologija i marksizm* (pp. 47–80). Leningrad: Gosudarstvennoe Izdatel'stvo.

Luria, A. R. (1925b). Russische psychoanalytischer Vereinigung (Sitzungsbericht). *Internationale Zeitschrift für Psychoanalyse*, 11: 136–137.

Luria, A. R. (1925c). Die Psychoanalyse in Russland. *Internationale Zeitschrift für Psychoanalyse*, 11: 395–398.

Luria, A. R. (1925d). Russische psychoanalytischer Vereinigung (Mitgliedverzeichnis). *Internationale Zeitschrift für Psychoanalyse*, 11: 142.

Luria, A. R. (1926a). Die moderne russische Physiologie und die Psychoanalyse. *Internationale Zeitschrift für Psychoanalyse*, 12: 40–53.

Luria, A. R. (1926b). Russische psychoanalytischer Vereinigung (Sitzungsbericht). *Internationale Zeitschrift für Psychoanalyse*, 12: 125–126.

Luria, A. R. (1926c). Russische psychoanalytischer Vereinigung (Sitzungsbericht). *Internationale Zeitschrift für Psychoanalyse*, 12: 227–229.

Luria, A. R. (1926d). Russland. *Internationale Zeitschrift für Psychoanalyse*, 12: 578.

Luria, A. R. (1926e). Psikhoanaliz, kak sistema monistischeskoj psikhologii. In: K. N. Kornilov (Ed.), *Problemy sovremennoj psykhologii* (pp. 244–252). Leningrad: Gosizdat.

Luria, A. R. (1926f). Principial'nye voproszy sovremennoj psykhologii. *Pod Znamenem Marksizma*, 4–5: 129–139.

Luria, A. R. (1926g). Moskovskij gosudarstvennyj institut eksperimental'noj psikhologii v 1924 godu. In: K. N. Kornilov (Ed.), *Problemy sovremennoj psykhologii* (pp. 244–252). Leningrad: Gosizdat.

Luria, A. R. (1927a). Russische psychoanalytischer Vereinigung (Mitgliedverzeichnis). *Internationale Zeitschrift für Psychoanalyse*, 13: 137.

Luria, A. R. (1927b). Russland. *Internationale Zeitschrift für Psychoanalyse*, 13: 248–249.

Luria, A. R. (1927c). Russische psychoanalytischer Vereinigung (Sitzungsbericht). *Internationale Zeitschrift für Psychoanalyse*, 13: 266–267.

Luria, A. R. (1928). Die moderne Psychologie und der dialektische Materialismus. *Unter dem Banner des Marxismus*, 4: 506–524.

Luria, A. R. (1929). Die Methode der abbildenden Motorik bei Kommunikation der Systeme und ihre Anwendung auf die Affektpsychologie. *Psychologische Forschung*, 12: 2–3.

Luria, A. R. (1932a). *The Nature of Human Conflicts: An Objective Study of Disorganisation and Control of Human Behaviour.* New York: Liveright.

Luria, A. R. (1932b). Krizis burzhuaznoj psykhologii. *Psikhologija, 1–2:* 63–88.

Luria, A. R. (1932c). Psychological expedition to Central Asia. *Journal of Genetic Psychology,* 40: 241–242.

Luria, A. R. (1936). K voprosu o geneticheskom analize psikhologichekikh funkcij v svjazi s ikh razvitiem. In: *Problemy nervnoj fiziologii i povedenija. Sbornik posvjashchennyi professoru I.S. Beritashvili* (pp. 361–367). Tblisi: Izdatel'svo Gruzinskogo Filiala Akademii Nauk SSSR.

Luria, A. R. (1940). Psikhoanaliz. *Bolzhaja Sovetskaja Enziklopedija,* 47: 507–510.

Luria, A. R. (1947). *Traumatic Aphasia: Its Syndromes, Psychology and Treatment.* The Hague: Mouton, 1970.

Luria, A. R. (1961). An objective approach to the study of the abnormal child. *American Journal of Orthopsychiatry,* 31.

Luria, A. R. (1966). *Human Brain and Psychological Processes.* New York: Harper & Row.

Luria, A. R. (1968a). The directive function of speech in development and dissolution. I: Development of the directive function of speech in childhood. II: Dissolution of the regulative function of speech in pathology of the brain. In: E. Miller (Ed.), *Foundations of Child Psychiatry* (pp. 273–282, 282–284). Oxford & New York: Pergamon Press.

Luria, A. R. (1968b). *The Mind of a Mnemonist: A Little Book about a Vast Memory.* New York: Basic Books.

Luria, A. R. (1972). *The Man with a Shattered World: A History of a Brain Wound.* New York: Basic Books.

Luria, A. R. (1973). *The Working Brain: An Introduction to Neuropsychology.* New York: Basic Books.

Luria, A. R. (1976a). *Basic Problems of Neurolinguistics.* The Hague: Mouton.

Luria, A. R. (1976b). *The Neuropsychology of Memory.* Washington, DC: Winston.

Luria, A. R. (1979). *The Making of Mind: A Personal Account of Soviet Psychology.* Cambridge, MA: Harvard University Press.

Luria, A. R. (1980). *Higher Cortical Functions in Man* (2nd edition). New York: Basic Books.

Luria, A. R. (1987). Mind and brain: Luria's philosophy. In: R. L. Gregory (Ed.), *The Oxford Companion to the Mind*. Oxford & New York: Oxford University Press.

Luria, A. R., & Majovski, L. (1977). *American Psychologist* (November): 959–968.

Luria, A. R., & Vygotsky, L. (1930). *Ape, Primitive Man and Child: Essays in the History of Behavior*. New York: Harvester, 1992.

Marshall, J. (1974). Freud's psychology of language. In: *Freud: A Collection of Critical Essays*, ed. R. Wollheim. New York: Anchor.

McCarley, R., & Hobson, J. A. (1977). The neurobiological origins of Freud's dream theory. *American Journal of Psychiatry, 134*: 1211–1221.

Mecacci, L. (1988). Review of A. R. Luria, *The Mind of a Mnemonist* and *The Man with a Shattered World*. *Journal of the History of the Behavioral Sciences, 24*: 268–270.

Mesulam, M.-M. (1981). A cortical network for directed attention and neglect. *Annals of Neurology, 10*: 309–325.

Mesulam, M.-M. (1985). Patterns in behavioral neuroanatomy: association areas, the limbic system, and hemispheric specialization. In: M.-M. Mesulam (Ed.), *Principles of Behavioral Neurology* (pp. 1–70). Philadelphia, PA: F. A. Davis.

Mesulam, M.-M. (1994). Neurocognitive networks and selectively distributed processing. *Revue Neurologique, 150*: 564–569.

Mesulam, M.-M. (1998). From sensation to cognition. *Brain, 121*: 1013–1052.

Meynert, T. (1884). *Psychiatry: Clinical Treatise on the Diseases of the Fore-Brain*, trans., B. Sachs. New York & London: G. P. Putnam, 1885.

Panksepp, J. (1985). Mood disorders. In: P. Vinken, G. Bruyn, H. Klawans, & J. Frederiks (Eds.), *Handbook of Clinical Neurology, Vol. 45* (pp. 271–285). Amsterdam: Elsevier.

Panksepp, J. (1998). *Affective Neuroscience: The Foundations of Human and Animal Emotions*. New York: Oxford University Press.

Panksepp, J. (1999). Emotions as viewed by psychoanalysis and neuroscience: an exercise in consilience. *Neuro-Psychoanalysis, 1*: 15–38.

Pappenheim, E. (1990). Psychoanalysis in the Soviet Union. *American Psychoanalyst, 24*: 4–5.

Passingham, H. (1993). *The Frontal Lobes and Voluntary Action*. Oxford: Oxford University Press.

Ramachandran, V. S. (1994). Phantom limbs, neglect syndromes, repressed memories, and Freudian psychology. *International Review of Neurobiology, 37*: 291–333.

Riese, W. (1959). *A History of Neurology*. New York: M.D.

Rodman, F. R. (1987). *The Spontaneous Gesture: Selected Letters of D. W. Winnicott*. Cambridge, MA: Harvard University Press.

Sacks, O. (1984). *A Leg to Stand On*. London: Duckworth.

Sacks, O. (1990). Luria and "Romantic Science". In: E. Goldberg (Ed.), *Contemporary Neuropsychology and the Legacy of Luria* (pp. 181–194). Hillsdale, NJ: Lawrence Erlbaum Associates.

Schore, A. (1994). *Affect Regulation and the Origin of the Self: The Neurobiology of Emotional Development*. Hillsdale, NJ: Lawrence Erlbaum Associates.

Schott, H. (1981). "Traumdeutung" und "Infantile Cerebrallähmung": Überlegungen zu Freuds Theoriebildung. *Psyche, 35*: 97.

Solms, M. (1994). "The Limbic System and the Internal World." Unpublished lecture delivered at the New York Psychoanalytic Institute, 2 April 1994.

Solms, M. (1995a). New findings on the neurological organization of dreaming: implications for psychoanalysis. *Psychoanalytic Quarterly, 64*: 43–67.

Solms, M. (1995b). Is the brain more real than the mind? *Psychoanalytic Psychotherapy, 9*: 107–120.

Solms, M. (1996a). Was sind Affekte? *Psyche, 50*: 485–522.

Solms, M. (1996b). Towards an anatomy of the unconscious. *Journal of Clinical Psychoanalysis, 5*: 331–367.

Solms, M. (1997a). *The Neuropsychology of Dreams: A Clinico-Anatomical Study*. Mahwah, NJ: Lawrence Erlbaum Associates.

Solms, M. (1997b). What is consciousness? *Journal of the American Psychoanalytic Association, 45*: 681–778.

Solms, M. (1998a). Preliminaries for an integration of psychoanalysis and neuroscience. *Bulletin of the British Psycho-Analytic Society, 34* (9): 23–38.

Solms, M. (1998b). Psychoanalytische Beobachtungen an vier Patienten mit ventromesialen Frontalhirnläsionen. *Psyche, 52*: 919–962.

Solms, M. (1998c). Auf dem Weg zu einer Anatomie des Unbewussten. In: M. Koukkou, M. Leuzinger-Bohleber, & W. Mertens (Eds.), *Erinnerung von Wirklichkeiten: Psychoanalyse und Neurowissenschaften im Dialog, Vol. 1* (pp. 416–461). Stuttgart: Verlag Internationale Psychoanalyse.

Solms, M. (1999a). Discussion of Hobson's "new neuropsychology of sleep". *Neuro-Psychoanalysis, 1*: 183–195.

Solms, M. (1999b). The deep psychological functions of the right cerebral hemisphere. *Bulletin of the British Psycho-Analytic Society, 35* (1): 9–29.

Solms, M. (2000). Freud, Luria and the clinical method. *Psychoanalytic History, 2*: 76–109.

Solms, M. (in press [a]). Dreaming and REM sleep are controlled by different brain mechanisms. *Behav. Brain Sci.*

Solms, M. (in press [b]). Proceedings of the Neuro-Psychoanalysis Center of the New York Psychoanalytic Institute. *Neuro-Psychoanalytic Dialogues, 1.*

Solms, M. (in press [c]). Do unconscious phantasies really exist? In: J. Schacter et al. (Eds.). [New Library of Psychoanalysis.] London: Routledge.

Solms, M., & Nersessian, E. (1999a). Freud's theory of affect: questions for neuroscience. *Neuro-Psychoanalysis, 1*: 5–14.

Solms, M., & Nersessian, E. (1999b). Concluding remarks. *Neuro-Psychoanalysis, 1*: 91–96.

Solms, M., & Saling, M. (1986). On psychoanalysis and neuroscience: Freud's attitude to the localizationist method. *International Journal of Psycho-Analysis, 67*: 397.

Solms, M., & Saling, M. (1990). *A Moment of Transition: Two Neuroscientific Articles by Sigmund Freud.* London: Karnac Books & The Institute of Psycho-Analysis.

Stewart, W. (1969). *Psychoanalysis: The First 10 Years.* London: Allen & Unwin.

Van der Veer, R., & Valisiner, J. (1991). *Understanding Vygotsky: A Quest for Synthesis.* Oxford: Blackwell.

Vygotsky, L., & Luria, A. R. (1925). Foreword to S. Freud, *Po to storonu principa udovol'stvija* (pp. 3–16). Moscow: Sovremennye Problemy.

Weitzner, L. (1987). Psychoanalytic reflections on the diagnosis of aphasia in a young boy. *Bulletin of the Anna Freud Centre, 10*: 145–161.

Winnicott, D. W. (1960). The theory of the parent–infant relationship. *The Maturational Process and the Facilitating Environment* (pp. 37–55). London: Hogarth Press & The Institute of Psycho-Analysis.

INDEX

Printed in the United States
By Bookmasters